Teaching and Learning Geometry

Related titles:

Teaching and Learning Geometry

Issues and methods in mathematical education

Doug French

continuum
LONDON • NEW YORK

Continuum International Publishing Group

The Tower Building	15 East 26th Street
11 York Road	New York
London SE1 7NX	NY 10010

www.continuumbooks.com

First published 2004

British Library Cataloguing-in-Publication Data
A catalogue record for this book is available from the British Library.

Library of Congress Cataloging-in-Publication Data
A catalog record for this book is available from the Library of Congress.

ISBN: 0 8264 7361 X (hardback)
     0 8264 7362 8 (paperback)

Typeset by RefineCatch Limited, Bungay, Suffolk
Printed and bound in Great Britain.

Contents

Preface   vi

1. The Role of Geometry   1

2. Learning Geometry   12

3. Beginnings: Experimental Geometry   30

4. Polygons: Symmetry and Angle Properties   40

5. Constructions and Congruence   55

6. Perimeter, Area and Volume   65

7. Enlargement and Similarity   77

8. The Theorem of Pythagoras   91

9. The Circle   104

10. Linking Geometry and Algebra   119

11. Polyhedra   136

12. Vector Geometry   149

Bibliography   162

Index   167

Preface

Geometry has always been a great source of interest and fascination to me. I can recall the delight of making a set of polyhedra as a homework task from school when I was about 12 years old. I also remember finding a copy of *Elementary Geometry* by Godfrey and Siddons (1903) in the school library during the first year of my teaching career. It has been a source of many interesting problems and good teaching ideas that have influenced me as a teacher over the years. I also consider myself fortunate as a teacher to have encountered the textbooks of the *School Mathematics Project* (SMP 1965, 1966) at an early stage because they provided a different perspective on geometry through their use of symmetry, transformations, vectors and matrices in contrast to the geometry in the style of Euclid and the conic sections of coordinate geometry that I had encountered at school.

These two strands have provided me with a rich geometrical background so that I am saddened by the rather sparse knowledge of geometry that I now find in the students I train to be mathematics teachers. This has arisen from the attempt to bring together the two influences on school geometry resulting in a neglect of geometry as a source of good problems which require independent thought and as a context for developing the idea of proof in mathematics.

Geometry does, however, seem to be in a state of flux in many countries with questions being asked about the role of proof, the degree of formality that is appropriate and the place of real-world applications. The availability of powerful computer software is another significant influence and I would rate the opportunity to explore geometrical configurations with dynamic geometry software as another important, but much more recent, influence on my own enjoyment of geometry and on my teaching.

The present book is a companion to my earlier book *Teaching and Learning Algebra* (French 2002). Writing it has presented a very different set of challenges. Algebra is more procedural than geometry and there is an abundance of writing and research about the problems of teaching it, so that in many respects it is easier to suggest how it should be approached in school, even though it may be difficult to change what happens in practice. Geometry is very different. There is a rich array of writing about geometry itself, but there is far less material about teaching and learning the subject. Perhaps because solving geometrical problems and generating proofs is less procedural and more dependent on intuition, it seems to be less easy to identify what is involved in learning it successfully. However, I have tried to distil from my reading and my classroom experience some reflections on the subject which will, I hope, provide food for thought and have some influence on classroom practice.

I must acknowledge the debt I owe to the students I have worked with over many years, both in school and university, because my ideas could not have been developed without a wealth of classroom experience. Equally, I am immensely grateful to colleagues in school and university and in the Mathematical Association and to many other contacts who have been a constant source of ideas and inspiration. Finally, I should like to thank Alexandra Webster of Continuum for her help and encouragement during the preparation of the book for publication.

Doug French
University of Hull
d.w.french@hull.ac.uk
September 2003

Chapter 1

The Role of Geometry

WHY LEARN GEOMETRY?

Geometry has an immediate intuitive appeal at a simple level. From an early age children play with shapes, noting their obvious properties and seeing how they relate to each other. They also observe a wide variety of both simple and sophisticated geometrical configurations in their surroundings and acquire some of the language associated with them. They learn informally to recognize shapes such as circles, squares and triangles and they begin to understand words like horizontal, vertical and parallel. The first steps in the study of geometry are concerned with naming, describing, classifying and making links to measurement, position and movement. Describing and classifying are not necessarily trivial tasks, as becomes very evident when, for example, we look at the properties of all the different quadrilaterals and the links between them. Moreover they lead on to the more demanding requirements of defining and deducing. Measurement is clearly of immense practical importance and establishes students' under-standing of the ideas of length and angle and associated ideas like area and volume, but the essence of geometry and the source of its endless fascination is the way in which deduction plays a central role in proving results that are often both simple and surprising.

An excellent classroom example which encapsulates this element of surprise is illustrated in Figure 1.1. Students are asked to draw any quadrilateral, to mark the midpoints of the edges and then to join those four points to form another quadrilateral. Comparing the many examples that are produced suggests that the result is always a parallelogram. This can be demonstrated very dramatically by constructing the configuration on a computer screen using dynamic geometry software and observing what happens as the shape of the quadrilateral is changed as its vertices are dragged to different positions.

  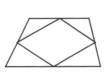

Figure 1.1 *Why is it a parallelogram?*

The result itself has an immediate appeal, but the proof which explains why it is true also has its own distinctive appeal by virtue of the simplicity of the argument. In the right-hand diagram of Figure 1.1, one of the diagonals of the initial quadrilateral has been constructed. The midpoint theorem, or an equivalent argument based on enlargement, tells us that the diagonal is parallel to and double the length of the two edges that lie on either side of it. This pair of opposite sides are therefore both parallel and equal in length, thus proving that the quadrilateral formed by joining the midpoints is a parallelogram. This result, known as Varignon's theorem, features as one of the 'desert island theorem' in *The Changing Shape of Geometry*, edited by Pritchard (2003), a fascinating collection of articles which celebrates a century of geometry and geometry teaching.

Geometrical problems can be approached in a variety of ways: it can be an experimental, practical subject where problems are solved by measurement and calculation, but to a mathematician geometry is essentially a deductive subject which either uses purely geometrical reasoning or embraces algebraic procedures as well. Algebra had no place in geometry until the seventeenth century, when Descartes established the notion of coordinates as a way of describing the position of a point in space leading to the idea of equations to describe lines and curves. Since that time geometry has been subdivided into two broad strands. Pure or synthetic geometry employs geometrical reasoning alone in a style which was formalized two thousand years ago in Euclid's *Elements* (Heath 1967), but which has subsequently been simplified and made more accessible. Analytic or coordinate geometry harnesses the power of algebra to geometrical problems by using equations for curves and by employing vectors and matrices. At school level there is an obvious progression from experimental to pure to analytic geometry, but there are difficulties about deciding the relative importance of each and the balance between pure and analytic in the later years of secondary schooling.

The arguments for including geometry in the mathematics curriculum are closely linked to the reasons why mathematics as a whole is studied, but it is interesting to note that geometry, in the form of a close study of Euclid's *Elements*, had a dominant place in the curriculum in the United Kingdom and was a prerequisite for university entrance, until the end of the nineteenth century. During the twentieth century it has been increasingly recognized that mathematics should have a central place in the education of all school students and that geometry in some form has a vital role in the wider mathematics curriculum. Three broad reasons for including geometry can be identified:

- to extend spatial awareness
- to develop the skills of reasoning
- to stimulate, challenge and inform

Spatial awareness is a rather vague, but nonetheless important, idea concerned with our ability to perceive and manipulate geometrical objects. We recognize the utilitarian role of having a sense of shape and space in a whole range of situations in simple everyday tasks like erecting shelves in the home or reading a map and in more sophisticated activities like those of the builder, architect, navigator and graphic designer. Also within mathematics itself geometrical representations are significant tools for dealing with numerical and algebraic problems. We only have to look at the sequence of triangle numbers, shown in Figure 1.2, to see how a geometrical representation can provide both insight and appeal.

It is commonly argued that mathematics, and geometry in particular, are valuable components of the school curriculum because they provide a context for developing students' reasoning skills. While there may be some truth in this it does not provide a sufficient justification for the dominant place that mathematics is given at school because these skills in a general form can be learnt through other subjects. However, if it is accepted that mathematics is important for other reasons related to its utility and the intellectual challenge and stimulation it can provide, then geometry can be seen as offering an important way of establishing what

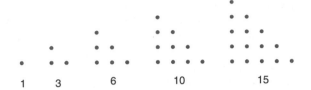

Figure 1.2 *The triangle numbers*

Goldenburg, Cuoco and Mark (1998) refer to as mathematical 'habits of mind'. These 'habits' relate to the ways of thinking that become habitual to the mathematician: the constant urge to pose and solve problems, to seek patterns, to note links and connections and above all to prove conjectures. Geometry, particularly in its pure or synthetic form, is particularly appropriate as a way of developing these qualities because it is rich in problems and theorems which both have an intuitive appeal and require arguments that may often be simple, but are not as routine or procedural as is often the case with a purely algebraic approach. That is not to underrate the importance of algebra, because it has an important role in geometry and there is much to be gained from the interplay between different perspectives on a problem.

The third of the reasons for learning geometry is that it can stimulate, challenge and inform. This embraces the idea that geometry is an intrinsically interesting subject in its own right which is worth engaging with for its aesthetic and intellectual appeal and because it is part of developing an informed background to so many aspects of our world: the symmetry of so many objects around us, the ubiquity and utility of the circle and other geometric figures, the parabolic path taken by a projectile, the elliptical orbits of planets and so on. Moreover there are geometrical results, of which the theorem of Pythagoras is a towering example, which are of vital practical significance and yet also a source of great intrinsic interest. Geometry is worth doing because it is enjoyable, but that enjoyment is often lost because the subject is so often presented in school merely as facts to remember and procedures to be followed to solve standard problems, rather than as something to be explored and puzzled over in an endeavour to understand and make sense of its riches.

An interesting example which illustrates many of the key characteristics of geometry is provided by Figure 1.3. The problem is to construct three mutually touching circles when their centres are given. This is used in Oldknow and Taylor (2000) as an example of the use of dynamic geometry software in mathematics teaching and the problem is particularly effective when it is posed in that context, but it can equally well be presented as a problem to be solved on paper with ruler and compasses. The configuration that is required is shown in the left-hand

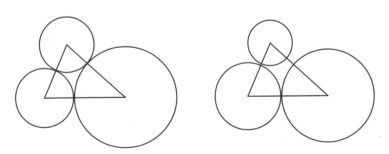

Figure 1.3 *Constructing three touching circles*

diagram of Figure 1.3, where the centres of the circles are taken as the vertices of a given triangle. The right-hand diagram shows an abortive attempt to draw such a configuration by trial and error. It is easy to construct two touching circles: the problem is to find the right place for them to touch so that the third circle precisely touches the other two. This can certainly be achieved by experimentation for a particular triangle using dynamic geometry, but as soon as one of the vertices is moved the construction fails. It is necessary to analyse the problem to find a general method and that provides a good exercise in geometrical thinking.

A first step is to make a rough diagram of the result we are seeking to obtain and to explore its key features. These are indicated by the additional lines in Figure 1.4. The requirement that the circles touch means that there is a common tangent to two circles at each touching point and we can then see that determining their point of intersection would be a useful step. Joining that point to the vertices of the triangle tells us that the point of intersection of the tangents is also the point of intersection of the angle bisectors of the triangle. Thinking about this in different terms, we see that the intersection point is the centre of the inscribed circle of the triangle and

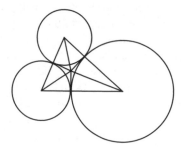

Figure 1.4 *Finding where the circles touch*

that the three touching points correspond to the points at which that circle touches the triangle. We now have a procedure for determining the position of the three points where the circles touch:

- Construct the bisectors of two of the angles of the triangle.
- From their point of intersection, drop a perpendicular to one of the sides of the triangle.
- Draw the two circles that touch at that point.
- Construct the third circle.

If this is done using dynamic geometry software the triangle can immediately be varied to see that the construction always works. If it is done on paper using ruler and compasses, students can draw several diagrams using different triangles. Solving the problem requires a carefully reasoned approach which is clearly dependent on a background of geometrical knowledge about tangent properties. It has the considerable virtue that the thinking results in an exact procedure whose effectiveness can be demonstrated.

Many people, particularly if they do not have a strong background in geometrical thinking, prefer to approach geometrical problems algebraically. With the touching circles problem an algebraic approach does provide a simple procedure which leads intriguingly to an alternative geometrical construction.

If we denote the lengths of the sides of the triangle by a, b and c and the radii of the circles by x, y and z, we have three equations:

$$x + y = a, \quad y + z = b, \quad z + x = c$$

Adding these three equations gives

$$2(x+y+z)=a+b+c \quad \Rightarrow \quad x+y+z=\tfrac{1}{2}(a+b+c)=s$$

where s is the semi-perimeter of the triangle. From this last equation we can express the three radii in terms of the semi-perimeter and the sides of the triangle, as follows:

$$x=s-b, \quad y=s-c, \quad z=s-a$$

To take a particular example, consider a triangle with sides of 5, 7 and 8 units. The semi-perimeter is then 10 units and the values of the three radii are found to be 5, 3 and 2. It is not difficult then to determine which vertex to use for the centre of each circle. This point is clarified in Figure 1.5 which shows an alternative geometrical construction based on these algebraic results.

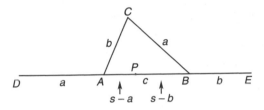

Figure 1.5 *An alternative construction for the touching circles problem*

To find the position of one of the touching points, we need to construct a length corresponding to the perimeter. In Figure 1.5 this has been done by producing the side AB of the triangle in both directions, so that the lengths AD and BE are equal to the other two sides, BC and AC respectively. The midpoint, P, of the line DE is then the required point on AB. The diagram shows clearly how AP and BP correspond to the required radii, $s-a$ and $s-b$.

While this alternative construction to the touching circle problem is not as straightforward as the first method using the centre of the inscribed circle, it does illustrate neatly the interplay between algebra and geometry, with an algebraic result suggesting a geometric procedure.

It should be clear that geometry has an important place in the mathematics curriculum, because it has many characteristics that can contribute to students' general intellectual development as well as to their mathematical development. In addition it provides practical skills and knowledge that have useful applications in everyday situations and in a wide variety of occupations. This leads on to the next two sections of this chapter which examine what should be taught – the geometry curriculum – and the all important question of how the subject should be taught and learnt.

THE GEOMETRY CURRICULUM

While there is much common ground between different countries, there are greater contrasts in content and emphasis with geometry curricula than are to found with arithmetic or algebra. Hoyles, Foxman and Küchemann (2002) in a comparative study of geometry curricula in a representative group of countries found a considerable contrast between, for example, the Netherlands where geometry is linked strongly to the real world and France, Japan and Singapore where there is little emphasis on the real world. There are also marked differences in how procedural and formal the approaches are and the extent to which the idea of proof is given emphasis. There are also significant differences between countries in the relative emphasis given to transformations, vectors and coordinate geometry as compared to synthetic geometry in the style of Euclid. The extent to which the use of computers is encouraged or expected varies very widely. There is clearly much interest and concern in many countries about the geometry curriculum so the situation is far from static. The ICMI study, Mammana and Villani (1998), reflects this widespread concern as does the report on geometry produced jointly by the Royal Society and the Joint Mathematical Council in the United Kingdom, RS/JMC (2001).

In England the mathematics curriculum is determined by the National Curriculum, DfEE/ QCA (1999). In response to growing concerns the current version has specified in a much clearer way than earlier versions the precise geometrical content that is required. The key headings below indicate the range of topics that are expected for students aged between 11 and 16 years:

> properties of triangles and other rectilinear shapes, properties of circles, specifying transformations, properties of transformations, coordinates, vectors, measures, construction, mensuration, loci.

The curriculum does specify particular definitions, theorems and constructions which students are expected to know. For example, three typical detailed statements are as follows:

> recall the definitions of special types of quadrilateral, including square, rectangle, parallelogram, trapezium and rhombus;

> prove and use the facts that the angle subtended by an arc at the centre of a circle is twice the angle subtended at the circumference, the angle subtended at the circumference by a semicircle is a right angle, that angles in the same segment are equal, and that opposite angle of a cyclic quadrilateral sum to 180°;

> use straight-edge and compasses to do standard constructions including an equilateral triangle with a given side, the midpoint and perpendicular bisector of a line segment, the perpendicular from a point to a line, and the bisector of an angle.

Interestingly we find the statement 'understand, recall and use Pythagoras' theorem' without any suggestion that students should encounter any proof of this important result. This is surprising in the light of the expectation, as indicated above, that proofs are expected of the circle theorems which, although of obvious interest and value, are much less fundamental and lack such a rich range of applications and alternative possibilities for proof.

Turning to the United States, the geometry curriculum has been strongly influenced by the *Curriculum and Evaluation Standards for School Mathematics*, NCTM (1989) and the more recent revised document *Principles and Standards for School Mathematics*, NCTM (2000b). These documents are not so prescriptive as the English National Curriculum, but the range of topics and the underlying ideas have many similarities. They do make very specific references to the particular value of geometry as 'a rich context for the development of mathematical reasoning', NCTM (2000b, p. 232), whereas the English National Curriculum does not explicitly give geometry a special place as a vehicle for developing reasoning. However, the statements in DfEE/QCA (1999) are clearly aimed at giving greater emphasis to proof within the geometry curriculum as compared to earlier versions of the curriculum.

The other noteworthy contrast between England and the United States is the greater emphasis that is given in the latter to approaching geometry through real world contexts. This is evident in the two standards documents, NCTM (1989, 2000b) and is a very striking feature in many of the curriculum projects, described in Senk and Thompson (2003), that have been set up since 1989 in response to those standards. There is little attempt in English textbooks to relate geometry to the real world in other than trivial ways, so that geometry appears for the most part as an abstract study in the same way as is evident in France, Japan and Singapore, referred to previously. This is clearly an issue where there is little consensus. There does not appear to be any research about the relative effects on attainment and attitudes of presenting geometry in terms of real-world contexts, as compared to presenting it as a relatively abstract study of configurations with an intrinsic interest of its own. The stance adopted in this book is that geometry is worth studying for its own sake and that it is particularly attractive both because it has an immediate visual appeal and because it offers a variety of challenges at different levels. Links should be made on occasion to simple real-world applications, but not in the false belief that students' motivation is necessarily or only increased by appeals to utility.

There is much common ground between geometry syllabuses across the world in terms of topics. Variations occur in the emphasis and timing of different elements and in the relative importance accorded to practical approaches, proofs and applications, resulting in wide differences in the formality of style of presentation that is adopted. Similarly there are variations in the relative importance accorded to synthetic and analytical geometry and the extent to which algebra and trigonometry, and symmetry, transformations, matrices and vectors are involved.

The objects upon which the study of geometry is based are listed below, but even at this simple level there is a lack of consensus about the relative importance to be accorded to each item. The properties of polygons and some aspects of circles are a common feature of all geometry curricula, but the role of the third and fourth items in the list varies greatly.

- polygons and their properties, giving particular emphasis to triangles, quadrilaterals and regular polygons
- circles and their properties related to chords, tangents and angles
- three-dimensional figures such as polyhedra and the sphere, cylinder and cone
- other curves, such as the parabola and ellipse, and their properties

In conjunction with these objects there are the ideas that are used in looking at their properties and relationships with similar variations in the emphasis that is given to each:

- measurement and calculation of length, angle, area and volume
- symmetry and transformations
- the use of algebra
- the theorem of Pythagoras and trigonometry
- congruence and similarity
- coordinates and equations of straight lines, curves and surfaces
- matrices and vectors

Finally we have the place of reasoning and the importance to be accorded to proof. Linked to that there are questions as to what should be accepted as 'self-evident' and what it is reasonable to expect students to be able to deduce or prove. This issue is discussed by Barnard (2002) who contrasts a deductive system based on a 'minimal set of axioms' with a collection of isolated facts that lack 'the logical connections that are intrinsic to geometry'. The sense that 'one thing follows from another' and that geometrical results are linked together in an essentially hierarchical way is an important one to develop, but it is necessary to be clear what are to be taken as starting points. For example, we can deduce that vertically opposite angles are equal on the assumption that the angles on a straight line sum to 180°. We are then able to deduce that alternate angles are equal by taking the equality of corresponding angles as the defining property of parallel lines.

Developing the reasoning skills of students has been discussed in the first section of this chapter as one of the major reasons for including geometry in the mathematics curriculum. The urge to prove what has been suggested by intuition or experiment is one of the characteristic activities of a mathematician. Finding a proof is not just a matter of verifying that a conjecture is true, although that can certainly be a powerful motivation. Additional reasons for learning about proof are advocated by de Villiers (1998, 1999), including explanation and discovery, and the element of challenge with the fulfilment that comes from successful resolution of a problem. A proof can add greatly to our understanding of a theorem, whose truth we already accept, by providing a deeper or alternative explanation. Furthermore the process of proof finding can lead to the discovery of new results and, certainly at a higher level, it has been a major motivation for developing new mathematical ideas. The proof of Varignon's theorem discussed at the beginning of this chapter leads readily to the discovery of the further result that the area of the parallelogram formed by joining the midpoints of any quadrilateral is half the area of the quadrilateral. That is not something which is instantly obvious from the diagrams illustrating the theorem.

The problem illustrated in Figure 1.6, referred to by Duval (1998), is a good example of a geometrical result that is not intuitively obvious. It can be proved in several contrasting ways which show how different approaches provide different insights. The point *P* is a variable point on the diagonal *AC* of rectangle *ABCD* and the line segments *EG* and *FH* through *P* are drawn parallel to the sides of the rectangle. The surprising fact is that the two shaded rectangles, *BEPH* and *DFPG*, have the same area and the problem is to explain why. It is necessary to identify pairs of triangles which form subconfigurations of the diagram which then lead to various ways of proving the area property. Three alternative approaches are considered here.

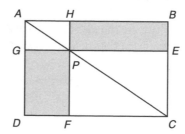

Figure 1.6 *Why do the rectangles have the same area?*

- There are three pairs of congruent triangles: *AHP* and *AGP*, *PEC* and *PFC* and the large pair *ABC* and *ADC*. In each case the three pairs of corresponding sides are equal because each pair of triangles is created by drawing the diagonal of a rectangle. The rectangles are obtained by subtracting two smaller triangles form a larger triangle as follows:

$$\text{Rectangle } BEPH = \Delta ABC - \Delta AHP - \Delta PEC$$
$$\text{Rectangle } DFPG = \Delta ADC - \Delta AGP - \Delta PFC$$

Since the corresponding pairs of triangles are congruent, and therefore equal in area, the two rectangles have the same area.

- The six triangles mentioned above are all similar. Focusing on triangles *AGP* and *PFC*, we have a pair of equal ratios leading to a pair of equal products that correspond to the areas of the two rectangles:

$$\frac{AG}{PF} = \frac{GP}{FC} \quad \Rightarrow \quad AG.FC = PF.GP$$

Since *AG* = *HP* and *FC* = *PE*, the product *AG.FC* is the area of rectangle *BEPH* and that has been shown above to be equal to the product *PF.GP*, the area of the rectangle *DFPG*.

Using pairs of letters to denote lengths of sides can make the algebraic steps of geometrical arguments look unnecessarily daunting. In this case it looks much simpler if the lengths *AG*, *PF*, *GP* and *FC* are denoted on the diagram by single letter variables *a*, *b*, *c* and *d*, so that the argument can be presented as:

$$\frac{a}{b} = \frac{c}{d} \quad \Rightarrow \quad ad = bc$$

Alternatively the argument can be given a trigonometrical form by using the tangent to determine equal ratios. Denoting the equal angles *APG* and *PCF* by θ, that gives:

$$\tan \theta = \frac{a}{c} = \frac{b}{d} \quad \Rightarrow \quad ad = bc$$

- An alternative trigonometrical argument uses the same pair of similar triangles as above. With the angles *APG* and *PCF* denoted by θ, as above, and letting the lengths *AP* and *PC* be *p* and *q*, we have:

Sides of rectangle *BEPH*: $p \sin \theta$ and $q \cos \theta$

Sides of rectangle *DFPG*: $q \sin \theta$ and $p \cos \theta$

It follows then that the area of both rectangles is given by the same expression $pq \sin \theta \cos \theta$

These varied ways of approaching the same problem draw on different geometrical ideas, together with some algebra and trigonometry, and provide a good example of the rich range of possibilities that arise with even a simple problem. Specifying the topics and ideas of a curriculum is only part of ensuring that students have a fruitful encounter with geometry. The type of problems to which the ideas are applied and the spirit and style in which they are approached are also a crucial element.

TEACHING AND LEARNING GEOMETRY

Many examples in school geometry involve calculating angles. These are a valuable exercise in mathematical thinking because their solution requires a knowledge of the properties of the figures involved together with an ability to find and communicate a chain of reasoning that takes you from what you know to what you are asked to find. Figure 1.7 shows two regular polygons, a hexagon and an octagon, which share an edge. The problem, which appeared in an examination paper for 16 year old students, is to determine the angle between the two polygons as shown in the left hand diagram. The question could be posed as 'find the angle' or

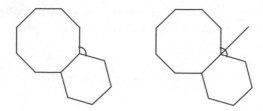

Figure 1.7 *What is the angle between the hexagon and the octagon?*

alternatively as 'show that the angle is 105°'. The latter has the advantage that the focus of the student's response has to be on the explanation rather than the numerical result.

There are two obvious strategies for solving the problem. One is to subtract the respective interior angles from 360°: 360° − (120° + 135°) = 105°. Another method, suggested by the right-hand diagram, is to add the two exterior angles to give the required angle directly: 60° + 45° = 105°.

The essence of the problem for the student lies in realizing that either the interior or the exterior angles of the two polygons have to be found. The problem for the teacher is to help a student who lacks a way forward to think what is required and then to find ways of calculating the necessary angles. There are two questions to ask: 'What do you need to find?' and then 'What do you know about finding the angles of polygons?' That involves remembering, or reinventing, the usual methods for finding such angles, which are discussed in detail in Chapter 4. Another approach to the problem of helping the student to see a strategy, assuming an earlier familiarity with the software, would be to ask: 'How could you draw this diagram with LOGO?' That would focus attention on the exterior angle property and shows how initial exploration of geometrical ideas with computer software can be drawn upon at a later stage to help students solve problems. It is not necessary to actually use the software to create a diagram, but thinking about how it could be done with LOGO provides one possible key to a solution.

To learn geometry successfully requires a knowledge of facts, an ability to reason and a less definable ability of seeing the essential features of a configuration that provide clues to solving a problem or proving a theorem. Skemp (1976) identified two broad types of understanding: instrumental and relational. Instrumental understanding is knowing how to carry out procedures, whereas relational understanding involves knowing why a procedure works as well as how to carry it out. The report of the RAND Mathematics Study Panel in the United States, RAND (2003), speaks of 'mathematical proficiency' as that which is needed in order to be competent in mathematics. The first two of five strands of this proficiency are 'procedural fluency' and 'conceptual understanding' which are closely allied to Skemp's two types of understanding, but in addition 'strategic competence' and 'adaptive reasoning' are identified. These embrace the ability to reason and how to search for ways of approaching problems. The fifth strand is to have a 'productive disposition' which is concerned with motivation, which comes through seeing mathematics as a worthwhile study, confidence in one's ability to make sense of the subject and a willingness to be persistent.

It is, of course, relatively easy to state what is required to learn geometry successfully, but far less clear how this is to be put into practice when a teacher is faced with a class of students. Perhaps there are some clues in the notion of mathematical proficiency if we take the five elements in reverse order by recognizing first that little is achieved if students do not have a productive disposition towards geometry and that requires careful thought about presenting geometry in ways which engage students' attention. Strategic competence and adaptive reasoning cannot be developed independently of conceptual understanding and procedural fluency, but it seems to be a common assumption that these should precede rather than be developed alongside the all-important thinking skills. In fact, as the RAND study RAND (2003) suggests, all the strands need to be intertwined, mutually reinforcing each other:

> Because the five strands are interdependent, the question is not which ones are most critical but rather when and how they are interactively engaged. The core issue is one of balance and completeness, which suggests that school mathematics requires approaches that address all of the strands.

This description of mathematical proficiency can usefully be coupled with observations of good mathematics teaching in countries, like Hungary and Japan, which come out well in international comparisons. Andrews and Sinkinson (2000) have listed some of the characteristics of successful mathematics teaching in such countries and, in particular note that:

Mathematics is presented as a problem-solving activity.

Relatively few problems are completed each lesson.

They characterize the problems that are used as ones that are chosen 'to exemplify generality', 'to generate discussion, proof and justification' and 'to help learners make links between topics'. One of the secrets of success would seem to lie in choosing good problems which offer some intrinsic motivation and using them as the focus for lessons where understanding, fluency and thinking skills can be developed together. Geometry is particularly rich in good problems at all levels as I hope the few examples in this chapter have demonstrated. The purpose of this book is to look at different aspects of geometry, always with problems at the centre, but making constant reference to the essential factual knowledge, conceptual understanding and thinking skills and strategies that are required to develop a good mathematician's 'habits of mind'.

Chapter 2

Learning Geometry

THE INFLUENCE OF EUCLID

Until the early years of the twentieth century in the United Kingdom, geometry only featured as part of the school curriculum for the small minority, largely male, who had the good fortune to be able to continue with their education beyond an elementary level. The geometry curriculum was determined exclusively by Euclid's *Elements* which was commonly seen as a text to be learnt by rote, so that the theorems and their proofs could be produced verbatim in the order and the form prescribed by the book. This inevitably led to failure on the part of many with success only for those few students who were able to appreciate the purpose and meaning of Euclid's work in spite of such a narrow approach to learning. Even the talented minority who were successful within these constraints acquired a very restricted view of geometry. Students had little opportunity to exercise their creative talents through solving problems or relating the ideas to wider perspectives involving a wider range of mathematical techniques, particularly algebraic methods, or relating the ideas to applications drawn from the world outside mathematics.

Concern among teachers about the effects of this rigid adherence to Euclid on the teaching of geometry led to the founding of the Association for the Improvement of Geometrical Teaching in 1871 whose name was later changed to become the Mathematical Association in 1897, as interests extended beyond geometry. Little progress could be made until the entry requirements of the universities of Oxford and Cambridge, and bodies such as the civil service and the army, were relaxed so that a verbatim knowledge of Euclid ceased to be expected. The later years of the nineteenth century saw a mounting campaign to encourage a more practical introduction to geometry in schools and a less rigid adherence to the precise form and the prescribed order of the proofs in Euclid. These developments are described in detail in Price (1994) and Howson (1973, 1982). Two names that are particularly associated with this pressure for reform are Professor John Perry (1850–1920) and Charles Godfrey (1873–1924), a public school master. They came from two very different perspectives to become major influences on the way in which school geometry developed over the fifty years or so that followed the relaxation by the universities in 1903 of the requirement to adhere rigidly to Euclid. Perry advocated a much more practically based school geometry course with far less emphasis on the deductive proofs of Euclid whereas Godfrey advocated a practical stage as a prelude to developing many of the theorems that feature in Euclid, but allowing a variety of methods of proof and giving greater emphasis to 'riders' – problems linked to the theorems.

The first few years of the new century produced a flurry of activity with many new geometry textbooks being published of which *Elementary Geometry* by Godfrey and Siddons (1903) was perhaps the most significant, remaining in print for many years and offering a much richer view of geometry than that presented by Euclid. The deductive aspects followed on from more experimental activities involving measuring, cutting and folding and informal demonstrations of results which are considered as well as formal proofs.

The proposal that deductive geometry should be preceded by informal experimental work appears in the first report on geometry teaching produced by the Mathematical Association (1923) which introduced the idea that there should be three stages in learning geometry: Stages A, B and C. The idea of three stages were further developed in the Association's second report, Mathematical Association (1938), and this was a major influence on geometry teaching and textbook writers until at least the 1960s, when other more radical changes were proposed and began to be adopted.

Stage A is an experimental stage where students engage in a range of practical work involving measurement, cutting and folding to investigate geometrical properties and begin to acquire an intuitive feel for geometrical objects and relationships. For example, the fact that the angle sum of a triangle is 180° is established experimentally by measuring the angles with a protractor or by tearing the three corners from a paper triangle and placing them together to see that the three angles appear to lie on a straight line. This contrasts with earlier teaching based on Euclid where measurement was not used and students did not learn to use a protractor or compasses in their geometry lessons. The rationale for stressing the importance of Stage A approaches is summed up in the second geometry report, Mathematical Association (1938), in a message which is still valid today:

> One of the great mistakes in the teaching of mathematics, and one to which we are always liable, is that of presenting abstractions familiar to ourselves to minds unprepared for them.

Stage B is a deductive stage where ideas are defined precisely and results are presented as theorems and proved in a formal way. However, unlike the presentation of geometry based rigidly on Euclid, there is flexibility about the precise order in which theorems are presented and about the mathematical tools that can be used in proofs, in particular allowing the use of algebra. The move to Stage B did not preclude a return to a Stage A approach initially when a new topic such as the circle theorems was encountered. The final Stage C is a systematizing stage in which a more global view of the subject is taken bringing out the links between theorems, considering a logical order of presentation of results and clarifying initial assumptions by making reference to axioms. This last stage always had a rather shadowy existence and was, and is, perhaps only relevant to a small minority of students.

The early years of the twentieth century also saw many other changes in school mathematics together with an increase in the proportion of both boys and girls having access to secondary education through increased state provision of grammar schools. The introduction of graphs and trigonometry into school mathematics were two curriculum changes at this time that were significant in providing additional tools that could be applied to geometrical proofs and problems. Familiarity with graphs led to coordinate geometry, particularly linked to a study of the conic sections, becoming a common feature of mathematics courses in the final years of secondary education.

CURRICULUM CHANGE FROM THE 1960s

The 1960s were characterized by a period of intense curricular development in many countries: an informative account will be found in Cooper (1985) of some aspects of these changes in England. Although this movement for change was international, the form it took varied between different countries. It was variously referred to as 'new' or 'modern' mathematics and influenced both the content of the curriculum and the way it was taught. The changes to teaching methods that were encouraged were in the direction of more experimental and exploratory approaches building to some extent on the Stage A approach to geometry that had its origins about fifty years before. Content changes included the introduction of sets and matrices, probability and statistics, some reference to computers, and transformation geometry as an alternative to the traditional deductive geometry with its strong Euclidean influence. The emphasis on sets was controversial at the time and was given much greater emphasis in the United States than in the United Kingdom, but has had little long-term effect on the curriculum. Probability and statistics have become a ubiquitous, although sometimes controversial, feature of school mathematics such that it seems surprising today that they were only introduced into the curriculum fifty years ago. Early attempts to use computers in school mathematics were very limited and it was not until the 1990s that their use began to become widespread, although there is considerable variation both across schools and between different countries. The impact of computers in mathematics teaching is very varied and there is limited consensus about the precise role they should play, although there is widespread recognition of the potential value of software such as LOGO and dynamic geometry.

The changes to the geometry curriculum in the United Kingdom that arose in the 1960s have been very significant, particularly through the influence of the School Mathematics Project (SMP) founded in 1961. The publication of the first book in the project's main school course, SMP (1965), and the subsequent books in the series provided a substantial contrast to the then current mathematics textbooks, where geometry was very much in the style of Godfrey and Siddons' *Elementary Geometry* with Stage A activities leading to a formal deductive approach to a range of standard theorems and their application to 'riders'. SMP retained and developed Stage A approaches to the basic properties of geometrical figures, but included the informal study of transformations such as reflection, rotation, translation and enlargement. Standard results such as the angle sum of a triangle, the angle properties of polygons and the theorem of Pythagoras all featured in the course, but with much less emphasis on the formal theorem followed by proof approach hallowed by Euclid. Congruent triangles were barely mentioned, but similarity was given an important place using the idea of a scale factor and the transformation of enlargement initially rather than the conceptually harder idea of equal ratios.

By the 1980s a widespread common curriculum had emerged where theorems and their proofs in the style of Euclid had very little place and the important Cockcroft report of 1982 on school mathematics could say: 'the differences between "modern" and "traditional" mathematics have become less marked', Cockcroft (1982). It is perhaps significant of thinking at that time that the words 'geometry' and 'proof' do not feature in the index of the report! Although elements of a transformation approach to geometry did feature in the curriculum elsewhere in the world, countries such as the United States, France and Japan have retained a geometry curriculum which is much more in the spirit of Euclid than has been the case in the United Kingdom. However, recent thinking, as reflected in the most recent version of the National Curriculum for England, DfEE/QCA (1999), and in the documents of the Key Stage 3 National Strategy, DfEE (2001), is moving the English curriculum firmly back in the direction of a more deductive approach to geometry. In the United States, where school geometry was not so strongly influenced by the changes of the 1960s and has retained a traditional Euclidean form, the standards produced by the National Council of Teachers of Mathematics, NCTM (1989, 2000b), seem to be moving curricular thinking in directions which give more emphasis to informal approaches and greater links between areas of mathematics, while not losing the essential deductive element.

STAGES IN LEARNING GEOMETRY

The three-stage model for teaching geometry from the geometry reports of the Mathematical Association (1923, 1938) can be seen as a precursor to more sophisticated models of how students learn geometry developed in more recent times. Inhelder and Piaget (1958) describes the shift in students' thinking from concrete operations to formal operations whereby the focus moves from the consideration of particular examples to the ability to reason in more general and abstract terms. This should not be interpreted to mean that a transition from concrete to formal operations takes place at a particular time or that the transition is in any way a smooth one. Neither should it be assumed that the move cannot be influenced by the nature of the classroom tasks that the teacher sets up. Indeed the evidence from the work on cognitive acceleration described in Adey and Shayer (1994), which is linked to Piaget's ideas, suggests that students' ability to think at higher levels can be strongly influenced by classroom tasks specifically structured to develop their general thinking skills.

More specific to geometry, the five levels proposed by van Hiele (1986) are a significant attempt to describe a hierarchy of stages through which students go in learning geometry and as such provide a guide to how a geometry course might be structured. Van Hiele (1986) proposed five levels as follows:

- Level 1. Shapes are recognized as 'wholes' without any strong perception or recognition of their parts or properties. Thus a young child will recognize a circle or a square without any strong sense of their particular features or any ability to distinguish them from ellipses or rectangles that do not diverge too much from the special cases.
- Level 2. At this stage students become aware of the individual properties of shapes and are able to describe them in terms of those properties. Thus a square is seen as having four equal sides and right angles at each of its corners and, if attention is drawn to them, there is recognition of the equal diagonals intersecting at right angles. However, the relationship of the square to the rhombus or rectangle will not be seen or accepted readily.
- Level 3. Here there is an increasing appreciation of the definitions of shapes and their relationship to other shapes. The distinction between a definition and a listing of properties is becoming clear and a sense of the relationship between shapes is evident so that the student recognizes, for instance, that the square is a special case of either the rhombus or rectangle and that these in turn are special cases of the parallelogram, as shown in Figure 2.1.
- Level 4. This is the stage at which deductive competence is established so that students can make sense of local chains of reasoning to prove geometrical results with some awareness of their initial assumptions. They are thus able to distinguish between properties that define a shape and properties that can be deduced. For example, the equality of the opposite angles of a rhombus is a property that can be derived from the fact that a rhombus is defined as a quadrilateral with four equal sides.
- Level 5. The final stage is linked to an understanding of the role of axioms in a systematic development of a geometry characterized by an interlinked system of theorems derived from a minimal set of initial assumptions.

Like all attempts to characterize learning the van Hiele levels are of necessity a very simplified version of the reality they are seeking to describe by seeming to imply a smooth progression between levels and not taking account of the varying conceptual difficulty of different ideas. In practice any learner moves backwards and forwards between different levels according to their

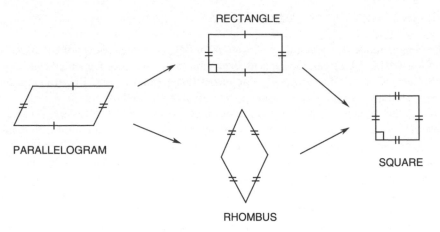

Figure 2.1 *The relationship between some quadrilaterals*

depth of knowledge of the particular ideas being considered. Thus a student who is generally quite happy operating at level 4 with familiar material may revert back to earlier levels when faced with making sense of new ideas. The same sort of thing happens whenever the solution of a problem is causing difficulty when it is frequently a good strategy to explore the ideas in an experimental manner initially reflecting the approach of a student operating at level 2.

While van Hiele's levels do provide a description of the sort of progression that a teacher may expect as students develop their geometrical understanding, they are perhaps more useful in thinking about how a curriculum should be structured than in offering advice to the teacher planning a particular lesson or dealing with a student's specific difficulties with a topic. They do not offer a model of how to develop student's thinking and understanding beyond the rather obvious fact that the ability to make sense of ideas is dependent on the extent to which particular modes of thinking have been developed at an earlier level.

SPATIAL AWARENESS AND GEOMETRICAL INTUITION

As noted in Chapter 1 one of the common aspirations of school geometry is to develop students' spatial awareness. This is perceived to be relevant to many aspects of the real world in terms of employment where, for example, builders, architects, surveyors and navigators obviously require some kind of geometrical sense. There is a similar perceived relevance to everyday tasks in the home such as constructing shelves or making curtains and making sense of maps when planning a journey or finding a place in a town. However, any link between these practical applications and what happens in the classroom is far from clear. While we may reasonably surmise that activities involving spatial skills might improve performance with such tasks, it is inevitably difficult to separate the influence of out of school learning from what happens in the classroom. Thus, for example, childhood experiences with constructional toys may be more influential than school geometry, and they are likely to contribute in some measure to success with school geometry as well.

The essence of a Stage A and B approach to geometry and of van Hiele's levels is that success in using deduction in conjunction with geometry is dependent on a variety of appropriate practical experiences giving a feel for the elements involved. Fischbein (1982), in discussing intuition in relation to proof, speaks of 'the quality of self-evidence, which is the basic characteristic of an intuition'. He contrasts the self-evident equality of vertically opposite angles with mathematical truths that are not self-evident like the theorem of Pythagoras, where the result is surprising and not at all intuitively obvious. Learning geometry involves both intuitive and analytical elements. Intuition is involved not only in seeing obvious features of geometrical figures, but also in the creative task of spotting critical hidden features of figures, making productive conjectures and identifying useful constructions when solving geometrical problems.

While analytical skills – the ability to reason – can be to some extent learnt systematically, it is much less clear how intuitive skills can be developed, although they are certainly a product of our experiences of geometrical configurations of all kinds arising in many different contexts. It is certainly clear that school geometry should aim to develop geometrical intuition by providing a rich experience through observing, handling, manipulating, linking, discussing and describing shapes as well as seeking to develop analytical skills.

MISCONCEPTIONS IN GEOMETRY

The idea of angle is a fundamental geometrical concept. Understanding angles is an essential requirement from an early stage in learning geometry. There is much evidence concerning students' misconceptions about angles and all teachers are aware of the difficulties students encounter in mastering how to measure angles with a protractor. Figure 2.2 shows an example taken from APU (1987) where a large sample of 11 year old students were asked to indicate which statement they thought was correct. The percentages show the proportion of responses for each statement. The two angles are in fact the same size, but the second most popular response suggests that many respondents were seduced by the length of the arms or the 'space' or 'distance' between the arms into deciding that one angle was larger than the other. Other evidence from the same source confirms the influence of these extraneous factors.

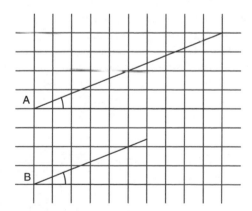

Angle A is bigger than angle B. (33%)
Angle B is bigger than Angle A. (4%)
Angle A and Angle B are the same size. (52%)
You can't tell. (4%)

Figure 2.2 *Which is the bigger angle?*

The two angles have been drawn on a square grid as a simple means of making the gradient, and hence the angle, the same for each, but with the arms approximately doubled in length in one case. Since over half the respondents made a wrong response this sophisticated way of seeing that the angles are equal clearly had no influence on many of them, although we have no evidence as to how the correct responses were derived. However, it is likely that many made their judgement on the basis of the angles looking about the same rather than through any reasoned approach. A lot of evidence suggests that many students do not fully appreciate the nature of angles as a measure of turning or rotation, something that is no doubt hindered by the frequent occurrence of angles in static diagrams rather than in contexts where a rotation can be observed. Practical approaches in the early stages of learning geometry over many years, reinforced in recent times by a variety of opportunities provided by computer images, have sought to link the idea of angle to the idea of turning, but the difficulties persist.

Returning to the example of Figure 2.2, one way to follow up such errors is to ask students to measure the pair of angles, assuming that they have learnt how to use a protractor correctly. For those who responded incorrectly to the original question the equality of the measurements produces an element of conflict, because they have to reconcile the evidence of their measurements with their incorrect intuitive sense that one angle is bigger than the other. Creating this sense of conflict between an intuitive sense and the evidence provided by measurement is one step in helping students to modify their ideas by drawing attention to the inadequacy of their current thinking. Adey and Shayer (1994) emphasize the importance of cognitive conflict as a means of helping students to develop their cognitive skills. They describe cognitive conflict as 'an event or observation which the student finds puzzling and discordant with previous experience or understanding'. Errors and misconceptions can be a valuable source of situations involving conflict between the students' perception of a situation and the accepted interpretation.

Another frequent source of difficulty is the confusion between perimeter and area and, at a later stage, between surface area and volume. At one level there may simply be a confusion of language – the meaning of the words – but there is certainly very often a deeper misconception at work which makes students think that perimeter and area are linked in a simple way so that an increase in one is thought to lead to an increase in the other. It is valuable for students to consider examples which conflict with this notion, like the various rectangles in Figure 2.3 which show that constant perimeter does not imply constant area and vice versa. However, like many misconceptions, this confusion about area and perimeter is very persistent and will not necessarily be eliminated by making reference to a single counter-example or through a single lesson task investigating the perimeter of rectangles of constant area. It requires frequent

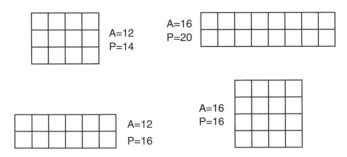

Figure 2.3 *Misconceptions about perimeter and area*

encounters through a variety of examples which draw out the conflict between faulty intuition and geometrical truths.

At a simple level conflicts may arise through misunderstanding the meaning of words. Fielker (1973) gives an interesting example based on a diagram with three parallel lines labelled *a*, *b* and *c* as in Figure 2.4. Eleven year old students happily told him that '*a* is parallel to *b*, and *b* is parallel to *c*', but when Fielker said 'then *a* is parallel to *c*', they said 'no, because *b* is in the way!' Clearly the students had a restricted view of the meaning of parallel which required the lines to be adjacent to each other. Perhaps this is induced by the usual examples that teachers draw upon, invariably using pairs of lines such as railway track or the opposite sides of rectangles. Railway track may be a deceptive example in another way because the effect of perspective makes the lines appear to meet at a distant point. Another misconception was noted by Kerslake (1979), who observed that young children were less likely to see a pair of lines as parallel if the two segments differed significantly in length. These examples make very clear that, even with a seemingly simple idea like parallel lines, surprising misconceptions can occur. Similar difficulties arise with the idea of perpendicularity, discussed by Gal and Vinner (1997). In contrast to parallel lines, if *a* is perpendicular to *b* and *b* is perpendicular to *c*, it is not true in two dimensions that *a* is perpendicular to *c*. With both these concepts students need to experience a wide variety of examples over time and teachers need to be alert to the possibility of unexpected and surprising misinterpretations.

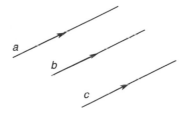

Figure 2.4 *Three parallel lines*

Many words have mathematical meanings which are different to their everyday meanings: the word 'similar' is an obvious example. A striking example concerning the word diagonal is given by Pimm (1987). A student was asked to find the number of diagonals in various polygons – two of the responses are shown in Figure 2.5. The student thinks that the rectangle has no diagonals, but that the triangle has three, so there is clearly a strange misconception at work here. Eventually light dawns and we see that the student is counting the number of sloping edges using the more everyday meaning of diagonal to describe a line that is sloping rather than horizontal and vertical.

My own favourite example of this sort of misunderstanding of mathematical words, which is

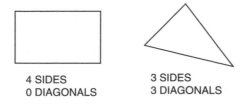

4 SIDES
0 DIAGONALS

3 SIDES
3 DIAGONALS

Figure 2.5 *A misconception about diagonals*

also referred to in Pimm (1987), arose in a lesson I was observing where the teacher had asked the twelve year old students to illustrate and name all the different types of triangles and other polygons that they could think of. One boy, acting in a supremely logical way, had decided as shown in Figure 2.6, that right should be seen in opposition to left rather than as an indication of perpendicularity.

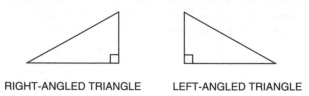

RIGHT-ANGLED TRIANGLE   LEFT-ANGLED TRIANGLE

Figure 2.6 *What does 'right'-angled mean?*

Mathematical words often acquire an erroneous 'default' meaning which excludes general cases. Figure 2.7 shows a variety of different pentagons. Typically, when the word pentagon has become familiar, it becomes attached to a regular pentagon. Moreover a request to draw a pentagon will invariably result in a regular pentagon being drawn with a horizontal edge at the base. However, pentagons do not have to be regular, their sides do not have to be of the same length, one edge does not have to be horizontal and the pentagon does not even have to be convex. The selection of pentagons illustrated in the figure all have equal edges, but only the first is regular and that has been drawn in the usual 'default' position. Examples like these are also useful in drawing attention to the meaning of 'regular' where the polygon not only has all its sides equal but also all its angles. Constructing a pentagon with five equal plastic rods freely jointed at the ends, or an equivalent construction using dynamic geometry software, is a good way of emphasizing that a regular polygon has equal angles.

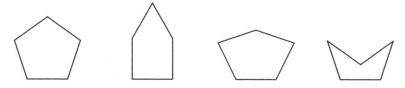

Figure 2.7 *Some pentagons with equal sides*

Difficulties often arise because assumptions are made about relationships on the basis of a particular diagram. Figure 2.8 shows two related examples. In the first case it is easy to assume that the median bisects the angle of the triangle, but that is incorrect except when the triangle is isosceles with the median positioned between the equal sides. Conversely in the second diagram it is easy to assume wrongly that an angle bisector bisects the opposite side if the triangle is not too far from being isosceles. In each of these cases investigating a few cases by drawing or using

Figure 2.8 *Misleading conclusions from inappropriate diagrams*

dynamic geometry is sufficient to highlight the error and warn of the dangers of arguing from one particular diagram which may have special features.

Figure 2.9 shows the two diagonals from one vertex of a regular pentagon, which appear to trisect the angle. Here we have a problem where intuition does lead to a correct result, but intuition is not sufficient to be sure that the result is correct. The fact that the angle is trisected can be proved readily by calculating angles in the three isosceles triangles in the figure or, interestingly, by seeing the pentagon as inscribed in a circle and recognizing that the three angles at a vertex are angles subtended by arcs of equal length.

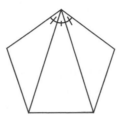

Figure 2.9 *Why is the angle in a regular polygon trisected by the diagonals?*

A further area of misconception arises through the difficulty of interpreting two-dimensional diagrams of three-dimensional objects. A simple example arises with the typical depiction of a cube shown in Figure 2.10, which can equally well be seen as a two-dimensional picture of three rhombuses forming a hexagon. It is clear that many people have considerable difficulty 'seeing' three-dimensional objects through conventional mathematical diagrams. Whether the ability to visualize three-dimensional objects from such representations can be improved by using suitable classroom tasks is an open question. However, it is certainly important for the teacher to be aware of the difficulty that many students have and to give them frequent access to actual objects and models to help their appreciation of the shapes that are being depicted and discussed.

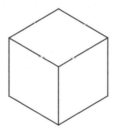

Figure 2.10 *Is it a cube or three rhombuses in a hexagon?*

Similar difficulties arise when diagrams of the nets of solids are depicted or students are asked to design such nets. Figure 2.11 shows two configurations of six squares: the first will be recognized as the conventional net for a cube, but the second is not a net for a cube because when folded up two of the squares will overlap. For many people it is not an easy matter to visualize how the net will fold up in order to determine which creates a cube and which does not. Practical experience through the use of suitably designed tasks should improve powers of visualization.

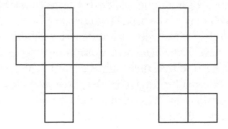

Figure 2.11 *Possible nets for a cube?*

LEARNING ABOUT PROOF

Proof in mathematics is commonly presented as a means of verifying the truth of conjectures, but it is usually something that is pursued after evidence has established that a conjecture is at least plausible, if not so convincing that the possibility of it being wrong seems very improbable. Mathematical proof involves a certainty, subject to agreement on initial premises, that does not apply to proofs in a scientific or legal context, where the argument hinges upon the evidence that is available and is always subject to revision if new evidence emerges.

For students mathematical proofs often seem to serve little purpose. In their own terms they feel that they already know that a result is true either because it is in some way self-evident, as with the equality of the base angles of an isosceles triangle, or on the basis of experimental evidence, as with measuring the angles of a number of triangles to verify that the angle sum is 180°. This comment indicates two significant areas of difficulty in motivating students to learn about proof.

The first concerns what is taken to be self-evident. Deduction has to take place from agreed assumptions which may be some formal minimal set of axioms, but, much more acceptably for beginners, starting points which are accepted as true either because they have been deduced previously or because they will be widely accepted as self-evident. School geometry should give students an understanding of the geometrical ideas and language of these starting points together with an ability to follow chains of reasoning and to develop their own deductive arguments.

One of the difficulties arising from the traditional adherence to Euclid was that a result like the equality of the base angles of an isosceles triangle was deduced rather than taken as self-evident. The proof shown in Figure 2.12 uses the three-sides case of congruence, a result which itself might also be seen as self-evident although a proof is given in Euclid. Proving

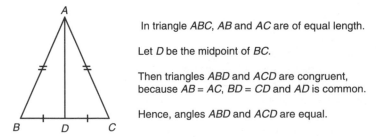

In triangle *ABC*, *AB* and *AC* are of equal length.

Let *D* be the midpoint of *BC*.

Then triangles *ABD* and *ACD* are congruent, because *AB* = *AC*, *BD* = *CD* and *AD* is common.

Hence, angles *ABD* and *ACD* are equal.

Figure 2.12 *Proving that the base angles of an isosceles triangle are equal*

such facts in a formal way is demotivating for most students because there seems little purpose in showing why something that is so obvious is true. The two examples are obvious results that should be taken as true on the basis of a combination of intuition and experiment. That does not preclude helping students see that the equal side property defines an isosceles triangle whereas the equal angle property is a derived property, but that distinction is best made by considering the information needed to construct an isosceles triangle accurately. At a later stage, it may be instructive for some students to see how congruence can be used to prove the result in the style of Figure 2.12. The congruence of the triangles also implies that the median bisects the angle at the vertex *A* and is perpendicular to the base *BC*. However, for most students such properties should be taken as self-evident features which arise from the symmetry of isosceles triangles.

The second difficulty is making the distinction between a deductive proof and acceptance of a result on the evidence of appearance or measurement, referred to as 'naïve empiricism' by Balacheff (1988). The fact that the angle sum of a triangle is 180° is not a self-evident fact, but making measurements does provide strong, although not conclusive, evidence that it is true, so that there is a more obvious place for deductive argument in such a case. However, since students will only meet such an argument after they have come to accept that the result is true, they may still fail to see purpose in a proof. Hoyles (1997) speaks of developing in students 'an inner compulsion to understand why a conjecture is true if they have first engaged in experimental activity where they have "seen" it to be true', because a proof is more than an argument to demonstrate the truth of a proposition for, as suggested by de Villiers (1998), it offers explanation and insight into the ideas involved. Moreover, the ingenuity or neatness of the argument can often be intriguing in its own right. When proofs are discussed with students we are seeking to encourage them to think as mathematicians, to extend their conceptual understanding and to respond to the insights and stimulation provided by mathematical arguments and results.

As with solving problems, appreciating and developing proofs requires more than an understanding of the geometrical ideas involved and an ability to reason. Having failed to find a proof of a proposition or to solve a geometrical problem, it is a common subsequent experience to follow somebody else's argument with no difficulty and then either to be surprised that you missed some obvious feature or to wonder how the solver came to think of their solution strategy. Students need to be equipped with a range of strategies which enable them to explore different avenues, to view geometrical figures in different ways and to make links to other ideas.

THE ROLE OF COMPUTERS

The continuing rapid development of a wide range of powerful computer hardware and software has led to a dramatic extension of ways of exploring and presenting geometry. Two broad styles can be identified and each is linked to two styles of teaching: these are indicated by the two-way table of Figure 2.13.

Computers can be used, typically in a dedicated room, with students working individually or in small groups or a single computer can be used as focus for work with a whole class. Each type of use has possibilities and limitations, both practical and pedagogical. Dedicated rooms are expensive and are commonly in high demand, but they do provide individual experience, a feature that may increasingly become more widely available in ordinary classrooms as powerful portable computers for educational use become cheaper. When an individual mathematics

	WHOLE CLASS	INDIVIDUAL OR SMALL GROUP
OPEN		
CLOSED		

Figure 2.13 *Two dimensions for classroom computer use*

classroom is equipped with a single computer with projection facilities, alone or in conjunction with an interactive whiteboard, there is abundant scope for frequent use which may often only be for short periods of time to illustrate a point quickly or to try out an idea.

The other dimension of Figure 2.13 relates to the style of use, specified in broad terms as open or closed, which refer to the nature of the tasks that students work on. Closed tasks are based on precise instructions and routine exercises whereas open tasks involve more exploratory problem-oriented activities which require initiative and creative skills. The same characterization can be applied to whole-class activity, depending on the extent to which it involves presentation and practice of skills with closed questions or more open-ended discussion drawing on students' ideas. The two categories are extremes of a spectrum, because many lessons will have elements of both. Software and accompanying resources are commonly designed with particular styles of use in mind.

Software can be placed in a number of broad categories:

- Small software is a term used to refer to items designed to develop a particular skill or to reinforce ideas about a specific process or topic. This often allows students to practise skills in interesting ways which are self-checking and may involve puzzles and games incorporating several levels of difficulty.
- Generic software can be used for a wide range of different tasks. Widely used examples are LOGO, dynamic software packages like Cabri Geometry and Geometer's Sketchpad and graph plotters, such as Omnigraph and Autograph, which, besides plotting graphs, allow transformation geometry to be explored. Increasingly these features are becoming available on graphical calculators, although the small screen and poor resolution are much less clear and attractive than a computer screen.
- Teaching and resource packages. Typically these are available on DVD or CD ROM and vary from material presented like a textbook with varying degrees of interactivity to collections of resources of a more imaginative and flexible nature.

In addition the internet is a vast, varied and continually growing source of information and ideas, which includes examples of all the previous types of resources.

As an example of small software, Figure 2.14 shows a sample screen taken from one of the components of a software package on symmetry and transformations produced by SMILE. This displays half of a figure with a line of symmetry on a square grid on the screen. Students are asked to complete the picture by inserting line segments in appropriate places. Other items in the same package involve inserting lines of symmetry and finding centres of rotation, with each offering tasks at different levels of difficulty. Details of software produced by SMILE will be found at www.smilemathematics.co.uk.

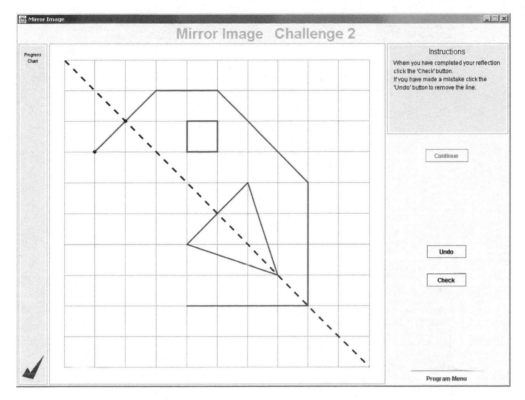

Figure 2.14 *Symmetry and transformations. a SMILE program*

MSW LOGO, a version of the programming language LOGO, is available free from www.softronix.com. The software provides a simple and versatile means of enabling students to draw geometrical figures using a small, but powerful set of commands that are very easy to learn. The example in Figure 2.15 shows an eighteen-pointed star created by drawing a segment 200 units in length, turning through an exterior angle of 140° and then repeating those two commands 18 times to give two lines at each of the vertices. This is an extension of one of the simplest uses of LOGO to explore the properties of regular polygons, a topic that is discussed in detail in Chapter 4.

Dynamic geometry packages allow geometrical figures to be drawn on the screen and then modified by dragging points in the figure. Figure 2.16 shows a Cabri Geometry screen where the three medians of a triangle have been constructed. If any of the vertices of the triangle are dragged the triangle changes its shape, but the medians are still seen to intersect in a common point. As shown the software can also display lengths of segments so that the division of each median in the ratio 2:1 can be demonstrated as a prelude to proving the result, which is discussed in Chapter 7. Cabri Geometry is published by Texas Instruments and further details will be found at education.ti.com. The software originated at the University of Grenoble in France and some interactive examples will be found at www-cabri.imag.fr. The Geometer's Sketchpad, published by Key Curriculum Press, is another widely used dynamic geometry package. Further details can be found at www.keypress.com/sketchpad.

As well as their main function of plotting graphs, most graph plotters have a facility for plotting shapes and applying standard transformations to them. Figure 2.17 shows a screen

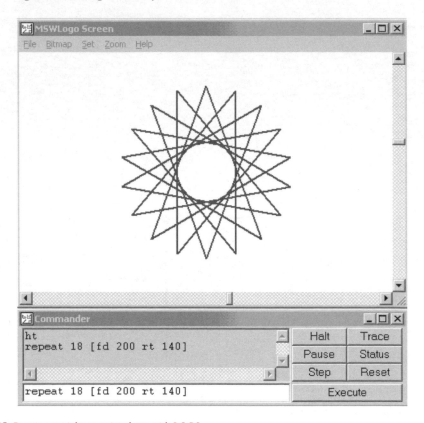

Figure 2.15 *Drawing an eighteen-pointed star with LOGO*

produced using Autograph. The triangle in the first quadrant has been reflected in the *y* axis and then the image has been reflected in the line *y* = *x*. It is easy to see that the pair of reflections is equivalent to a single rotation of 90° clockwise about the origin. Carrying out the two transformations in the reverse order does not produce the same result. The single equivalent transformation is a 90° rotation about the origin as before, but it is anti-clockwise. The same result as previously can be obtained by reflecting the triangle in the first quadrant in the line *y* = *x* first and then by reflecting the image in the *x* axis rather than the *y* axis.

Further details of the graph plotting software, Autograph, will be found at www.autograph-maths.com. Omnigraph, published by Spa Software, is another widely used graph plotter and details of that will be found at www.spasoft.co.uk.

As an example of the vast range of material available on the internet Figure 2.18 shows an interactive geometry page taken from the website www.mathsnet.net. A point, *A*, with its mirror image, *B*, in a line are displayed together with a point, *X*, which can be moved on the line. The points *A* and *B* can also be moved and the distances *AX* and *XB* are displayed. The student is asked to choose between three assertions about the situation, the correct one stating that *X* moves along the perpendicular bisector of *AB*. This website presents other geometrical situations in a similar style with a range of other mathematical resources. It is but one example of this ever-growing source of ideas and resources for learning mathematics readily accessible to both teachers and students. The author's website at ces.hull.ac.uk/people/DougFrench includes classroom resources and links to other sites of interest.

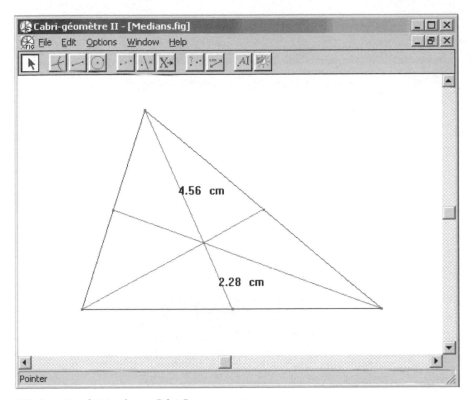

Figure 2.16 *Properties of a triangle on a Cabri Geometry screen*

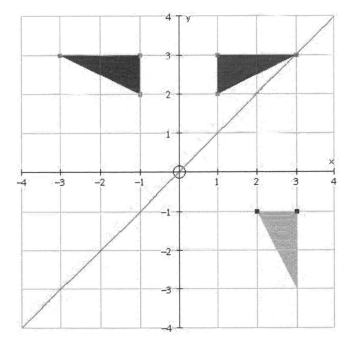

Figure 2.17 *Transformations on an Autograph screen*

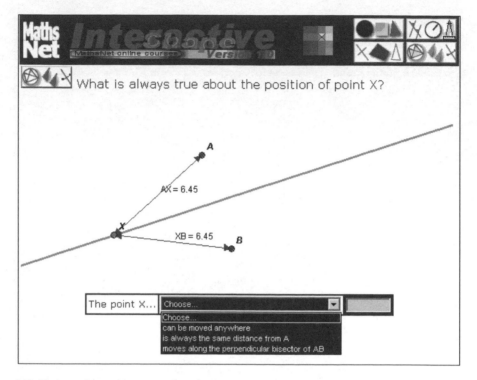

Figure 2.18 *Mathsnet: Interactive geometry from the internet*

CONCLUSION

Geometry in nineteenth-century schools, through slavish adherence to Euclid, was characterized by an exclusive emphasis on deduction with little attention to providing any underlying intuitive feel for the geometrical elements involved. The first half of the twentieth century saw an increased emphasis in the United Kingdom on introductory practical experiences, but it was still the case until at least the 1960s that many students experienced geometry as a dull routine of mysterious theorem-proving and impossible problems. In the latter half of the twentieth century there has been a strong swing against the deductive side of geometry with the result that the practical and experimental aspects, and to a lesser extent algebraic approaches, have tended to become more dominant. To a varying extent the same has been true in many other countries with moves towards greater emphasis on the practical. There is widespread debate about the future of geometry and in the United Kingdom there has been a move back towards giving greater emphasis to reasoning and proof.

The use of computers is increasingly becoming a feature of geometry teaching, but there is little consensus about the precise role that they should play or their effectiveness beyond the experimental stage of learning geometry. However, there is a strong sense that they are a potentially valuable resource that can significantly enhance students' motivation and develop understanding when used thoughtfully.

Success in learning and doing geometry requires a blend of intuition and deduction. Intuition is founded on a wide range of experience of geometric figures and their properties developed both by practical activities and by discussion of their features. The art of deduction is learnt by seeing it in action through a wide variety of examples presented by teacher and text, accompanied by commentary and discussion of what is being stated and why. Alongside this students need abundant opportunities to develop their own arguments by working on tasks tackled individually or in collaboration with peers with guidance from sympathetic teachers.

Teachers need to be clear about the respective roles of experiment and deduction, to be aware of the many sources of conceptual difficulty and to be alert to issues of misunderstanding linked to the use of technical language. Links between exploratory activities and deductive approaches should be strong so that each reinforces the other. Helping students to see the richness of possibilities in a geometrical figure and providing them with ways of thinking about novel situations requires more than practice in solving routine problems or involvement in unregulated investigation. The rest of this book looks at many of the key aspects of school geometry and offers advice to the teacher about appropriate introductory tasks, common sources of difficulty and ways of extending students' ability to solve problems and generate proofs.

Chapter 3

Beginnings: Experimental Geometry

EXPERIMENTAL GEOMETRY

Students' early encounters with geometry will be linked with van Hiele's early stages of visualization and the beginnings of analysis and deduction through examining the properties of shapes and beginning to classify them. Up to about the age of 11, shape recognition and acquiring vocabulary, both the names for shapes and words used in describing their properties, position and movement together with learning to measure length and angle will be dominant activities. As they engage in exploring shapes in a variety of ways, besides learning appropriate language and skills they will also be enhancing their spatial sense and laying the foundations for a more analytical, deductive approach to geometry.

Measurement plays an important part in experimenting with geometry: length measurement is developed first before moving on to the conceptually harder ideas of angle, area and volume. It is a simple matter to compare two lengths by placing them alongside each other without reference to a ruler: comparison comes before measurement. The same applies to angles: two angles in a figure can be compared by superimposing them and that should precede making measurements with a protractor. Comparisons of areas and volumes can be made at a simple level by using plane figures made with squares and solids made with cubes. Making comparisons by fitting together or superimposing shapes is a step towards reasoning and deducing general results, whereas measuring, while of obvious immense practical importance, focuses attention on particular cases rather than encouraging a search for generality.

This preliminary work requires a wide range of experimental activities involving drawing, looking at diagrams and pictures, cutting out, folding and fitting together. Card or plastic polygons of all kinds are particularly valuable: the Mathematical Activity Tiles (MATs), produced by the Association of Teachers of Mathematics (see www.atm.org.uk) and described in Pinel (1993), are a very useful and attractive tool for exploring the properties of shapes. Plastic cubes that can be linked together are a useful resource for investigating three-dimensional objects. Computer software such as SMILE, referred to in Chapter 2, which enables shapes to be moved and compared on screen, provide another format for developing awareness of shapes.

Most mathematical activity brings together many different ideas simultaneously so that tasks and problems will often not be purely geometrical, but involve other ideas such as counting, calculation and, at a later stage, algebra. Absorbing this richness and making links between different ideas is vital if students are to progress with mathematics in general and geometry in particular. While it is important to focus narrowly on specific ideas from time to time, ideas make much better sense when they are interrelated and used in a variety of interesting contexts. In the sections that follow I look at various activities under the general headings of shape recognition, symmetry, angles, accurate drawing, tessellations and transformations, and illustrate how each provides opportunities to learn important words, to develop key ideas and to take steps towards being able to reason and explain rather than guess and assert.

RECOGNIZING SHAPES

Figure 3.1 shows a square in two different orientations. It is not uncommon to find that young students recognize the left-hand diagram as a square, but not the second, which they will often suggest is a diamond. This is shown in the following piece of dialogue which is not untypical of the sort of discussion that can take place between teacher and student.

T: What is this shape?
    [Shows a square with an edge placed horizontally]
A: A square.
T: If you turn it like this, what is it?
    [Shows the same square turned through 45° so that it stands on one vertex.]
A: A diamond.
T: But you said it was a square before.
A: Now it is a diamond.

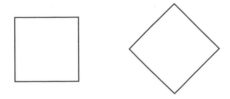

Figure 3.1 *A square or a diamond?*

Quite apart from the use of the word diamond instead of rhombus which is excusable at this level, there is a very real difficulty in not accepting that a physical square is still a square regardless of its orientation. The default image of a square has an edge placed horizontally and that image is held so strongly that squares are not necessarily recognized when placed in a different orientation. This is no doubt compounded by the fact that in this case the shape in the second position is like a diamond in its default position and by the misconception that a shape cannot be two things at once – both a diamond and a square. Similar difficulties arise when, for instance, it is suggested that a square is special case of a rectangle or that a rectangle is a special case of a parallelogram.

These difficulties can be overcome as students acquire greater familiarity with shapes through having opportunities to talk about their properties. They are helped to use appropriate vocabulary and to see the links between shapes by classifying them according to their properties. Merely naming examples and providing simple definitions is not sufficient. Handling actual shapes and manipulating computer images accompanied by thoughtful discussion is needed to build understanding and reduce confusion. As their thinking develops they can then begin to appreciate that a definition is a statement of the minimum requirements for a shape, and that other properties can be derived from it.

A rich task involving triangles, illustrated by Figure 3.2, is to ask students to create triangles by joining points on a 3 by 3 square grid either on a pinboard (or geoboard) or directly on paper with a square grid. The initial task, which I first encountered in SMP (1968), is to see how many different triangles can be found. Figure 3.2 shows six different triangles: students need to be challenged to see if they can find all the different triangles (there are more than the six shown). That may result in some debate about what is meant by the word 'different'. Students

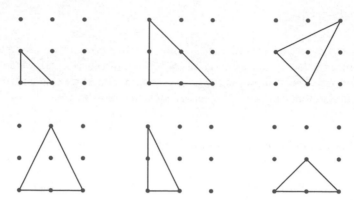

Figure 3.2 *Triangles on a 3 by 3 pinboard*

may suggest that the same triangle in different orientations is different, the same issue as discussed above with squares. Being sure that all the possibilities have been identified and that the same triangle has not been repeated in a different orientation is a challenging task.

The set of triangles provides opportunities to identify isosceles triangles and right-angled triangles and to realize that a triangle may be both isosceles and right-angled. Students will often suggest that the triangle at bottom left is equilateral: that gives an opportunity to discuss why that is not so and to help them to see that they can be sure without making any measurements.

The second task associated with triangles on a pinboard is to determine in how many positions each triangle can be placed. This is a counting exercise which requires a systematic approach, but it also involves geometrical skills related to transformations. Reflection, rotation and translation can be invoked as a way of describing the relative positions taken up by a particular triangle. For example, the small triangle at top left can be arranged in four different ways in each square of the grid making 16 possible positions in total.

The pinboard task has all sorts of possible extensions: the same question can be asked about quadrilaterals or other polygons and a square grid of larger size or an isometric grid offer further possibilities.

Another task is to give students a pair of identical triangles and ask them to find and record as many shapes as possible where the pair are placed edge to edge. They are then asked to describe the quadrilaterals that they have created. Figure 3.3 illustrates the six possibilities with a general triangle. For each common edge there are two possibilities which arise by reflecting in the edge or by making a half turn about the midpoint of the edge. The first gives a kite and the second a parallelogram. Since a triangle has three edges and there are two possible quadrilaterals for each that gives a total of six configurations.

Other possibilities arise by using triangles with special features – isosceles, equilateral, right-angled and obtuse-angled. Each of these gives rise to further points for discussion. Allowing the two triangles to overlap produces a very different set of examples to consider.

SYMMETRY

The diagrams of Figure 3.4 have each been created by placing four small right-angled isosceles triangles on a 3 by 3 grid. There are many other possible arrangements which students can be

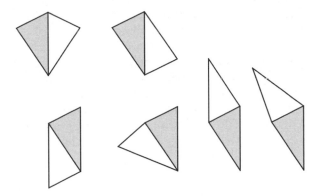

Figure 3.3 *Shapes with a pair of triangles*

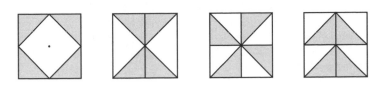

Figure 3.4 *Observing line symmetry*

asked to suggest. Diagrams like these can be used to improve students' ability to describe and to form mental images of shapes and to decide how many lines of symmetry there are. The dialogue below, referring to the left-hand diagram, suggests some points for students to consider:

T: Tell me about this shape.
A: It's a small square in a bigger square.
B: There are four triangles at the corners.
T: What can you say about the triangles?
C: They are all the same size.
D: They have right angles.
T: Anything else?
E: They are isosceles triangles.
T: How much of the diagram is shaded?
F: Half of it.
T: How do you know?
G: Because four of the triangles will fit in the square in the middle.
T: Is there a line of symmetry?
H: Yes, down the middle – straight up and down.
I: And going across from side to side, so there are 2.
T: Any other ideas?
J: You could go from corner to corner.
K: And the other corners. So there are four lines of symmetry.

The third diagram does not have a line of symmetry, something which is not necessarily obvious to students. They need to experiment with an arrangement like this to really convince themselves before the idea of rotational symmetry is introduced in an informal way. Of course, it is important to realize that some arrangements will display no symmetry at all and that varying the colours of the components of designs like these may alter the symmetry.

Similar discussions can take place with other arrangements and students can be asked to find their own, possibly designed to fulfil particular conditions. For example, they could be asked to find a configuration which just has a horizontal line of symmetry or one that has no symmetry at all, neither line symmetry nor rotational symmetry.

Folding and cutting paper are very useful ways of examining symmetry by providing opportunities to ask students to predict what will happen by visualizing a mental image and examining the properties it has. The left-hand diagram is a square of paper folded in half. The right-hand edge in the diagram is the fold and a triangle has been cut out. Students are asked to predict the form that the hole takes when the paper is opened out.

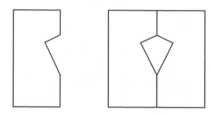

Figure 3.5 *Symmetry by paper folding*

T: I have folded this piece of paper and cut out a triangle on the fold. What shape will the hole be when I open it out?
A: It will have four sides.
T: How do you know that?
B: Because the two sides you have cut are on both sides of the paper.
T: What do you call the shape you get?
C: A square.
D: No the sides are not the same. It's a rectangle.
T: Does anybody disagree with that?
E: The top two sides are short and the bottom two are longer, so it can't be a rectangle.
F: It's a kite.
T: Is that right?
    [Opens out the folded paper to reveal the kite as in the right-hand diagram.]

Again this offers a rich variety of possibilities for experimentation and discussion. The shape that is cut out can be varied and the number of folds can be increased. Various possibilities are suggested below:

- Make two folds at right angles. What shapes do you get for the hole if you cut these shapes from the corner:

  square, rectangle, isosceles triangle, any other triangle, quadrilateral, kite

- Make three folds at 45°. What shapes do you get for the hole if you cut these shapes from the corner:

  isosceles triangle, right-angled triangle, any other triangle

Making folds at 60° or 30° and cutting out an assortment of holes creates attractive snowflake patterns like that shown in Figure 3.6. These are much appreciated by young students and make

Figure 3.6 *A snowflake pattern*

attractive classroom displays. They can lead to useful discussions about symmetry as well as developing spatial sense when attempts are made to obtain particular effects.

ANGLES

The idea of angle is a much more difficult concept than that of length. It should be related to turning from an early stage so that a right angle is related to a quarter turn and a straight angle to a half turn. These can be linked to the commands 'right turn', 'left turn' and 'about turn', but the language is a potential source of difficulty here. The link between right turns and right angles might suggest that there is such a thing as a left angle! Right and left as turns relate to turning clockwise and anti-clockwise, whereas right, as a description of an angle, is used irrespective of the direction of turning, which is often not specified or particularly significant. More facetiously perhaps there is also the contrast between a right angle and a wrong angle!

Angles based on quarter turns should be explored with young students by asking them to make bodily movements and by looking at the many examples of turning that they can see all around them – turning a door handle or a steering wheel, unscrewing the lid of a jam jar or toothpaste tube, moving the hands on a clock face and so on.

LOGO is a particularly valuable piece of software for developing this sense of angle as rotation and it can provide an introduction to degree measure well before students are ready to learn how to measure accurately with a protractor. Figure 3.7 shows the first two sides of a square produced by moving the cursor (often referred to as a 'turtle') forward 100 units, turning right through 90 degrees and then moving forward another 100 units. The commands for this – fd 100, rt 90, fd 100 – appear in the window at the bottom of the screen.

Some of the misconceptions that students have with angles have been considered in Chapter 2. One of the key ideas to emphasize is that an angle is linked to the idea of turning or rotation. The way in which students learn to use a protractor should draw on and reinforce this link to turning. Two difficulties that are encountered in using a protractor are significant here. Firstly it is necessary to align the centre and the zero line of the protractor correctly. This is not a major problem with a 360° protractor, but students often incorrectly place the bottom edge of a semi-circular protractor along an arm of the angle they are measuring. Secondly, and much more importantly, is the problem of deciding which scale of the protractor to read the number of degrees from. Textbooks and teachers vary in the advice they offer about this. Experienced users

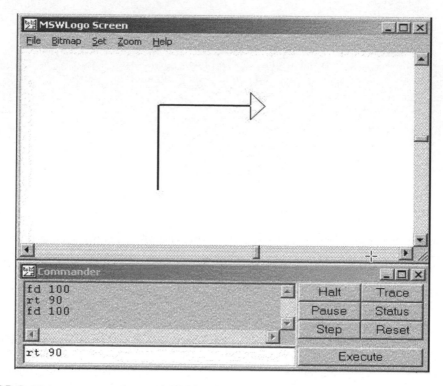

Figure 3.7 *Creating a square or a staircase with LOGO*

see which value is appropriate by unconsciously sensing whether the angle is acute or obtuse, but this may not be the best approach with novices who may confuse the two words. It reinforces the idea of angle as turning if they are encouraged to start from zero and count round to obtain the angle they require, a procedure that becomes redundant as they become confident about estimating the size of the angle as a guide.

It is not difficult to provide interesting tasks which reinforce measuring skills. After a few initial practice examples on measuring and constructing angles, these skills can be related to practical situations and used to develop further geometrical ideas. Scale drawings can be used to solve simple problems. For example, measuring the angle of elevation to find the height of a tree or using a pair of angles measured from two positions to determine the distance of a distant object. Figure 3.8 shows how angles of 38° and 47° from two points *A* and *B*, 100 metres apart on an east–west line, to a distant object, *P*, can be used to produce a scale drawing from which the distance of the object can be determined. Ambiguity about what is meant by the distance of

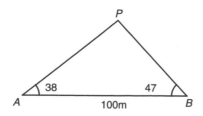

Figure 3.8 *Determining the position of distant object*

the object can be discussed – do we mean the lengths *AP* and *BP* or the perpendicular distance from *P* to *AB*?

Besides learning to measure lengths and angles, students should also learn to use a pair of compasses to mark off lengths in producing accurate drawings. They can then learn to perform constructions with straight-edge and compasses which are such an interesting feature of the study of geometry.

Figure 3.9 shows the traditional 'flower' pattern that students encounter as an early exercise in using a pair of compasses. The striking fact that it is so simple to construct six equally spaced points round a circle makes it easy to draw a regular hexagon. The two other diagrams link this to equilateral triangles. The right-hand diagram prompts interesting questions like determining what fraction the area of the hexagon in the middle is of the area of the six-pointed star or of the larger circumscribing hexagon. It also invites the idea of drawing another six-pointed star in the smaller hexagon and then another yet smaller one and so on – an introduction to the wonders of the infinitely small!

Figure 3.9 *Constructions using six points on a circle*

TESSELLATIONS AND TRANSFORMATIONS

Tessellations provide another attractive medium for developing spatial awareness and exploring the properties of shapes. Figure 3.10 shows two tessellations of triangles. Creating such patterns either with individual card or plastic triangles or by drawing is a valuable exercise in itself. Observing and describing what is seen in the tessellation extends understanding of shapes and the use of language. It is interesting to pick out other shapes in the tessellations: in both cases it is easy to identify rows of parallelograms: in one case they are all facing the same way and in the other facing in different directions on alternate rows. In the top example there are also sets of parallelograms running diagonally whereas in the second case two rows of kites running horizontally in opposite directions can be seen. Modifying the triangles so that they are equilateral, isosceles or right-angled will offer other possibilities and, of course, there are a whole range of possibilities using other polygons.

Figure 3.11 illustrates the three important transformations of reflection, rotation and translation which students should meet in an informal way at an early stage as a way of describing properties of shapes and of exploring them. The tessellations considered above have involved translations, and reflection and rotation lie at the heart of the two kinds of symmetry mentioned previously. Exploring the effect of mirrors on both everyday objects and geometrical shapes begins to develop the properties of reflection in an informal way.

Placing two mirrors at 60° and placing some objects between them emulates the effect of a kaleidoscope by creating attractive patterns like that of Figure 3.12. The figure was created with Cabri Geometry using the reflection command: it is a straightforward matter to produce

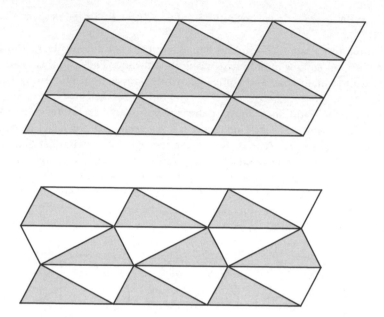

Figure 3.10 *Two tessellations of triangles*

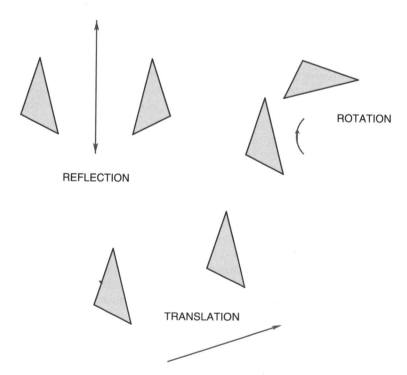

Figure 3.11 *Transformations: reflection, rotation and translation*

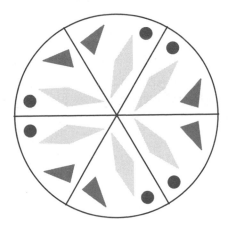

Figure 3.12 *A kaleidoscope pattern*

such patterns on a computer screen. Moreover being able to move any one of the initial motifs of the pattern by dragging them has the interesting effect of moving all its reflections, thereby drawing attention to key properties of the transformation.

CONCLUSION

The early stages of learning geometry should provide students with an ability to recognize shapes and to begin to explore their simpler properties while learning the names and other language associated with them. The visual attractiveness and the practical investigations involved make the subject very motivating. It is important though that time spent making diagrams attractive and in doing practical work does not hinder the development of language and the power to observe, describe and to classify shapes and the ability to measure and produce clear and accurate diagrams as well as sketches which identify key features of a shape.

The long-term aim is to develop students' ability to think deductively as well as to build their powers of visualization and geometrical intuition. Deductive thinking has its beginnings in expecting students to explain why something is true and to make sense of the explanations given by their peers and by their teachers. This requires discussion, as well as practical and written work, and a developing sense of the importance of explanation and justification alongside practical skills and factual knowledge.

This chapter has highlighted some important initial ideas and skills to do with recognizing shapes and some of their properties, the importance of symmetry and the related transformations of reflection and rotation. The idea of angle is a crucial one, but it is a frequent source of difficulty. The use of simple tasks with LOGO allied to actual bodily movements and learning to measure with a protractor in a way that reinforces the link with turning are both valuable aids in developing understanding.

In subsequent chapters these ideas and others will be developed further and placed in a context where reasoning becomes increasingly important. Nonetheless there is always a role for experiment in learning geometry at any level. When a new idea or a particular difficulty is encountered measurement, cutting and folding, making models and other experimentation all have their place in aiding understanding and developing geometrical intuition.

Chapter 4

Polygons: Symmetry and Angle Properties

SYMMETRY: REFLECTION AND ROTATION

Symmetry, which has been discussed in Chapter 2, is an immediate and often appealing feature of a wide range of geometrical figures and an abundance of familiar examples can be found, including trademarks, symbols and a variety of artefacts, as well as those from the natural world, such as flower heads, snowflakes and the human face. Many examples of symmetry are, of course, three-dimensional, but for the purposes of this chapter we shall confine our attention to two dimensions and in particular to polygons, because it is easier to restrict attention initially to plane shapes when developing a more formal approach to geometry.

Bilateral or line symmetry, linked closely to the idea of reflection, is a simpler and more immediately accessible property than rotational symmetry. A wide collection of examples provides a valuable source which can be drawn upon and added to in order to recognize the important properties of bilateral symmetry, as well as to recognize that there are figures which display a different kind of symmetry or no symmetry at all. The key feature of bilateral symmetry, implicit in the word bilateral meaning two-sided, is the presence of one or more lines of symmetry each dividing the figure into two identical, but reversed halves. At a simple level a line of symmetry is a line along which the shape can be folded with the two halves coinciding precisely or, alternatively, a mirror line where one half of the figure is the mirror image of the other. Bilateral symmetry is thus linked closely to reflection, a familiar idea and an important geometrical transformation.

In studying bilateral symmetry, students need to engage in extensive exploration involving folding, working with mirrors and other practical tasks, which include the key problems of determining the position and number of lines of symmetry exhibited by a variety of different figures. Figure 4.1 shows some typical classroom tasks aimed at this type of exploration.

Examples which do not display symmetry are an important source of insight: it is not always immediately obvious to students that a capital letter N or a parallelogram do not exhibit bilateral symmetry, because the intuitive feeling that they are symmetrical in some way is very strong. Attempting to fold a paper parallelogram in half in different ways as shown in Figure 4.2 is very instructive in helping students to see that there is no line of symmetry.

Typically, reflection in horizontal or vertical lines of symmetry or mirror lines is not problematic: students can see such lines in a figure and given an object or half a figure they have no difficulty drawing the reflection. Difficulties arise when the line of symmetry or mirror line is on a slant. The illustrations in Figure 4.2 showed misconceptions about the possibility of lines of symmetry for a parallelogram. There are obvious parallels with common errors that arise when 'completing the figure' tasks involve a slanting mirror line, as shown in Figure 4.3. Errors of this kind are discussed at length in Küchemann (1981).

Clearly, students need to develop an analytical approach based on an understanding of the properties of reflection to counter the tendency to make incorrect intuitive leaps in solving such

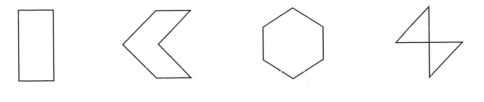

Draw all the lines of symmetry of each shape.

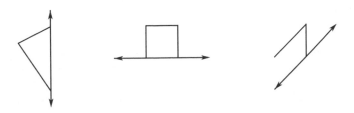

Complete the shapes with the mirror line as shown.

Figure 4.1 *Classroom tasks on symmetry*

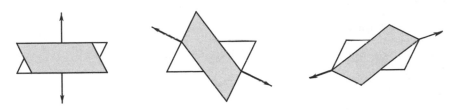

Figure 4.2 *Folding a parallelogram: no line of symmetry!*

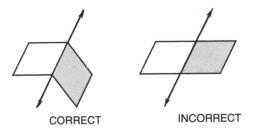

CORRECT   INCORRECT

Figure 4.3 *Reflecting in a slanting mirror line*

completion problems. The key properties are illustrated in Figure 4.4. The corresponding object and image points are on a line perpendicular to the line of symmetry or mirror line, and they are at equal distances on each side. Alternatively, we can say that the mirror line is the perpendicular bisector of the line joining object and image.

A task which draws on these ideas is to construct the image of a simple shape in a given mirror line or equivalently to complete a figure when the part on one side of a line of symmetry is given. This can be done either as a pencil and paper exercise or by using software like Cabri Geometry or Geometer's Sketchpad. Using dynamic geometry software is much more

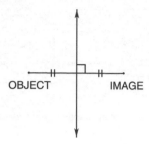

Figure 4.4 *Key properties of reflection*

impressive since both the object and the mirror line can be moved to observe the effect on the image. Determining how to construct the image of a point is a valuable exercise in geometrical thinking, providing a good focus for class or small group discussion. The following dialogue, linked to Figure 4.5, is illustrated with dynamic geometry software, but little modification is required if a chalkboard or an overhead projector is used as the display medium with students doing pencil and paper tasks with a straight-edge and compasses.

> T: How can we find the image of *P* in the mirror?
> A: It must be the same distance on the other side.
> T: How can we get it in the right place?
> B: Draw a line at right angles to the mirror.
> T: How?
> C: Draw a circle with centre at *P* and see where it crosses the mirror.
> T: Why do that?
> A: The two points *A* and *B* on the mirror are the same distance from *P*.
> T: What next?
> B: Two more circles from these points with the same radius as before.
> T: Now what?
> C: The image *Q* is where those circles cross.
> T: Why is that?
> A: Because it is the same distance from the points on the mirror.

Figure 4.5 *Constructing the image given by a reflection*

With dynamic geometry we can look at the effect of moving the point *P* and discuss why the construction ensures that *Q* is the image of *P*. The fact that the two triangles *ABP* and *ABQ* are congruent isosceles triangles, because corresponding sides are equal, explains why *P* and *Q* are mirror images. When the diagram is complete the construction lines can be hidden and then additional points and their images can be constructed so that the effect of moving a whole shape like a triangle can be demonstrated and discussed.

Rotational symmetry can be discussed in a similar way, although there is the added complication of measuring angles or constructing angles of the same magnitude. The essential feature of the discussion is to involve students in the reasoning behind the construction rather than just give them a set of instructions to produce an end result.

ANGLE PROPERTIES AND TRIANGLES

The properties of angles arising from intersecting and parallel lines and the angle sum of a triangle are examples of properties that can be established empirically by measurement before being justified by a reasoned argument. Angles at a point and angles on a straight line provide early examples where unknown angles can be found by reasoning rather than measurement. These lead readily to vertically opposite angles – angles on opposite sides of a vertex – and the angles between parallel lines. These simple general results can be established by reasoning as shown in the two examples of Figure 4.6. In both examples the algebraic argument will make better sense to most students if it is preceded by applying the same argument to a variety of numerical cases.

Vertically opposite angles

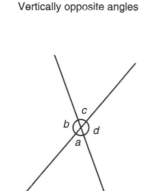

Angles between parallels

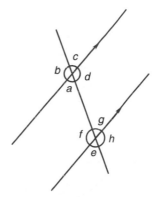

Using angles on a straight line:
$$\left. \begin{array}{l} a + b = 180 \\ b + c = 180 \end{array} \right\} \Rightarrow a = c$$

$a = e$ (corresponding angles)
$e = g$ (vertically oppposite angles)
$\Rightarrow a = g$ (alternate angles)

Figure 4.6 *Deducing simple angle properties*

Let us consider briefly some of the elementary properties of triangles. It is instructive for students to say what they think a triangle is and then to help them to refine their definition. This both refines their use of language and helps them to appreciate the need for precision. Typically a discussion might involve statements from students where the teacher responds with diagrams as shown in Figure 4.7. This leads to a progressive refining of ideas about what defines a triangle eventually leading to a statement of the form: 'a triangle is a closed shape with three straight sides'.

The name 'triangle' suggests three angles and that in turn suggest three corners or vertices. It is interesting here to note the inconsistencies in the language we customarily use for polygons with three, four and five sides. Some of the words suggested in Figure 4.8 are never used and with others usage varies between countries, as with quadrilateral in the United Kingdom and quadrangle in the United States.

It has three sides.   They have to be joined up.   They have to be straight.

Figure 4.7 *Defining a triangle*

3 sides	4 sides	5 sides
Triangle	Quadrangle	Pentangle
Trilateral	Quadrilateral	Pentalateral
Trigon	Quadragon	Pentagon

Figure 4.8 *Words for polygons with 3, 4 and 5 sides*

The three types of triangle – equilateral, isosceles and scalene – and their immediate properties present little difficulty, with the last two providing an opportunity to distinguish between acute, right- and obtuse-angled triangles. Creating tessellations of triangles of different types, referred to previously in Chapter 3, is an interesting elementary task with an attractive end result. A tessellation like Figure 4.9 can be used to draw attention to angle properties. The

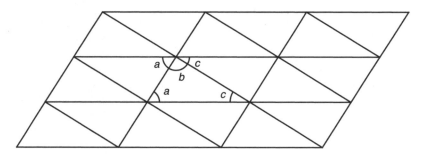

Figure 4.9 *A tessellation of triangles*

lettered angles suggest that the angle sum of a triangle is 180° and provide a step towards a proof.

Proving that the angle sum of a triangle is 180° is usually the first encounter that students have with an argument that is referred to as a proof, although it should certainly not be the first time that they have encountered a simple chain of reasoning either to establish a new fact or to solve a simple problem. They need to see that measurement can never provide an exact result: how do we know that the sum is not actually 179° or 179.873° or some similarly awkward number? In Figure 4.10 a line parallel to the base of the triangle has been constructed to pass through the top vertex. This results in two pairs of alternate angles which are equal. The angle sum property then follows directly from the fact that the angles on a straight line have a sum of

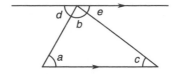

$a = d$ and $c = e$ (alternate angles)
Since $d + b + e = 180°$, then $a + b + c = 180°$.

Figure 4.10 *To prove that the angle sum of a triangle is 180°*

180°. Using dynamic geometry to produce the illustration makes it possible to vary the triangle to emphasize that the argument applies to any triangle and is not restricted to the particular triangle shown by a static diagram.

Figure 4.11 illustrates a simple, but important, property of the isosceles triangle, namely that the exterior angle opposite to the two equal angles is equal to double one of those angles. This is an immediate consequence of the angle sum of a triangle and is a special case of the fact that in any triangle the exterior angle is equal to the sum of the two opposite interior angles. Since isosceles triangles arise so frequently, particularly in conjunction with circles, it is useful to be aware of a simple result like this. It is a straightforward exercise to verify this using numerical values for the base angles of the triangle and constructing a line through B parallel to AC, as in the right-hand diagram, provides a simple proof.

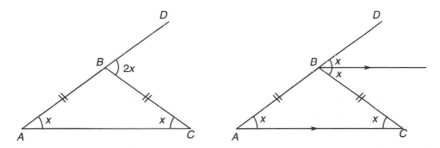

Figure 4.11 *Exterior angle of an isosceles triangle*

Figure 4.12 shows a nice problem involving isosceles triangles based on a configuration referred to in Andrews and Sinkinson (2000). The diagram consists of two line segments AF and AG with three isosceles triangles constructed between them as shown. It is instructive to construct the diagram using dynamic geometry software and to observe the effect of varying the angle between the two lines. The problem is to determine the relationship between the angle between the two initial lines and the other angles. The interesting property is that the angles indicated are multiples of the initial angle denoted by x in the diagram.

For students it is useful to start by posing the problem with a particular value for the angle BAC and to ask them to determine all the other angles in the diagram. Repeating the calculations with other values will rapidly lead students to the conjecture that angles DCE and EDF are respectively three and four times the initial angle. The conjecture can then be proved by denoting angle BAC by x and expressing the other angles in terms of x. This can be done in a straightforward way by applying the fact that the exterior angle of a triangle is equal to the sum of the two opposite interior angles to each of the triangles ABC, BCD and CDE in turn. A

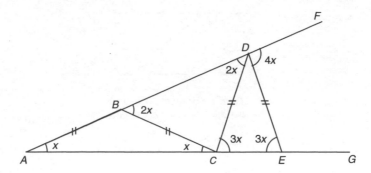

Figure 4.12 *A problem with isosceles triangles*

feature which investigation with dynamic geometry will highlight is the special case when the points *C* and *E* coincide. This happens when the angles *DCE* and *DEC* become right angles and, since they are each three times the angle *BAC*, the special case arises when the angle between the initial lines is 30°.

The angle properties associated with angles on a straight line, parallel lines and triangles, especially isosceles triangles, can be used to solve a rich variety of simple problems and to prove simple properties, often making use of algebra in a meaningful way. The use of dynamic geometry provides a useful medium for posing and exploring problems by exhibiting the generality which is lacking in a static diagram.

PROPERTIES OF QUADRILATERALS

Some quadrilaterals become very familiar to students from an early age, particularly the square, rectangle, rhombus and kite, although the second and third names may not be familiar and the recognition of the shape may depend on its orientation, as the dialogue concerning a square which becomes a diamond in Chapter 3 suggested.

A rhombus provides a good starting point for considering the properties of a quadrilateral because compared to squares and rectangles it is neither too familiar nor too special. The essential defining characteristic of a rhombus is that it is a quadrilateral – a four-sided shape – with all its sides equal. Students often have difficulty in recognizing the same shape in different orientations and in accepting that a particular shape may be a special case of a shape with more general properties. The rhombuses shown in Figure 4.13 are a good example of this, showing that a square is a special kind of rhombus with right angles and that a rhombus is a parallelogram with equal sides.

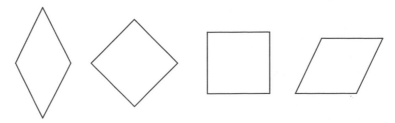

Figure 4.13 *Varying a rhombus*

A detailed look at a rhombus will identify the following properties:

- Four equal sides.
- Two lines of symmetry.
- Both pairs of opposite sides are parallel.
- Both pairs of opposite angles are equal.
- The sum of adjacent pairs of angles is 180° which follows immediately from the fact that the angle sum of any quadrilateral is 360°.
- The diagonals bisect each other at right angles, which is a consequence of the four congruent triangles created within the rhombus by the diagonals, as shown in Figure 4.14.

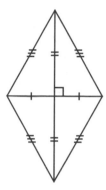

Figure 4.14 *The diagonals of a rhombus*

Students need frequent experience of shapes being constructed, varied, moved and fitted together using a variety of different media: diagrams on paper, chalkboard and overhead projector screen, card or plastic shapes that they can handle, framework models which can be varied in the same way as the rhombuses in Figure 4.13, and images created by dynamic geometry and other software. Examples need to be discussed to draw out the defining properties and the links between each particular type of quadrilateral. As a further illustration of this, Figure 4.15 brings out the contrast between the properties of the parallelogram and kite.

Parallelogram	Kite
Two opposite pairs of sides equal.	Two adjacent pairs of sides equal.
No lines of symmetry.	One line of symmetry.
Rotational symmetry of order 2.	No rotational symmetry.
Diagonals are not equal.	Diagonals are not equal.
Diagonals are not perpendicular.	Diagonals are perpendicular.
Diagonals are both bisected.	One diagonal is bisected.
Diagonal do not bisect angles.	One diagonal bisects angles.

Figure 4.15 *Contrasting the properties of a parallelogram and a kite*

Tessellations of quadrilaterals are both attractive and instructive. It is a striking fact that all quadrilaterals tessellate because they have an angle sum of 360°. Figure 4.16 shows such a tessellation: marking the angles with letters or colours makes it easier to fit a set of congruent quadrilaterals together and draws constant attention to the angle sum property. It is instructive to construct examples of tessellations of different quadrilaterals using a variety of media. A general quadrilateral is obviously not the simplest starting point! Tessellations of squares and rectangles are very simple and familiar. Tessellations of rhombuses or parallelograms demonstrate clearly that adjacent pairs of angles have a sum of 180°. Kites and arrowheads, which are concave kites, also make attractive tessellations.

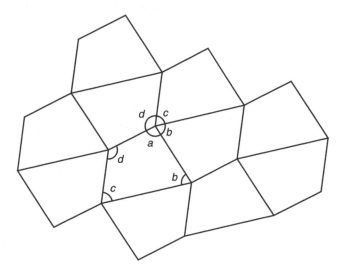

Figure 4.16 *A tessellation of quadrilaterals*

POLYGONS

Regular polygons, and perhaps some that are not regular, are encountered at an early stage because they are an obvious source of examples displaying symmetry and they have simple, but significant angle properties. The angle sum of a convex polygon with n sides can be determined by dividing the polygon into triangles either by drawing all the diagonals from one vertex, giving $n - 2$ triangles, or by joining an interior point to each vertex, giving n triangles. Each triangle contributes 180° to the angle sum of the polygon, but in the second case the additional 360° contributed by the angle at the interior point has to be subtracted. These two approaches give the two equivalent results shown in Figure 4.17.

Having determined the angle sum it is a simple matter to calculate the interior angle of a regular polygon by dividing by the number of sides to give:

$$180 - \frac{360}{n}$$

However, starting from the important exterior angle property leads directly to the same result. The sum of the exterior angles of any polygon is 360°, a fact that can be demonstrated

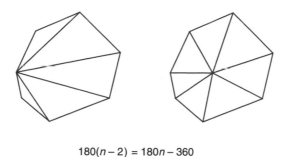

$$180(n-2) = 180n - 360$$

Figure 4.17 *The angle sum of a polygon*

dramatically by asking a student with an arm pointed forwards to walk round a polygon drawn on the floor. It is very clear that the pointing arm has turned through a full circle when it has turned through each of the exterior angles.

LOGO, which has been referred to in Chapters 2 and 3, is particularly useful for exploring the angle properties of regular polygons and provides a very good motivation for looking at the exterior angle property. Starting with the simplest case, a square is drawn by repeating four times the commands FD 100 RT 90 (or something similar depending on the version of LOGO that is used), where 100 is a convenient length for the sides and 90 is the angle in degrees. This can be written as the brief statement: REPEAT 4 [FD 100 RT 90].

Once students are happy about how to draw a square with LOGO and before making mention of the exterior angle property, it is interesting to ask them how to create an equilateral triangle. It is a common experience to find that students – even, in my experience, student teachers meeting LOGO for the first time – suggest or try: REPEAT 3 [FD 100 RT 60]. They are surprised to get a diagram like Figure 4.18 – the extended lines and the angles have been added to the three lines that would appear in the LOGO diagram. The picture creates a clear case of cognitive conflict which motivates the student to think what has gone wrong and how to rectify the situation. This is a much more effective learning experience than would be achieved by just giving a set of instructions which obtained a correct result immediately.

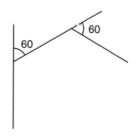

Figure 4.18 *Not an equilateral triangle!*

Figure 4.19 shows a plan for a typical lesson with a combination of class discussion and individual or small group work which uses LOGO to introduce the external angle property of polygons.

A useful exercise, which follows on from the homework task of Figure 4.19, is to draw graphs of exterior and interior angles of regular polygons against the number of sides. The two

Objectives

Exterior angle property of polygons
Relation between exterior and interior angle
Use of REPEAT command in LOGO

Starter (5 minutes)

Oral questions reviewing angle properties: on a straight line, at a point and in a triangle.

Discussion (15 minutes)

Class grouped round a single computer or a projected display.
How do we draw a square on the screen?
Do: FD 50 RT 90 FD 50 RT 90 FD 50 RT 90 FD 50 RT 90
Discuss and do: REPEAT 4 [FD 50 RT 90]
Remind about clearing screen (CS).
How do we draw an equilateral triangle?
Discuss: REPEAT 3 [FD 50 RT ??]. What angle?
If they suggest 60˚, display it! So, what should it be?
Discuss exterior angle property.
Demonstrate sum as 360˚ by walking round a polygon on the floor.

Task (20 minutes)

Students to work in pairs.
Record command(s) entered in each case.
Construct a regular pentagon (5 sides), a regular hexagon (6 sides) and a regular octagon (8 sides).
Construct three regular hexagons round a point.

Final Discussion (15 minutes)

Check on exterior angles for the three polygons.
Summary: exterior angle = 360˚ ÷ number of sides.
Oral questions: angles for decagon, nonagon and dodecagon.
Back to pentagon: what is interior angle? Other polygons?
Summarize: interior + exterior = 180˚.

Homework Task

Complete a table for regular polygons from 3 to 12 sides.
Headings: name, number of sides, exterior angle, interior angle.
Find out names of all the polygons.

Figure 4.19 *An introductory lesson on regular polygons using LOGO*

graphs shown in Figure 4.20 display a number of significant features to discuss with students. There is the obvious symmetry in the line through 90° and the reason for it. The behaviour of the angles as the number of sides increases indefinitely introduces the idea of a limiting process as a regular polygon tends towards a circle. Then there is the technical point that the graphs are not continuous: they only consist of discrete points starting with the case of $n = 3$. It is always worth pointing out that polygons with 2 sides or $3\frac{1}{2}$ sides are not possible, although it could perhaps be argued that a 2-sided polygon has an interior angle of 0° and an exterior angle of 180°!

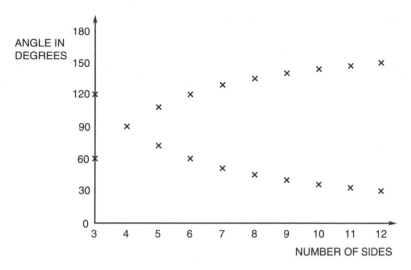

Figure 4.20 *Graphs of the interior and exterior angles of a regular polygon*

AN EXAMPLE WITH A REGULAR DODECAGON

A regular dodecagon can be dissected into 12 equilateral triangles and 12 rhombuses as shown in Figure 4.21. This dissection is referred to as Kürschak's tile in a fascinating article by Alexanderson and Seydel (1978). It has many interesting classroom possibilities, which I have expanded on in French (1998). These draw on and reinforce in an attractive way the elementary geometrical ideas relating to angles, shapes and symmetry discussed in this chapter.

All the edges of the rhombuses and triangles forming the dodecagon are clearly of the same length. Since the angles at the centre are $\frac{1}{12}$ of $360° = 30°$, each rhombus has two angles of $30°$ and two of $150°$. As an alternative approach, we can calculate the obtuse angle of the rhombus as $\frac{1}{2}(360° - 60°) = 150°$ by noting the angles at each of the interior points where an equilateral triangle and two rhombuses meet. It then follows that each interior angle of the dodecagon is

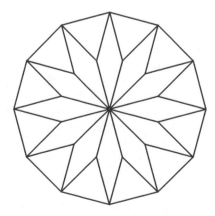

Figure 4.21 *A dissection of a regular dodecagon*

$60° + 30° + 60° = 150°$. It is interesting then to note that two consecutive edges of the dodecagon will neatly contain one of the rhombuses.

Drawing the dissection on paper or with dynamic geometry provides a variety of challenges. Using straight-edge and compasses or the equivalent it is not difficult to construct an angle of 30° by bisecting the 60° angle of an equilateral triangle. The diagram can then be built up by constructing the angles around the centre.

One of the most striking features of this dissection is that the 12 triangles and 12 rhombuses can be rearranged in a variety of ways to give dodecagons which display different symmetry properties. For example, Figure 4.21 has 12 lines of symmetry and rotational symmetry of order 12. Neither of the two diagrams of Figure 4.22 have line symmetry, but both have rotational symmetry: order 6 on the left and order 4 on the right.

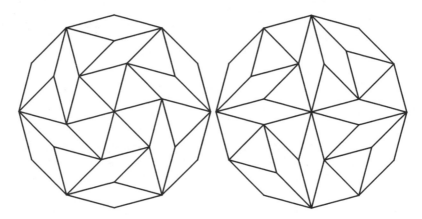

Figure 4.22 *Symmetry properties of a dissected dodecagon*

It is worth seeing how small modifications can change the symmetry by introducing one or more lines of symmetry or by destroying the symmetry completely. Students can readily explore and describe the symmetries of a variety of dissections of the dodecagon using a set of appropriately coloured card or plastic shapes.

Another interesting feature of the dissection is that it gives a simple way of calculating the area of a regular dodecagon. Figure 4.23 shows how the addition of some equilateral triangles and some triangles obtained by cutting the same rhombuses along their longer diagonal creates a square containing the dodecagon. By comparing the number of triangles and rhombuses in the square and the dodecagon it is easy to see that the dodecagon is $\frac{3}{4}$ of the area of the square. If r denotes the radius of the circle which circumscribes the dodecagon, then the area of the square is $4r^2$ and, hence, the area of a regular dodecagon is $3r^2$, slightly less than πr^2, the area of the circumscribing circle.

As a final curiosity Figure 4.24 shows Lindgren's dissection, taken from Frederickson (1997), where a regular dodecagon is dissected into five pieces which can be reassembled to make a square. Since the area of the dodecagon is, $3r^2$, where r is the radius of the circumscribed circle, the edges of the square are of length $\sqrt{3}r$. This can be checked independently by calculating the length of the diagonal of the dodecagon which forms the edge of the square.

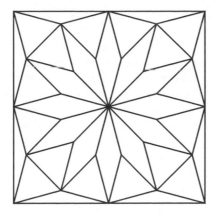

Figure 4.23 *What is the area of a regular dodecagon?*

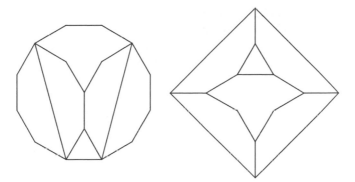

Figure 4.24 *A square from a regular dodecagon*

CONCLUSION

This chapter has been concerned with the second and third of van Hiele's levels where the properties of shapes are observed and students begin to learn how to reason about their properties. Description, classification, definition and deduction are all involved in this, with measurement and other practical modes of experimentation, including the use of computer software, helping both to provide motivation and to develop an intuitive feel for the ideas.

As students explore shapes and their properties they will encounter appropriate language and will begin to acquire knowledge of useful relationships concerning angle properties and the procedures for applying them to solving problems. While some obvious relationships will be accepted as self-evident, it is of the essence of geometry that results are arrived at through a process of reasoning and so it is important to use experimental work as a step towards using deduction to arrive at results. Problems where angles have to be calculated numerically are very valuable in developing reasoning skills, where an argument from what is given to what is wanted has to be constructed and where each step has to be justified. When these skills are combined with the use of algebra, general arguments can be developed so that students can begin to appreciate the nature of a proof as something that both verifies and explains. The interplay between geometry and algebra should reinforce understanding in both these key areas of mathematics.

It is clearly important to spend time practising the procedures needed to calculate angles in common situations, but that practice is likely to be much more effective if it arises frequently in the context of solving more challenging problems, where students are encouraged to think for themselves and apply the results and procedures that they are learning. Besides problems involving number and algebra, examples involving constructions with ruler and compasses are valuable in developing the students' skills of accurate drawing and their reasoning skills if discussion is focused on explaining why particular procedures achieve the desired result and they are encouraged to develop construction procedures of their own. LOGO and dynamic geometry software have a valuable role to play here.

The goal is to develop students' reasoning skills: remembering important facts and procedures is a necessary part of this, but it is not sufficient, because success in solving problems and coming to appreciate and generate proofs is dependent on a willingness and an ability to think independently. That requires an ethos where students are expected to think for themselves and where learning mathematics is not seen just as a matter of remembering facts and procedures. Learning to understand and generate simple chains of reasoning in geometry is a splendid vehicle for this because geometrical configurations have an intriguing and attractive quality that stimulates curiosity and encourages involvement.

Chapter 5

Constructions and Congruence

TRIANGLE CONSTRUCTION AND CONGRUENCE

The three transformations, translation, reflection and rotation, known as isometries, all preserve the shape and size of a shape, but change its position and, in the case of reflection, its orientation. The transformations are thus linked closely to the idea of congruence, which is used to describe shapes which are identical in all respects except for position and orientation. At a simple level students begin to acquire a feel for congruence as they explore the properties of the three transformations in superimposing one shape on another. This can be done experimentally with actual shapes, tracing paper or acetate, using paper folding in the case of reflection, and offers plenty of scope for using dynamic geometry software in related ways.

First thoughts about congruence are based on our intuition that two shapes fit exactly on top of each other. We then move on to making measures as a check on such intuitions. Finally, following the realization that measurement is never exact and that it is highly useful to make statements that are generalizable, we move into arguments based on reasoning to prove that two shapes are congruent. Being able to construct geometrical configurations accurately is a valuable skill in itself whether it is done on paper, employing ruler, protractor and a pair of compasses, or on a computer screen with an appropriate software package. The underlying principles are similar whatever the medium. One key idea is present as soon as students are asked to draw a triangle with three given sides: having drawn one side, how do they find the position of the third vertex? Using a pair of compasses to create intersecting arcs or dynamic geometry to create two intersecting circles is a simple, but fundamental, procedure whose rationale merits discussion rather than being presented simply as a recipe to remember. The following dialogue, illustrated by Figure 5.1, illustrates the ideas that the teacher should seek to draw out.

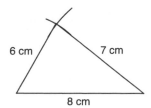

6 cm   7 cm

8 cm

Figure 5.1 *Drawing a triangle with sides of 6 cm, 7 cm and 8 cm*

T: How can we draw accurately a triangle with sides of 6 cm, 7 cm and 8 cm?
A: Draw one side first.
   [Draws 8 cm side.]
T: How are we going to draw the other sides?
B: Use a ruler. Draw 7 cm.
   [Draws a line 7 cm long from one vertex.]

T: What next?
C: Draw in the other side.
T: Is that right?
D: Yes. No, it might not be 6 cm.
   [Measures it and finds that it is more than 6 cm.]
T: How can we get it right?
A: Use compasses. Draw a part of a circle from one end – radius 7 cm. Then 6 cm radius from the other end.
T: What next?
B: Join the points where the circles (arcs) meet to each end of the first line.
   [Lines drawn in to complete the triangle.]
T: How do you know the third point is in the right place?
C: All the points on this circle (arc) [indicates which] are 7 cm from that point. And all the points on the other one are 6 cm from the other end. So that point is 7 cm from one end and 5 cm from the other.
T: Is that the only way to do it?
D: You could do the 7 cm at the other end.
T: Would that make any difference?

Appreciating that all triangles created in this way are congruent, although possibly positioned and orientated differently, is the key idea involved in understanding the three sides (SSS) case of congruency, the essence of Proposition 7, in Book 1 of Euclid's *Elements*, Heath (1967). Intuitively this is completely obvious to most students and can be reinforced by asking several of them to draw a triangle with given sides, cut them out and see that they can all be super-imposed. It is less obvious that some sets of three lengths will not give a triangle: students should be asked to try creating triangles with sides of say 8 cm, 6 cm and 2 cm or 8 cm, 6 cm and 1 cm to help them appreciate the limitations.

The situation is less clear when the initial information involves both sides and angles. An interesting challenge is to ask students to create triangles when they are given two sides and an angle without initially specifying the position of the angle. Figure 5.2 shows the four different

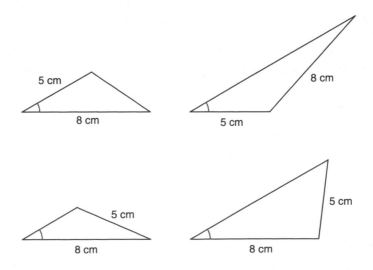

What happens if the shorter side is 4 cm or 3 cm?

Figure 5.2 *Triangles with sides of 5 cm and 8 cm and an angle of 30°*

triangles that can be created using such data. Arriving at these will give rise to discussion and lead firstly to the case of congruency involving two sides and the included angle (SAS). The other positions of the angle require thought about the method for constructing the second given side and the possibility that there may be two positions for that side or, indeed, that it may be impossible to construct a triangle with a particular specification. The extent to which these more subtle issues are discussed will depend on the stage that students have reached and the immediate objectives of a particular lesson. Similar issues meriting experiment, reasoning and discussion arise with the other two standard cases of congruence: one side and two corresponding angles (ASA) and a right angle, hypotenuse and one other side (RHS). One might ask, following on from the examples of Figure 5.2, under what other circumstances two sides and a non-included angle (SSA) gives congruence.

It rapidly becomes evident that only three pieces of data are required to construct a triangle. Quadrilaterals provide an interesting contrast: students' first thoughts are likely to be that a unique quadrilateral can always be drawn when they are given the lengths of four sides. Experimentation using four rigid strips of card or plastic freely linked at their ends to make a quadrilateral or four line segments similarly linked using dynamic geometry software soon makes it clear that four given sides do not in fact give a fixed quadrilateral. A linkage of four line segments is not rigid and moreover the order in which four segments are placed is significant, so the situation is much more complicated. If four sides are given in a particular order then an angle between a particular pair is needed as well: five pieces of data are in fact sufficient. Clearly other combinations of five pieces of data could be explored and the question of how much data is required extended to polygons with more sides, but appreciating the case of triangles is the most important because they are the key building block for all geometrical configurations and their rigidity is crucial to their use in the real world in structures of all kinds.

CONSTRUCTIONS WITH STRAIGHT-EDGES AND COMPASSES

The art of constructing geometric figures using a straight-edge and compasses and its modern manifestation in dynamic geometry software has come down to us from the Greeks through the propositions of Euclid. Constructing triangles with given measurements provides an introduction to the role of circles and compasses in creating given lengths. Certain standard constructions are useful tools to have available in investigating geometrical properties. As with triangle construction students should be challenged to produce methods for themselves which can be discussed and refined rather than be presented straight away with a recipe to remember.

The National Curriculum for England (1999) identifies four constructions of this type, illustrated in Figure 5.3, with which students should be familiar:

- perpendicular bisector of a line segment
- perpendicular from a point to a line
- perpendicular from a point on a line
- bisector of an angle

These constructions can be applied to a variety of interesting problems. Constructing the circumcircle of a triangle, illustrated in Figure 5.4, is a good example if it is used as a way of challenging students to solve the problem for themselves. It has the virtue of using

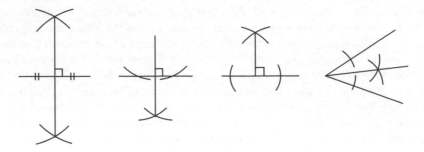

Figure 5.3 *Four standard geometrical constructions*

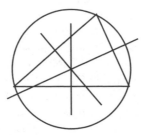

Figure 5.4 *Constructing the circumcircle of a triangle*

a construction to produce a significant result which can be checked by using the centre to draw the circle or to use it as a center for rotating the triangle. How do we get students to see how to think about this? A good problem-solving strategy is to look at a simpler problem. In this case finding a circle which passes through two given points is an obvious starting point. This leads to the fact that all circles through two points have their centre on the perpendicular bisector of the line segment joining the points. From a different perspective, that line is the locus of points that are equidistant from two given points. It is then a simple step to see that the intersection of the perpendicular bisectors of two sides of a triangle gives the centre of the circumcircle. It is always reassuring and satisfying to construct the third bisector and see that it does go through the same centre point.

One of the great virtues of using dynamic geometry with an example like this is that not only can the circumcircle be constructed as a check, but the original triangle can be altered by dragging one or more of the vertices of the triangle as shown in Figure 5.5. This demonstrates the generality of the construction in a striking way and prompts further questions such as the

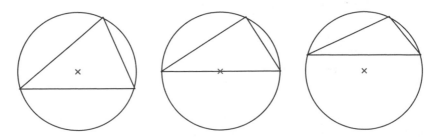

Figure 5.5 *Varying the position of the circumcentre of a triangle*

significance of whether the position of the centre is inside or outside or on one of the sides of the triangle.

Students need plenty of practice with the construction techniques in these first two sections of this chapter. These will be much more motivating and effective if they arise in a context where accurate diagrams are being drawn for a purpose, whether it be investigating the sets of data required to produce triangles and other polygons, creating scale diagrams, maps and plans, investigating the properties of figures or producing the nets for three-dimensional models like the polyhedra which are the subject of chapter eleven.

CONGRUENCE AND PROOF

Justifying constructions using straight-edge and compasses requires reference to congruent triangles. Moreover it has close links to deducing the properties of triangles and quadrilaterals and to the properties of reflections and rotations. In general identifying congruent triangles is often a significant part of proving a whole range of geometrical properties of varying levels of complexity.

At the simplest level we might consider an isosceles triangle, which is defined by its pair of equal sides from which it follows that the pair of base angles are equal. Interestingly this obvious property can be proved in three ways each using a different case of congruence as shown in Figure 5.6. Each proof rests on showing that the triangles ABD and ACD are congruent. In the first triangle D is the midpoint of BC giving the SSS case, in the second AD bisects angle BAC giving the SAS case and in the third AD is perpendicular to BC giving the RHS case. The fact that the property is obvious makes it doubtful whether it is a sensible starting point for applying the idea of congruent triangles! Students need to see, at an early stage, examples of congruence being used to derive less obvious truths.

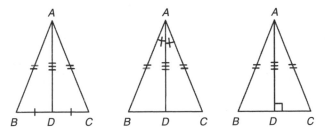

Figure 5.6 *Proving that the base angles of an isosceles triangle are equal*

The properties of the parallelogram and kite, pictured in Figure 5.7, were discussed in the previous chapter but no attempt was made there to distinguish between the properties used to define the figure and the properties that are derived. There is a choice with regard to defining properties and the reasoning leading to the corresponding properties will be dependent on that. For example a parallelogram could be defined as a quadrilateral with one pair of opposite sides both equal and parallel or it could be a quadrilateral with both pairs of opposite sides parallel or, again, a quadrilateral with both pairs of opposite sides equal. As with the example of isosceles triangles the other properties follow by showing that the two triangles created by including a diagonal are congruent and then considering the triangles that arise when the second diagonal is included. The same issues arise with a kite although there is less flexibility

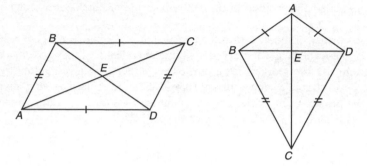

Figure 5.7 *Properties of the parallelogram and kite*

about the initial definition. In both cases there are obvious and immediate links to symmetry transformations: rotation for a parallelogram and reflection for a kite. The key property of the half-turn rotation displayed by the parallelogram is that a point and its image are equidistant and diametrically opposite to the centre of rotation at the intersection of the diagonals. For a reflection, illustrated by the kite, the mirror line is the perpendicular bisector of the line joining a point and its image. A rhombus, having features of both a parallelogram and a kite, displays both types of symmetry.

These examples involving properties of shapes are rather abstract and artificial to many students, so care must be taken not to give the impression that congruent triangles are only used to prove things that are already totally obvious. Two interesting examples are shown in Figure 5.8. These relate to simple practical situations and could indeed be used to estimate some actual distances.

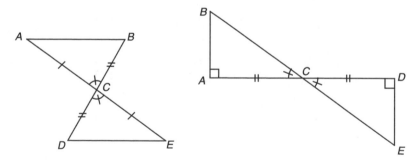

Figure 5.8 *Estimating the width of a pond and a river*

In the left-hand diagram of Figure 5.8 *AB* is the width of a pond which is to be estimated. We choose a point *C* accessible from both ends of the pond, measure the distance *AC* and then extend the line *AC* to *E* so that *AC* is equal in length to *CE*. Similarly, we measure the distance *BC* and then extend the line *BC* to *D* so that *BC* is equal to *CD*. The length of *DE* is then identical to that of *AB* and can therefore be measured to give the width of the pond. This can be explained by considering the triangles *ABC* and *EDC*, where we are given that *AC* is equal to *CE* and *BC* is equal to *CD* and angles *ACB* and *ECD* are equal because they are vertically opposite angles. The triangles are therefore congruent since two sides and the included angles are identical in each (SAS).

In the right-hand diagram of Figure 5.8, *AB* is the width of a river which is to be estimated. *A* and *B* are points on opposite banks of the river. A point *C* is chosen on the bank of the river so that angle *BAC* is a right angle. The distance *AC* is measured and then the line *AC* is extended to *D* so that *AC* and *CD* are equal in length. Next a point *E* on the perpendicular to *CD* from *D* is found so that the points *B*, *C* and *E* are in a straight line. The lengths of *DE* and *AB* are then equal. This follows because the triangles *ABC* and *DEC* are congruent. *AC* and *CD* are equal, the angles *BAC* and *EDC* are right angles and *ACB* and *ECD* are vertically opposite angles. The triangles are therefore congruent because one side and two corresponding pairs of angles are identical in each (ASA).

An example with an ingenious solution involves finding the minimum distance between two points. The story is that *A* and *B* are two boats moored in a harbour where *CD* is the harbour wall. The problem, as illustrated by the left-hand diagram in Figure 5.9, is to make a trip from *A* to pick up somebody at a point *P* on the wall and take them to *B* so that the distance travelled is a minimum. In other words, we seek the position of *P* on *CD* so that the total length *AP + PB* is a minimum.

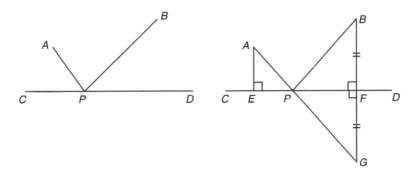

Figure 5.9 *A minimum distance problem*

The problem is solved by reflecting the point *B* in the harbour wall and joining its image, *G*, to A. *AG*, which is equal to *AP + PG*, is the shortest distance from *A* to *G* and *P* is the point where *AG* intersects *CD*. Since the triangles *PFB* and *PFG* are congruent with two sides and their included angle equal, it follows that *PB* and *PG* are equal and hence that *AP + PB* is the minimum distance.

Figure 5.10 shows how a rectangle of paper can be folded to create an equilateral triangle standing on the base of the rectangle. The first step is to fold the paper in half vertically creating the perpendicular bisector through the midpoint *D* of the base *AB*. A second fold is then made

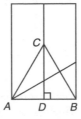

Figure 5.10 *An equilateral triangle by paper folding*

through *A* so that the point *B* falls on the perpendicular through *D*. That point is labelled *C* in the diagram. *ABC* is then an equilateral triangle. It is clear that *AB* and *AC* are equal from the way that the paper was folded, so we have to explain why *AC* and *BC* are equal. The two triangles *ACD* and *BCD* are in fact congruent because *CD* is common to both, *AD* is equal to *BD*, since *D* is the midpoint of *AB* and angles *ADC* and *BDC* are both right angles. Thus two sides and the included angle are the same in each triangle (SAS).

An attractive problem is created by joining two plastic strips of one length to two of another to make a parallelogram and then manipulating it to produce a crossed over quadrilateral as shown in the left-hand diagram of Figure 5.11. The two lengths *AC* and *BD* are equal as well as the marked sides *AD* and *BC*. The problem is to explain why the lengths *CE* and *DE* are equal avoiding vague references to symmetry. At first sight it would seem that the obvious way forward is to show that the triangles *AED* and *BEC* are congruent, but unfortunately it is only possible to show directly that one pair of sides and one pair of angles are equal. We need three facts! It is important to make false starts when looking at problems with students, whether they arise from suggestions prompted by them or engineered by the teacher, because they need to see that solutions are not always immediately obvious and that alternatives have to be tried until a fruitful way to proceed is found. The secret with solving geometrical problems often lies in adding an additional line or two to the figure: finding the right line to add is often the most creative part of a solution and not always obvious. In this case it is not too difficult to see that joining *C* to *D* creates two congruent triangles *ADC* and *BCD*. *CD* is common to both triangles, *AC* is equal to *BD* and *AD* is equal to *BC* because they are the original equal pairs of lengths. It then follows that the angles *BDC* and *ACD* are equal and hence that triangle *CDE* is isosceles with *CE* equal to *DE* as required.

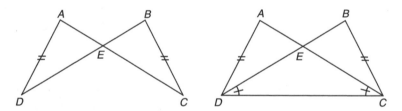

Figure 5.11 *The four-bar linkage*

The five problems illustrated by Figures 5.8 to 5.11 show a variety of examples where a procedure is explained by making reference to congruent triangles. The fact that they relate to situations that are presented as problems to solve or procedures to achieve some clear objective gives greater meaning and purpose both to the idea of proof and through that to the use of congruent triangles. In each case dynamic geometry can be used as a suitably dramatic way of viewing the situation by allowing the position of points and the whole configuration to be changed readily.

VAN SCHOOTEN'S THEOREM

Proving Van Schooten's theorem is a good example of a more demanding problem where congruent triangles provide a solution, which is obvious and simple once it has been pointed out, but very difficult to see for yourself. In the left-hand diagram of Figure 5.12 an equilateral

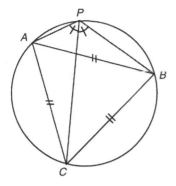 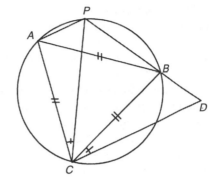

Figure 5.12 *Van Schooten's theorem*

triangle *ABC* is inscribed in a circle and *P* is a variable point situated on the minor arc *AB*. The theorem states the surprising and yet simple fact that $AP + PB = CP$.

A critical observation to make about the configuration is that the two angles *APC* and *BPC* are both equal to 60°, because each lies in the same respective segment as the angles *ABC* and *BAC* of the equilateral triangle. The secret of many geometrical proofs is often to add an extra line or two to the diagram to create a pair of congruent or similar triangles. In the right-hand diagram of Figure 5.12, the line *PB* has been produced and a line drawn from *C* to intersect it at *D*, so that angle *DCP* is 60°. The triangle *DCP* is then equilateral. If this diagram is constructed on a dynamic geometry screen, the point *P* can be moved and triangle *DCP* is seen to arise from rotating and enlarging the original equilateral triangle *ABC*.

The purpose of the construction is to create two triangles *ACP* and *BCD* which can be seen to be congruent. The lengths *AC* and *BC* are equal because they are sides of the original equilateral triangle. The angles *APC* and *BDC* are both 60° and the angles *ACP* and *BCD* are both equal to 60° minus the common angle *BCP*. It follows that the lengths *AP* and *BD* are equal, so that $AP + PB = DP$ and hence $AP + PB = CP$, because *DP* is equal to *CP*.

Of course, there are other ways of proving the theorem which may be shorter, such as using the cosine rule, but there is a certain attraction about a proof which can be seen directly in the picture, once some lines have been added. Although it may be a little cumbersome to put into words, the argument is very clear and elegant.

CONCLUSION

The study of congruent triangles is often seen as a rather obscure and difficult part of the geometry curriculum which is lacking in any purpose. This chapter has tried to meet both of these objections. The idea of proving two triangles to be congruent is made clearer by linking the different possible sets of measurements to the problem of making accurate constructions of triangles, something which can be referred back to from time to time when reference is made to a particular case of congruence.

The apparent lack of purpose often arises because the result that is being proved either seems to the student to be obvious or else too obscure to be worth considering. This points to the importance of well-chosen examples and to the need for discussion about the general purpose of proof which provides explanations as well as providing certainty. It is not appropriate at an early stage to use examples, like showing that the base angles of an isosceles triangle are equal, where the result is self-evident. Examples should often be chosen because they add insight to some key result or property like the angle sum of a triangle or because they explain an application or an intriguing feature of a configuration. Varying the format in which examples arise and are presented can add to the sense that there is something that is worth thinking about: the five examples in the main section of this chapter have been chosen to illustrate the variety that is possible which includes practical situations and the use of dynamic geometry software.

Geometrical problems can be very demanding and often rather frustrating when an obvious idea has been missed or a solution is presented as though it is easy to spot the critical idea that provides the key to a solution. It is important to discuss problems and help students see the sort of ways in which solution strategies emerge and how faulty lines of argument are exposed. Success comes from a combination of insight developed by experience and a thorough knowledge of necessary facts and procedures. Above all successful learning about congruence is dependent, as with every other part of mathematics, on developing a sense that explaining and proving things matters and is a stimulating part of learning mathematics.

Chapter 6

Perimeter, Area and Volume

THE CONCEPT OF AREA

The concept of area arises when we want to compare plane shapes either with each other or against a standard unit of measurement. Area has an obvious wide variety of direct practical applications: areas of floors in determining the number of floor tiles or the amount of carpet, areas of walls to determine quantity of paint, area of card for packaging, areas of fields to determine quantity of seed or the number of animals that can be grazed, area of land in relation to planning a building. Often these types of application will be linked with the idea of volume, as well as considerations that are not geometrical, such as mass or cost. At a more abstract level the area under a curve is the key conceptual idea underlying the integral calculus which opens up a wide range of more sophisticated applications including the strange notion that distance is represented by the area under a velocity–time curve.

Students' early ideas about area should be stimulated by asking which is the bigger of two shapes and by exploring the tiling properties of squares and shapes represented on grids. Whether a shape is an irregular one with curved boundaries or a simple rectangle, the essential idea of area is that of finding the number of squares that a shape covers. It is important that preliminary work explores this key idea to ensure that students do not focus on a single dimension, such as 'bigger because taller', and that they are helped to distinguish between the linked, but distinct, notions of area and perimeter. A premature recourse to the formula 'length times width' for the area of a rectangle often leads students erroneously to apply the result to situations not directly involving rectangles. Too much emphasis is commonly given to remembering and applying formulae at the expense of developing a clear understanding of their meaning and the strategic thinking needed to use them sensibly in solving problems.

The idea of counting squares to find an approximate area of an irregular shape, illustrated by Figure 6.1, is a valuable introductory task which can be linked to a real situation such as comparing the areas of hands or leaves or lakes. It introduces the need for a standard unit of measure such as square centimetre or a square metre. Besides providing a need to find strategies for counting accurately and recording results, such a square-counting task draws attention to the essentially approximate nature of measurement and provokes debate about how to ensure sufficient accuracy for a particular purpose. The difficulty is to decide what to do about squares which straddle the boundary of the shape where the usual rule of thumb is to count squares where more than half is within the shape. This can provoke demarcation disputes about what to do if, as a student might say, it is 'exactly half' and may lead to substantial inaccuracy if a majority of the boundary squares are 'more than half'. Issues of this kind are valuable points for discussion with students and should be used to encourage understanding and promote flexible thinking.

Carrying out the same exercise with a variety of polygons formed by linking points on a

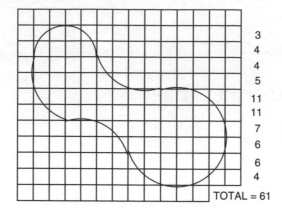

3
4
4
5
11
11
7
6
6
4
TOTAL = 61

Area of grid squares = 0.25 cm²
Approximate area of shape = 61× 0.25 = 15.25 cm²

Figure 6.1 *Area of an irregular shape*

square grid involves decisions about how to break the task into simple steps. Early examples need not involve triangles, but when these do appear part of the challenge for students is to find the area of a triangle using some informal method. Figure 6.2 shows two distinct strategies for finding such an area, which we might call 'subdividing and adding' and 'surrounding and subtracting'. It is not necessary with simple tasks of this kind to have any formal methods for calculating areas of rectangles and triangles, because the number of squares involved will be readily countable and in simple situations the triangles will be half of an obvious rectangle. Formulae are a potential by-product of such exercises, but the strategic thinking and the underlying understanding of the area concept are more important initially. Students should be encouraged to devise their own methods: comparing these acts as a check as well as a stimulus to further thinking about which strategies are best for a particular problem. Asking them to create their own polygons and then to find their areas will often stimulate more active interest and effort than a set of tasks from a textbook.

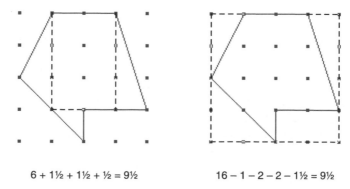

6 + 1½ + 1½ + ½ = 9½   16 − 1 − 2 − 2 − 1½ = 9½

Figure 6.2 *Two strategies for finding the area of a polygon*

RECTANGLES, PARALLELOGRAMS AND TRIANGLES

Shapes do not always come conveniently superimposed on a grid, but may be presented as a diagram with dimensions or, perhaps better, as a diagram or an actual object where appropriate lengths have to be measured. It is then necessary to begin to develop more formal approaches to finding the areas of standard shapes. The idea that the area of a rectangle is obtained by multiplying length by width is not one that presents much difficulty to students who are secure in their understanding of multiplying fairly small whole numbers. Difficulties clearly arise for some students when the numbers and multiplication techniques involved are less familiar, as with large numbers and fractions, but these are essentially arithmetical difficulties and our concern here is with geometrical considerations where ideas can often best be developed with lengths restricted to small whole numbers.

The area of a triangle may be approached by finding the area of a parallelogram and then showing that the area of any triangle is half that of a corresponding parallelogram. It may, however, seem more natural to observe that the area of many triangles can be found directly as half that of a corresponding rectangle, since that is a simple and familiar shape, whose area can be readily determined. Moreover the area of a parallelogram has also to be found by reference to a rectangle. The first two diagrams of Figure 6.3 illustrate straightforward cases of each

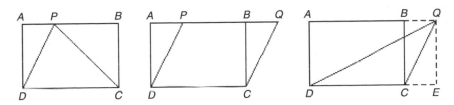

Figure 6.3 *Areas of parallelograms and triangles*

leading to the standard results for the triangle and parallelogram, but there are some examples like triangle *QCD* in the third diagram whose areas are more awkward to determine. A 'surround and subtract' strategy enables the area to be calculated as follows:

$$\text{Area of triangle } QCD = \tfrac{1}{2} \text{ rectangle } AQED - \tfrac{1}{2} \text{ rectangle } BQEC = \tfrac{1}{2} \text{ rectangle } ABCD$$

While that is a neat and instructive piece of reasoning it does not necessarily give students a good intuitive feel as to why the area should be the same as that of the first triangle.

Figure 6.4 shows how dynamic geometry software can be used to generate triangles on the same base with the same area by moving the vertex of the triangle along a line parallel to the base. A set of triangles with the same base and the same height, and hence the same area, are shown drawn on a square grid below. In terms of transformations the triangle has been given a shear, one of whose essential properties is to leave area invariant. It is perhaps easier to appreciate this by seeing a rectangle sheared to give a parallelogram rather like a pile of books being pushed across with lowest one not moving: it is intuitively clear why the area of the end of the pile, and indeed the volume, remain the same. The same idea is readily applied to triangles. The area invariance property of shearing involved here is sometimes referred to as Cavalieri's Principle and follows the sort of reasoning used by Archimedes in arriving at formulae for the volume of the cone and sphere.

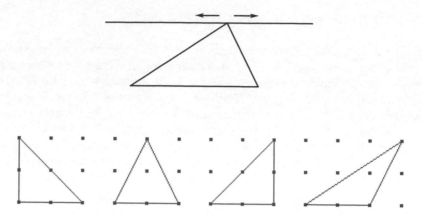

Figure 6.4 *Shearing to give triangles with the same base and height*

A particular conceptual difficulty that arises with triangles and parallelograms is the interpretation by students of the notion of height. It is very easy for the length of one of the slanting sides to be taken mistakenly as the height, when the base is in the standard horizontal position and students commonly find it difficult to identify what to take as the height when the base is in an oblique position. Exercises where students are given numerical values for base and height provide practice in evaluating a formula, but they do not build understanding of what the variables refer to. For this purpose students need to be put in a position where they have to make actual measurements of a shape so that they are required to think for themselves what the height is. This can also usefully draw attention to the fact that two different sides can be taken as the base for a parallelogram with different respective heights, and triangles have three possibilities for the base.

Since the triangle is a building block for all polygons, knowing how to determine its area is sufficient for solving a wide range of area problems. For instance, Figure 6.5 shows two ways in which the area of a trapezium can be determined by subdividing into simpler shapes: two triangles or a parallelogram and a triangle. The knowledge required is more than remembering that the area of a triangle is half the base multiplied by the height and being able to substitute numbers for the variables. The student needs a feel for how the formula has been derived, an understanding of the two variables base and height, an appreciation of the relationship between triangles and other polygons and confidence in applying various strategies to finding the areas of a variety of polygons presented in different forms.

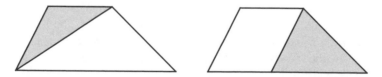

Figure 6.5 *The area of a trapezium*

PERIMETER AND AREA

As noted in Chapter 2, students commonly confuse the ideas of perimeter and area. This seems to be more than a mere confusion as to which word refers to each idea and it is more than forgetting which formula refers to which idea for a particular shape, something which is a particular problem with circles. There is a deeper problem to do with understanding the subtle relationship between the two ideas which requires an appreciation that changing one does not necessarily change the other. This is illustrated by the two contrasting sets of three diagrams of Figure 6.6. The first set shows a rectangle and then two copies of it with one square unit removed. Obviously in both cases the area is reduced by one unit, but in one case the perimeter is unchanged while in the other the perimeter is increased. In the second set a square is shown transformed on the right to a parallelogram by shearing so that the area remains the same, but the perimeter is increased. On the left the square has been transformed to a parallelogram (in fact it is a rhombus) by keeping all the edges and therefore the perimeter the same: in this case the area is decreased.

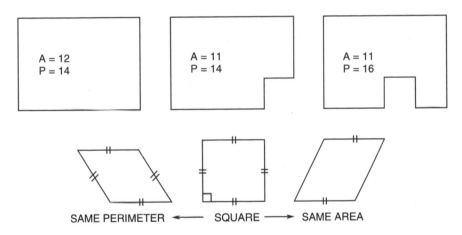

Figure 6.6 *Varying the area and perimeter of a rectangle*

Students can be asked to explore the relationship between area and perimeter by using exercises like the following where they are asked to produce shapes on a square grid and in the latter two cases to present the results graphically. These last two examples can of course be considered algebraically and calculus applied to finding the turning points of the graphs, but the purpose here is the simpler one of helping students to acquire a feel for the distinction between area and perimeter and the relationship between them.

- Draw a variety of different shapes with an area of 9 cm². Find the perimeter of each shape. Which shape has the minimum perimeter?
- Draw a variety of different shapes with a perimeter of 16 cm. Find the area of each shape. Which shape has the maximum area?
- Draw a variety of rectangles with a perimeter of 20 cm. Find the area of each rectangle. Tabulate the results and produce a graph of area against edge length. Which dimensions give the maximum area?

- Draw a variety of rectangles with an area of 16 cm². Find the perimeter of each rectangle. Tabulate the results and produce a graph of perimeter against edge length. Which dimensions give the minimum perimeter?

The third example is illustrated by Figure 6.7. Cabri Geometry has been used to draw a rectangle where the edge length can be varied, subject to the constraint imposed by the constant perimeter. The point on the slider that appears below the rectangle is moved to vary the length and width and the measures of each, together with the corresponding area, are stated alongside. In addition values have been tabulated on a spreadsheet and illustrated with a graph.

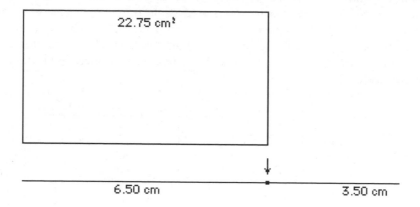

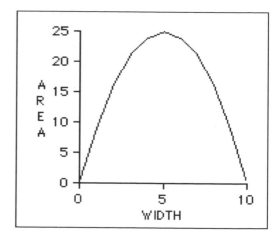

Width	Area
0	0
1	9
2	16
3	21
4	24
5	25
6	24
7	21
8	16
9	9
10	0

Figure 6.7 *Areas of rectangles with a constant perimeter of 20 cm*

CIRCLES

It is usual to arrive at the formula for the circumference of a circle, $C = \pi d$ by asking students to measure a number of circles and calculate the ratio of circumference to diameter and to observe that it seems to take a constant value that is just over 3. This value is then referred to as the constant π with comments that there are ways to determine it more accurately, but an approximation such as 3.14 or the value given by a calculator are fine for purposes of calculation. This provides an appropriate introduction which can be followed up by using the result to solve simple problems involving calculation which will bring in earlier ideas about perimeter.

Unlike polygons, which only involve the lengths of straight lines, the circumference of a circle involves a length along a curve which is awkward to measure accurately. It can only be calculated by recourse to a formula that is not intuitively obvious and involves the rather abstract and difficult idea of the constant π. The conceptual leap in coming to terms with the formula for the circumference of a circle and the further step to the area of a circle is considerable after the relatively easy ideas associated with rectangles and triangles. It is important therefore that suitable discussion and tasks are used to help students make sense of the underlying ideas alongside using the results to do calculations and solve problems.

It is useful to emphasize that the formula tells us that the circumference is a bit more than 3 times the diameter, so that there is always a simple way of estimating or checking an answer. In the case of the area formula, $A = \pi r^2$, the area is again roughly three times something and this time the something is a square given by r^2. The two diagrams of Figure 6.8 show a circle inscribed in a square and a square inscribed in a circle. In each case it is easy to express the area of the square in terms of a square on the radius of area r^2 and that tells us that the area of the circle lies somewhere between $2r^2$ and $4r^2$, so that it at least seems reasonable that the area is a little more than $3r^2$. A square counting exercise can provide further evidence. The area of a regular dodecagon, which is precisely $3r^2$ for a circumscribing circle of radius r, can be determined very simply using the method shown in Chapter 4 and that adds further to the plausibility of $A = \pi r^2$.

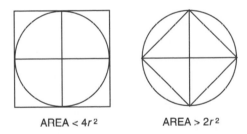

AREA < 4r^2 AREA > 2r^2

Figure 6.8 *Upper and lower limits for the area of a circle*

A more sophisticated argument is shown in the diagram of Figure 6.9. Any circle can be cut into a number of equal sectors which can be arranged to produce a shape which looks more like a parallelogram as the number of sectors is increased and the angle of each becomes correspondingly smaller. Eight sectors are shown in this particular diagram: it is easy to see that the corresponding parallelogram has a base of πr and a height of r giving an area of πr^2.

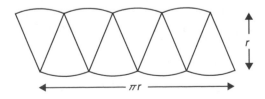

Figure 6.9 *The area of a circle*

After some initial practice in using πr^2 in routine situations, more demanding problems should be posed. These provide more practice of the routines, but also contribute to extending students' problem-solving skills and give them a sense that the ideas are useful and interesting. Solving an area problem involves the geometric step of 'seeing' the shapes involved and suitably subdividing the figures. That is then followed by arithmetical calculations or algebraic manipulation. Figure 6.10 shows four shapes where the perimeter and area are to be calculated. The shapes are displayed on a square grid so that students have to see for themselves the relevant lengths. In all four cases the perimeter of the curved sections is the same, namely the circumference of a circle with unit radius, with two straight sections to be added for shape D. The areas are more interesting: only in the case of A is significant calculation needed, because B, C and D can each be split into four pieces which fit together to make a rectangle of area 2 units. Shape A consists of a semi-circle with the remaining pieces forming a unit square so that the area is $\frac{1}{2}\pi + 1$.

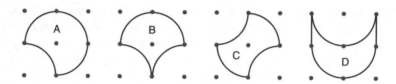

Which shape has the greatest area?
Which shape has the greatest perimeter?

Figure 6.10 *Shapes with circles*

To find the area of the segment in Figure 6.11, assuming a unit radius, the student has to devise an overall strategy and then to use various routine procedures to do the necessary

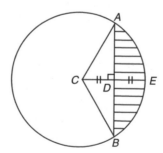

Figure 6.11 *The area of a segment*

calculations. One of these routine procedures is that of finding the area of a sector, which should be readily seen as a fraction of the area of the circle, not as another formula to be remembered. Four steps are involved in calculating the area of the segment:

- Observing that the area of the segment is found by subtracting the area of triangle ABC from the area of the sector ABC.
- Calculating the area of the triangle ABC: $AC = 1$ and $CD = \frac{1}{2}$, so that by Pythagoras $AD = \frac{1}{2}\sqrt{3}$. Then the area of the triangle is $\frac{1}{2}AB \times CD = AD \times CD = \frac{1}{4}\sqrt{3}$.

- Calculating the area of the sector, which involves finding the angle ACB: it may have become obvious that angle ACD is $60°$, but if not trigonometry can be applied to triangle ACD. The angle of the sector is then $120°$ so that its area is $\frac{1}{3}$ of the area of the circle. Since the circle has an area of π, the area of the sector is $\frac{1}{3}\pi$.
- Subtracting, evaluating and checking: $\frac{1}{3}\pi - \frac{1}{4}\sqrt{3} \approx 0.61$. This is a plausible answer because $\frac{1}{3}$ of the area of the circle is a approximately 1.

The first step of seeing how to break down the diagram to solve the problem is the crucial one, but there may be similar issues of seeing what is required in the sub-problems of finding the area of the triangle and sector. Fluency with the procedures for solving right-angled triangles and finding areas of simple shapes is necessary, but not sufficient.

Figure 6.12 shows another circle problem which has a surprising result. The two curves bounding the lune are arcs of circles. To find the area it is necessary to subtract the area of the segment standing on AB from the area of the semi-circle with AB as diameter. Taking the radius of the semi-circle as 1, the radius of the other arc is $\sqrt{2}$, giving areas of $\frac{1}{2}\pi - 1$ for the segment and $\frac{1}{2}\pi$ for the semi-circle. The lune then has an area of $\frac{1}{2}\pi - (\frac{1}{2}\pi - 1)$ which is 1, the same as the area of the triangle and without a π in sight!

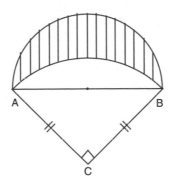

Figure 6.12 *The area of a lune*

VOLUMES OF CUBES, CUBOIDS AND PYRAMIDS

As with length times width for the area of a rectangle, the volume of a cuboid as length times width times height is not a problematic idea, but the idea of volume has its conceptual difficulties. One is the confusion between surface area and volume, which, rather like that between area and perimeter, needs to be met by tasks which draw attention to the discrepancies by looking at examples like those shown in Figure 6.13. The other significant difficulty is related to the difficulty of visualizing solid objects and interpreting two-dimensional representations of them. Working with actual objects is clearly useful here, as are tasks which ask students to draw objects on an isometric grid, like that shown in Figure 6.13, and to deduce information from the figures depicted. Our default view of the left-hand object in Figure 6.13 is that of a cube made up of 8 unit cubes, but in fact we can only see 7 of them. It may be that the volume should be given as 7, if the supposed hidden cube at the back is missing. Interestingly the surface area is still 24. Such debate becomes even more interesting if the default picture appears to be a cube made up of 27 unit cubes!

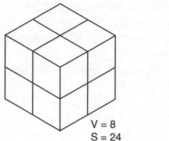
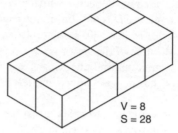

Figure 6.13 *Surface area and volume*

The volume of a pyramid as one third of the area of the base times the height is an important result and one that should be recognized as a general result that applies to all pyramids including the tetrahedron and cone. Figure 6.14 shows a cube on the left and then a skew pyramid formed by taking the point P as vertex and $ABCD$ as the base. The final right pyramid has been obtained by moving the point P on a plane parallel to the base $ABCD$ so that it is above the midpoint of the base. By Cavalieri's Principle, which states that the volume remains invariant for solids with the same altitude if the cross-sectional areas at each level are the same (discussed in Boyer and Merzbach (1991, p. 330)), the volume of the two pyramids is the same. Three of these skew pyramids fit together to make the cube. Each has P for its vertex with the other two having the front face and the right hand face of the cube respectively as base. Since three pyramids form the cube and the right pyramid has the same volume as a skew pyramid, this provides a nice demonstration that the volume of the pyramid is one third of the volume of the cube.

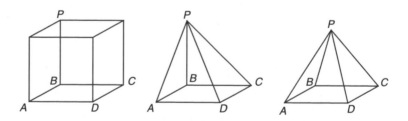

VOLUME OF PYRAMID = ⅓ AREA OF BASE × HEIGHT

Figure 6.14 *The volume of a pyramid*

It is particularly instructive for students to make models to demonstrate how the pyramids fit together. This is an interesting task in itself which is made more challenging if the students have to design the net as well. The skew pyramid can be constructed using the net shown in Figure 6.15. Another model with six square-based right pyramids with half the altitude of the cube provides another useful demonstration. This is linked to the polyhedron known as a rhombic dodecahedron which is depicted and discussed in Chapter 10.

Deriving the formula for the volume of a sphere, $\frac{4}{3}\pi r^3$, is difficult without using integration. It is instructive to demonstrate it experimentally, using suitable plastic containers of water or fine sand, to see that the volume of a cone and a sphere are respectively one and two thirds of the volume of a cylinder of the same diameter and height. Figure 6.16 shows a more

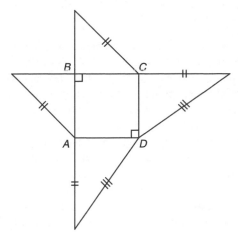

Figure 6.15 *A net for a skew pyramid*

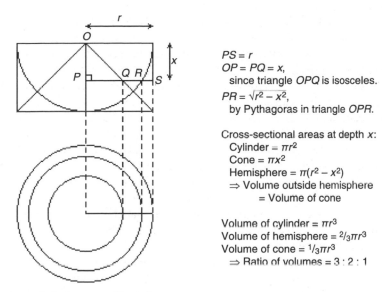

$PS = r$
$OP = PQ = x$,
 since triangle *OPQ* is isosceles.
$PR = \sqrt{r^2 - x^2}$,
 by Pythagoras in triangle *OPR*.

Cross-sectional areas at depth x:
 Cylinder $= \pi r^2$
 Cone $= \pi x^2$
 Hemisphere $= \pi(r^2 - x^2)$
 $\Rightarrow$ Volume outside hemisphere
   $=$ Volume of cone

Volume of cylinder $= \pi r^3$
Volume of hemisphere $= {}^2\!/_3 \pi r^3$
Volume of cone $= {}^1\!/_3 \pi r^3$
 $\Rightarrow$ Ratio of volumes $= 3 : 2 : 1$

Figure 6.16 *Volumes of cylinder, cone and hemisphere*

analytical approach which uses Cavalieri's Principle, with a cone and hemisphere in a cylinder, to show that the volume outside the hemisphere is the same as the volume of the cone. Since the volume of the cone is one third of the cylinder, it follows that the hemisphere occupies two thirds. The ratios of the volumes will be the same for a sphere and a cone in a cylinder of twice the height, but the formula for the volume of the sphere is, of course, twice that given for the hemisphere.

The three volumes can alternatively be obtained by integration as volumes of revolution, using the results for the cross-sectional areas given in Figure 6.16:

$$\int_0^r \pi r^2 \, dx = \pi r^3 \qquad \int_0^r \pi \, (r^2 - x^2) \, dx = \tfrac{2}{3}\, \pi r^3 \qquad \int_0^r \pi x^2 \, dx = \tfrac{1}{3}\, \pi r^3$$

CONCLUSION

Area and volume and the associated ideas of perimeter and surface area are of considerable practical as well as mathematical importance, with a resulting emphasis being given in the school curriculum to formulas and calculations. That emphasis is entirely appropriate, but it should arise in a context where students are encouraged to understand underlying ideas and to think for themselves in solving problems, rather than simply to remember formulas and procedures through relentless practice with routine examples.

Seemingly simple ideas like base and height of a triangle can become divorced from the reality that they describe if they are just seen as words in a formula. Presenting students with actual triangles and requiring them to make appropriate measurements is a simple step which ensures that the meanings of the variables in the formulas relate to a reality that makes sense to them. Similarly the common confusions between area and perimeter, and that between volume and surface area, need to be addressed directly by discussion and tasks that bring the pairs of ideas together and aim to counter false intuitions.

Understanding the derivation of formulas and seeing the links between them makes the key results easier to remember and encourages an attitude of mind that is willing to think things out when faced with a difficulty, rather than to rely solely on memory of particular procedures and previous examples. The formulas for the areas of a rectangle, parallelogram, triangle and trapezium are a good example of a linked set of results where each follows from its predecessor in the list. Awareness of the links makes it much easier to remember the results

The circle is of fundamental importance and the involvement π of means that the formulas for area and circumference can never be as intuitively obvious as corresponding results for triangles and quadrilaterals. However, some intuitive feel can be developed through the way in which the results are first derived and the derivation can be returned to at intervals to consider alternatives and place the ideas on a firmer footing. Configurations involving circles offer a rich variety of area problems of varying degrees of difficulty. Students need to be challenged to think for themselves about such problems and to be helped in developing solution strategies for themselves once they have mastered the simple application of standard results. Finding the area of a sector of a circle is a good example of a task that should be presented as a problem to be solved from first principles, rather than as something to be worked out using yet another remembered standard procedure.

Volume and surface area introduce the additional difficulty of visualizing three-dimensional objects from two-dimensional representations. The obvious message here is that students need to handle and to construct models to illustrate important properties and to link these to two-dimensional diagrams. The study of polyhedra is a fascinating and enlightening aspect of three-dimensional geometry which is considered at length in Chapter 10.

Area and volume are vital geometrical concepts which underlie many aspects of mathematics. They should be viewed, not just as a source of results to be remembered and procedures to follow, but as ideas to be understood and to be used in a wide variety of contexts.

Chapter 7

Enlargement and Similarity

ENLARGEMENT

Enlargement carries the idea of making something larger, although in a mathematical sense it may also refer to making a reduction in size, a process for which there is no widely accepted word. The technical term for all such enlargements is dilatation, but it is not a word that is commonly used so I shall use the word enlargement, but it is important to note that this ambiguity about the use of the word does need explaining to students if they are not to restrict its meaning to that of everyday usage.

Enlargement in this general sense is a ubiquitous feature of our world with its widespread use of maps, plans, scale drawings of all kinds, photographic enlargements, the use of photocopiers which enlarge and reduce and the corresponding facilities with text and images on a computer screen. There is no lack of examples on which to draw in helping students to appreciate the importance of the idea and its immense utility. For example, a map with a scale of 1:25,000 is an enlargement by a scale factor of two of a map with a scale of 1:50,000, while the real thing is 50,000 times larger than its depiction on the latter map. Another example is a standard sheet of A3 paper which is an enlargement by a scale factor of $\sqrt{2}$ of a sheet of A4 paper with the other paper sizes linked in a similar way.

Besides the difficulty of including reductions in size, students also need to understand that enlargement not only involves a change of size, but that various properties of a shape do remain unchanged, notably the angles between lines in a shape and the proportions of the shape. The first is not difficult to appreciate, but the second is a source of considerable difficulty which is linked to an understanding of ratio and proportion, which goes beyond its application to geometry. I have discussed this general issue at length in the chapter on proportionality in this book's companion volume, *Teaching and Learning Algebra* (French 2002b).

Students can explore the properties of enlargement as a transformation using a variety of drawing exercises on both plane and squared paper. Coloured interlinking cubes are particularly attractive for investigating enlargement at a simple level and enlargements of photographs can also provide a useful focus. Figure 7.1 poses the problem of what is meant by 'twice as big'. The three-square motif on the left has been made 'twice as tall' and 'twice as wide', but it is clear that the resulting pairs of pictures are distortions of the original and not enlargements in a

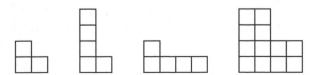

Figure 7.1 *Twice as big?*

mathematical sense. 'Twice as big' implies that all the dimensions have been doubled to produce the right-hand picture. The squares also enable students to see that making a shape 'twice as big' has the effect of making the area four times as big. Moreover, when interlocking cubes are used, this idea can be extended to volume where eight times as many cubes are required, because each unit cube is replaced by a cube with edges of two units. Discussions based on such simple configurations and pictures involving doubling are a first step towards the fundamental ideas of enlargement and similarity that angles and proportions are preserved, and that enlarging a shape with a scale factor k has the effect of enlarging the area by a factor of k^2 and the volume by k^3.

The challenge of constructing an enlarged version of a simple figure on plane paper leads to a diagram like Figure 7.2, where a triangle has been enlarged by scale factors of 2 and 3. A point is chosen as centre of enlargement and rays are drawn through each vertex of the triangle. Equal steps are then taken along each ray to give vertices for the enlarged triangles. Besides noting that angles and proportions are preserved it is also clear that corresponding edges of the triangles are parallel, another important property of a mathematical enlargement, although this is not necessarily a property that always applies when considering situations involving similar triangles. Besides making pencil and paper diagrams, dynamic geometry software can be used to explore enlargement by allowing both the initial shape of Figure 7.2 and the position of the centre of enlargement to be varied.

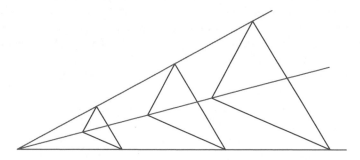

Figure 7.2 *Enlarging a triangle*

SIMILARITY

Students generally find proportionality problems straightforward when they involve doubling, but the idea becomes more difficult for scale factors which are larger whole numbers and substantially more difficult with fractional scale factors, because this involves the idea of ratio and the need to multiply by a fraction. This is a well-researched source of difficulty discussed in the wider general context of proportion in Hart (1981, pp. 88–101).

Figure 7.3 shows a pair of similar triangles, one with sides of lengths 4, 5 and 7 units and the other with its shortest side 6 units. The problem is to determine the lengths of the two unknown sides of the larger triangle, denoted by a and b. One common error is for students to say that the unknown sides are 7 and 9 because the lengths are 'two more' or because the sequence of lengths goes up by 1 and then by 2. Both errors involve the student using addition, whereas a proportional increase requires multiplication, often by a fraction, and the idea of multiplication is more difficult to understand than addition. Traditionally problems involving proportionality

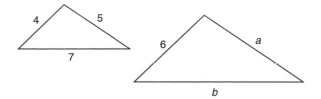

Figure 7.3 *Two similar triangles*

have been solved by equating equal ratios. For the triangles of Figure 7.3 that would give equations for each unknown length which are solved as follows:

$$\frac{a}{5}=\frac{6}{4} \quad\Rightarrow\quad a=\frac{5\times6}{4}=7\tfrac{1}{2} \quad\text{and}\quad \frac{b}{7}=\frac{6}{4} \quad\Rightarrow\quad b=\frac{7\times6}{4}=10\tfrac{1}{2}$$

Building on the idea of enlargement it would seem to be simpler conceptually to determine the scale factor of $\frac{6}{4}$ using the ratio of one pair of corresponding sides. This ratio obviously appears as part of the equal ratios procedure, but its significance is much clearer if it is first considered separately and simplified to $\frac{3}{2}$ or $1\frac{1}{2}$ or in a decimal form when the numbers are more awkward. It can then be used to find the other sides by multiplication, setting out the calculations along the following lines:

$$\text{Scale factor} =\frac{6}{4}=\frac{3}{2}= 1\tfrac{1}{2} \quad a = 1\tfrac{1}{2}\times 5 = 7\tfrac{1}{2} \quad b = 1\tfrac{1}{2}\times 7 = 10\tfrac{1}{2}$$

There are many simple applications of similarity relating to simple everyday situations, besides the more formal and theoretical applications which are part of pure geometry. Looking at examples drawn from real situations helps to give geometry a greater sense of meaning and purpose besides providing opportunities to develop the skills of problem-solving. Three examples are illustrated in Figure 7.4 and 7.5 and discussed below.

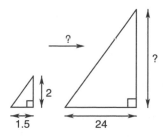

Figure 7.4 *Finding the height of a tree*

Figure 7.4 shows how the height of a tree or other tall object can be found on a sunny day by measuring its shadow and comparing it with the length of the shadow of a post whose height can be readily measured. In the diagram a post of height 2 metres has a shadow of length 1.5 metres and the tree has a shadow of length 24 metres. Assuming that the ground is horizontal and that both post and tree are vertical the two triangles are similar because the angle of elevation of the sun is clearly the same for both. So, we have:

$$\text{Scale factor} = \frac{24}{1.5} = 16 \quad \text{Height} = 16 \times 2 = 32 \text{ metres}$$

In Figure 7.5 the left-hand diagram shows an aircraft flying from east to west, C to D, observed in the distance through a south facing window, AB. An observer, O, stands 1.2 metres

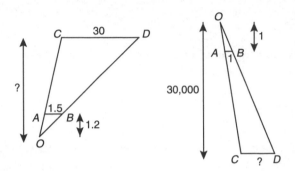

Figure 7.5 *Some problems using similar triangles*

away from the window, which is 1.5 metres wide, and notes, by observing the vapour trail, that the aircraft is visible for 3 minutes as it crosses the sky from C to D. The problem is to determine approximately how far away the aircraft is. As it stands the problem lacks sufficient data for a solution to be found, but that is in the nature of real problems and should lead students to think about what else we need to know. We could, for instance, presume that the aircraft is flying at about 600mph in which case it will travel 30 miles in 3 minutes. The two systems of units used here reflect how we often have to deal with real problems and do serve to make the valuable point that we only need to ensure that corresponding sides are measured in the same units, because it is the ratio between them that is important. The problem can then be solved as follows by referring to the two similar triangles OAB and OCD:

$$\text{Scale factor} = \frac{30}{1.5} = 20 \quad \text{Distance} = 20 \times 1.2 = 24 \text{ miles}$$

In the second problem the observer, O, is inside an aircraft looking down at the Earth 30,000 feet below and seeking to estimate the length of a lake denoted by CD. Again a mixture of units is used: if the observer holds her finger, which is 1 centimetre wide, 1 foot away from her eyes then her finger will cover a length of 30,000 centimetres on the Earth below and that is equivalent to 300 metres. The length of the lake can then be measured in finger widths. Again we have used two similar triangles, OAB and OCD, and created a situation where there is a simple scale factor of 30,000.

All three of these problems involve making all sorts of assumptions and approximations which is a valuable aspect of real applications. The resulting answers will be very rough, but they are nonetheless interesting because they relate to something which has a potential appeal in satisfying our curiosity about the world around us.

A more sophisticated example of similarity involving similar rectangles looks at the standard paper sizes, of which the A4 size is very familiar. A4 paper has the characteristic that when it is cut in half the resulting two pieces of paper, which are referred to as A5, are similar to the original, but, of course, they are each half the area. Sheets of A4 and A5 paper are shown in two different orientations in Figure 7.6.

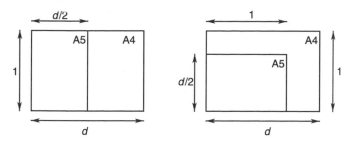

Figure 7.6 *A4 and A5 paper*

The sides of the A4 paper are taken as 1 and d in the two diagrams of Figure 7.6. It follows that the dimensions of the smaller rectangle are $\frac{1}{2}d$ and 1. Since the two rectangles are similar, the ratios of their sides are the same and that enables us to calculate the length d as follows:

$$\tfrac{1}{2}d : 1 = 1 : d \quad \text{or} \quad \frac{d}{2} = \frac{1}{d} \;\Rightarrow\; d^2 = 2 \;\Rightarrow\; d = \sqrt{2}$$

The system of paper sizes of which A4 and A5 form a part is based on similar rectangles whose sides are in the ratio $\sqrt{2} : 1$. The largest size is A0 with an area of 1 square metre and the smaller sizes are obtained by successively halving the area. A spreadsheet, as shown in Figure 7.7, can conveniently be used to do the calculations: the dimensions are in centimetres and square centimetres. The width, w, is found by putting the area equal to $\sqrt{2}w^2$ and solving the equation.

SIZE	AREA	WIDTH	LENGTH
A0	10,000	84.1	118.9
A1	5000	59.5	84.1
A2	2500	42.0	59.5
A3	1250	29.7	42.0
A4	625	21.0	29.7
A5	312.5	14.9	21.0

Figure 7.7 *Spreadsheet to show paper sizes in centimetres*

THE MIDPOINT THEOREM

Since students find similarity much simpler to understand when doubling and halving are involved, the midpoint theorem is an appealing and obvious result which has a variety of simple applications that often involve an element of surprise. The theorem is illustrated in Figure 7.8, where D and E are the midpoints of the sides AB and AC of a triangle ABC. Triangles ABC and ADE are similar because they have angle A in common and the ratios $AB{:}AD$ and $AC{:}AE$ are both 2:1. Alternatively, and perhaps more intuitively, triangle ABC is an enlargement of triangle

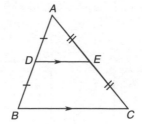

BC = 2DE and BC and DE are parallel.

Figure 7.8 *The midpoint theorem*

ADE with centre *A* and scale factor 2. It follows from the similarity of the triangles that *BC* is twice the length of *DE* and that *BC* and *DE* are parallel.

The midpoint theorem may be presented in several different forms, depending on which facts are taken as starting points, as follows for a triangle *ABC*:

- if *D* and *E* are midpoints of the sides *AB* and *AC*, then *BC* = 2*DE* and *BC* is parallel to *DE*
- if *D* is the midpoint of the side *AB* and the line through *D* parallel to *BC* intersects *AC* at *E*, then *E* is the midpoint of *AC* and *BC* = 2*DE*
- if *D* is the midpoint of the side *AB* and the line through *D* intersects *AC* at *E* such that *BC* = 2*DE*, then *E* is the midpoint of *AC* and *BC* is parallel to *DE*
- if *D* and *E* are points on the sides *AB* and *AC* such that *BC* = 2*DE* and *BC* and *DE* are parallel, then *D* and *E* are the midpoints of the sides

The last of these is the converse of the first: the list could be continued by including the converses of the second and third statements.

Varignon's theorem, referred to earlier in Chapter 1 and illustrated again here in Figure 7.9, is a particularly striking result that is easy to demonstrate. If the adjacent midpoints of the sides of any quadrilateral are joined, it comes as a surprise that the quadrilateral created is always a parallelogram. The result is easy to prove using the midpoint theorem, but as so often with geometrical proofs the critical difficulty for students is 'seeing' where to add an additional line or lines to a diagram to make a link with some known result. As shown in the right-hand

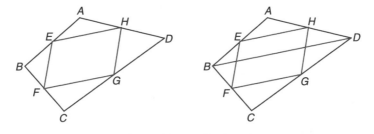

If *E, F, G, H* are the midpoints of the sides of any quadrilateral
ABCD, then *EFGH* is a parallelogram.

Using the midpoint theorem: *EH = FG* = ½*BD* and *EH* and *FG*
are both parallel to *BD*.

Figure 7.9 *Varignon's theorem proved using the midpoint theorem*

diagram of Figure 7.9, drawing in *BD*, one of the diagonals of the initial quadrilateral, provides the clue. Applying the midpoint theorem to triangles *ABD* and *CBD*, we can see that *EH* and *FG* are equal because both are $\frac{1}{2}$ BD and they are both parallel to *BD*. Since the opposite sides *EH* and *FG* are both equal in length and parallel, it follows that *EFGH* is a parallelogram.

Figure 7.10 shows another result involving the midpoints of one pair of opposite sides in a parallelogram. This can again be presented either by using drawing or dynamic geometry. *E* and *F* are the midpoints of the sides *CD* and *AB* of the parallelogram *ABCD*. *G* and *H* are the points where the line segments *DF* and *BE* intersect the diagonal *AC*. The points *G* and *H* trisect the diagonal *AC*. This is proved by seeing that the midpoint theorem in one of its forms applies to both the triangles *ABH* and *CDG*, since the two line segments *DF* and *BE* are parallel, because *DEBF* is a parallelogram. No additional lines are involved in applying the midpoint theorem: the difficulty lies in seeing the two relevant triangles in the diagram. Students can be helped to see by highlighting the triangles *ABH* and *CDG* with bold or coloured lines. The final step in the argument is to note that *AG* and *GH* are equal from triangle *ABH* and *GH* and *HC* are equal from triangle *CDG*. It then follows that all three lengths are equal and the diagonal is bisected.

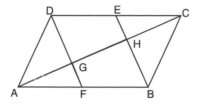

Figure 7.10 *Trisecting the diagonal of a parallelogram*

The fact that the medians of a triangle meet in a common point which divides each in the ratio 2:1 is another of those surprising results that abound in elementary geometry. The left-hand diagram of Figure 7.11 illustrates the result where a triangle *ABC* has *D*, *E* and *F* as midpoints of its three sides and the medians *AF*, *BE* and *CD* intersect in a common point *G*. Students can familiarize themselves with the result by drawing and measuring and by manipulating a dynamic geometry diagram.

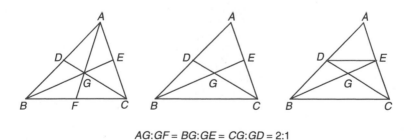

$$AG:GF = BG:GE = CG:GD = 2:1$$

Figure 7.11 *Median property of a triangle proved using the midpoint theorem*

The point of intersection is the centroid or centre of gravity of the triangle, something which can be demonstrated by suspending a triangle in a vertical plane freely from each of its vertices in turn with a plumb line denoting the median. The centroid is the point on which in theory it should be possible to balance a triangle in a horizontal plane.

There are two things that have to be proved here, namely the concurrence and the 2:1 division. Including additional lines is often a good strategy in finding geometrical proofs, but removing lines can be useful too. In this case it is simpler to remove one of the medians and show that the other two intersect in a point that divides each in the ratio 2:1. It then immediately follows that the same is true for any other pair of medians which must therefore share a common point. The middle diagram of Figure 7.11 shows the triangle ABC with just two medians, BE and CD, intersecting at G. Having removed a line, the presence of two midpoints suggests the midpoint theorem. If we draw in DE, as in the right-hand diagram, the midpoint theorem tells us that $BC = 2DE$ and that BC is parallel to DE. It follows that the triangles BGC and EGD are similar and hence that $BG = 2GE$ and $CG = 2GD$, so that the point G divides both medians in the ratio 2:1. Since a similar argument applies to the position of the point of intersection of any of the pairs of medians they must intersect in a common point.

Another way of stating the fact that G divides the medians in the ratio 2:1 is to say that $GF = \frac{1}{3} AF$ and similarly for the other medians. That means that the height of triangle BGC is one third that of triangle ABC. Since they have the same base BC, their areas have the same relationship and it then follows that the three triangles AGB, BGC and CGA have the same area because each is one third of ABC. It is, of course, then immediately obvious that the six triangles of the left-hand diagram of Figure 7.11 are equal in area, because each is half of the three triangles we have just shown to be equal. In fact we could have proved the original result about the medians by considering areas rather than similar triangles.

Finally, before leaving medians of a triangle for a moment, Figure 7.12 poses another problem to which our observation about areas provides an immediate solution. E, F, G and H are the midpoints of the sides of a quadrilateral $ABCD$ and the four line segments AG, AF, CH and CE form a quadrilateral $APCQ$. This time it is not a parallelogram, but we can show that the area of the quadrilateral $APCQ$ is one third of the area of the original quadrilateral $ABCD$. If the diagonal AC is drawn in we can see that triangle ACQ is one third of the area of triangle ADC using the properties of the medians in triangle ADC. Similar consideration of triangles APC and ABC completes the argument.

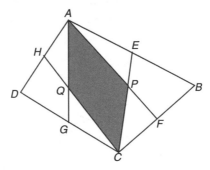

Figure 7.12 *A fraction of a quadrilateral*

THE INTERCEPT THEOREM

The intercept theorem might be seen as a more general version of the midpoint theorem. If a set of three parallel lines are cut by a pair of lines – transversals – then the corresponding line segments cut off on each are in the same ratio. With the transversals ABC and PQR in

Figure 7.13, this means that the ratios *AB:BC* and *PQ:QR* are equal. It is easy to see why this is so by looking at the two similar triangles, *ABS* and *BCT*, in the right-hand diagram, where AS and BT have been drawn parallel to the line *PQR*.

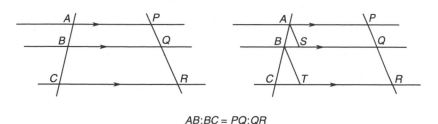

$$AB{:}BC = PQ{:}QR$$

Figure 7.13 *The intercept theorem*

Obviously the intercept theorem applies if there are more than three lines and it is particularly simple and powerful when the parallels are equally spaced. This is illustrated by an alternative proof of the medians property shown in Figure 7.14. The left-hand diagram is the triangle *ABC* with *D* and *E* as midpoints of *AB* and *AC* and *G* is the intersection of the two medians *BE* and *CD*. In the right-hand diagram *H* and *I* are the midpoints of *AE* and *EC* so that *AC* is divided into four equal segments. *F* is the midpoint of *BC*. The midpoint theorem tells us that *DH*, *BE* and *FI* are parallel and the three equal segments *HE*, *EI* and *IC* mean that *G* divides *CD* in the ratio 2:1. The presence of the parallel lines in the diagram displays the three equal segments on *CD* very effectively.

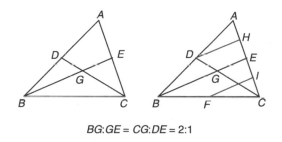

$$BG{:}GE = CG{:}DE = 2{:}1$$

Figure 7.14 *Median property of a triangle proved using the intercept theorem*

Imposing a set of equidistant parallel lines on a diagram often makes a particular property concerning the ratio of lengths stand out very clearly. In the diagrams of Figure 7.15 the midpoints *E* and *F* of the two sides *AB* and *BC* of the square *ABCD* have been joined to *D* and *A* respectively so that the square is divided into four parts. The problem is to determine what fraction each of the four parts is of the square. In the middle diagram a set of lines parallel to *DE* have been drawn passing through points on the sides *AB* and *CD* which divide them each into four equal segments. This divides the line AF into five equal parts and means that *AG* is $\frac{2}{5}$ *AF*. In a similar way, the right hand diagram shows that EG is $\frac{1}{5}$ ED. The height of triangle *AEG* is then $\frac{1}{5}$ if the edges of the square are taken to be of unit length. Since the base *AE* is $\frac{1}{2}$, the area of the triangle is $\frac{1}{2} \times \frac{1}{2} \times \frac{1}{5} = \frac{1}{20}$. Since both triangles *ABF* and *AED* have areas of $\frac{1}{4}$, the areas of *BEGF* and *AGD* are both $\frac{1}{4} - \frac{1}{20} = \frac{1}{5}$. Further calculation will show that the area of *CDGF* is $\frac{11}{20}$. So, the area of the square is divided in the ratio $1 : 4 : 4 : 11$.

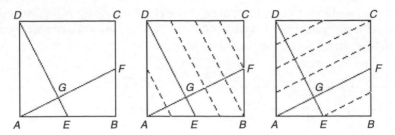

What fraction of the square is each of the four parts?

Figure 7.15 *A square problem*

The right-hand diagram shows a similar set of lines parallel to AF. It is interesting to observe that this shows that DG is $\frac{4}{5} DE$ whereas in the middle diagram we can see that FG is $\frac{3}{5} AF$. Since DE and AF are equal in length it follows that the lengths FG and DG are in the ratio 3:4 and because the angle at G is a right angle, triangle DFG is 3:4:5, which is certainly a surprising result. Indeed the reader might like to draw another diagram with parallels to show DF divided into five equal parts in the same way that AF and DE are divided in the middle and right-hand diagrams respectively.

Geometrical diagrams often exhibit considerable complexity and part of the art of solving a problem or proving a theorem may be to confine attention to one relevant part of the diagram only. The left-hand diagram of Figure 7.16 has been created by joining the midpoints of each side of the square to the two opposite vertices. The eight lines create an octagon inside the square. It is not a regular octagon because the angles are not all equal, although the sides are all of the same length.

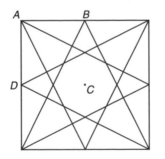
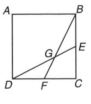

Figure 7.16 *The octagon problem*

The interesting question is to determine what fraction of the square the octagon occupies. This looks impossibly difficult at first and it is sensible to look for ways of making it look less complicated. The right-hand diagram shows the square $ABCD$ taken from the top left-hand corner drawn separately to include only the essential lines BF and DE where E and F are the midpoints of the sides DC and CD. The kite $CEGF$ is a quarter of the octagon we are interested in. Since the square $ABCD$ is a quarter of the big square, we only have to determine what fraction $CEFG$ is of $ABCD$. As with all good problems there are a variety of ways of proceeding, something about which I have written at length in French (2002b). Following on here from our earlier look at medians, it is perhaps simplest to see that G is the intersection of the medians of the triangle BCD. The height of triangle FCG, which is half the required kite, is thus $\frac{1}{3}$, if we take the square to have edges of unit length. The area of triangle *FCG* is then $\frac{1}{2} \times \frac{1}{2} \times \frac{1}{3} = \frac{1}{12}$, giving the area of the kite as double which is $\frac{1}{6}$. So, the octagon occupies $\frac{1}{6}$ of the large square.

THE GOLDEN RATIO

A golden rectangle was defined by the Greeks as one where removing a square from one end leaves a smaller rectangle similar to the original. It was thought to give a particularly pleasing shape for a rectangle and was a common feature of Greek architecture. The ratio of the length to the width of a golden rectangle is known as the golden ratio.

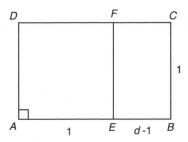

Figure 7.17 *The golden rectangle*

Figure 7.17 shows a golden rectangle, *ABCD*, with unit width and length *d*, which is therefore the value of the golden ratio. The rectangle is subdivided into a square *AEFD* with unit edges and a smaller golden rectangle, *EBFC*, with unit length and width $d - 1$. Comparing the lengths of the two rectangles we can see that the scale factor of the enlargement is *d*. This enables us to calculate the value of *d* by applying it as the scale factor to the widths, which gives its value as the positive root of a quadratic equation as follows:

$$d \times BE = AD \quad \Rightarrow \quad d(d-1) = 1 \quad \Rightarrow \quad d^2 - d - 1 = 0 \quad \Rightarrow \quad d = \tfrac{1}{2}(1 + \sqrt{5}) \approx 1.618$$

Figure 7.18 shows a regular pentagon with edges of unit length. Three of its five diagonals have been included to create a pair of similar isosceles triangles *ABF* and *CEF*. Since the two

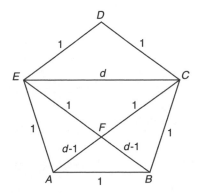

Figure 7.18 *The diagonals of a regular pentagon*

triangles *AEF* and *BCF* are also isosceles, the lengths of *EF* and *CF* are of unit length. With the length of the diagonals denoted by *d*, the lengths *AF* and *BF* are $d - 1$. We can then calculate the value of *d* in an identical way to the previous calculation for the golden rectangle:

$$d \times AF = EF \implies d(d-1) = 1 \implies d^2 - d - 1 = 0 \implies d = \tfrac{1}{2}(1 + \sqrt{5}) \approx 1.618$$

The diagonal length, or more generally the ratio of the diagonal to the edge, is the golden ratio. This connection between the golden rectangle and the regular pentagon is quite surprising and does have an interesting link to the regular icosahedron which is discussed in Chapter 11. It also provides a useful way of constructing a regular pentagon by using the edge and diagonal lengths rather than by measuring angles.

AREAS AND VOLUMES OF SIMILAR SHAPES

We have noted earlier the key fact that enlarging a shape with a scale factor of *k* has the effect of enlarging the area by a factor of k^2 and the volume by k^3. This idea can be developed at a simple level by considering simple shapes made up of squares and solids constructed with cubes. As with length, problems that involve doubling and halving provide simpler starting points than more general cases when considering area and volume.

Figure 7.19 provides a contrasting pair of problems where in one case the area of an isosceles triangle is halved by a line parallel to the base and in the other the volume of a cone is halved by a plane parallel to the base. In both cases the base is in fact at the top, but that allows us in the case of the cone to present the problem as finding the depth of water if a conical container is half full of water. The triangle could represent the cross section of a wedge of cheese which would be a triangular prism so that the area has to be halved to give two pieces of equal volume.

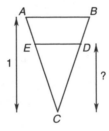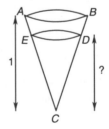

Figure 7.19 *Half a triangle and half a cone*

In both cases it is commonplace to find that students proceed by setting up equations involving the formulae for area of a triangle or the volume of a cone. These involve a number of variables and some relatively complicated looking algebra. It is much simpler to proceed by determining the scale factor for lengths from the respective area or volume scale factor of a half by taking the square or cube root, as follows:

- Triangle: Scale factor for area $= \dfrac{1}{2} \implies$ Scale factor for length $= \dfrac{1}{\sqrt{2}} \approx 0.71$

- Cone: Scale factor for volume $= \dfrac{1}{2} \implies$ Scale factor for length $= \dfrac{1}{\sqrt[3]{2}} \approx 0.79$

With a unit height as in the two diagrams the two scale factors of approximately 0.7 and 0.8 represent the actual height of the smaller triangle and cone, but in general, for an original height of h, the approximate heights required are approximately $0.7h$ and $0.8h$.

A POLYHEDRAL PROBLEM

Figure 7.20 displays a regular tetrahedron, a regular octahedron and a bigger regular tetrahedron surrounding the octahedron. It is very difficult for most students to see a three-dimensional shape and examine its properties from a two-dimensional picture, so some models made from card are essential to make sense of this problem. These are simple to make – all that is required is lots of identical equilateral triangles. Four of the triangles are taped together to make a regular tetrahedron which has three triangles meeting at each vertex and eight make a regular octahedron where there are four triangles at each vertex.

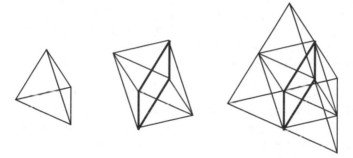

Figure 7.20 *Similar tetrahedra and an octahedron*

Careful examination of the octahedron will show that four of the edges form a square and, indeed, that there are three such squares since there are twelve edges. One of these squares is highlighted in the octahedron of Figure 7.20, but it does not, of course, look like a square. Moreover its orientation seems frustratingly to change as you look, for it may appear to be facing downwards to the right or upwards to the left. So, it is useful to look at a model from which you can also see that an octahedron is made of two square-based pyramids sharing the same square base.

The large tetrahedron is made by suitably placing four small tetrahedra on four of the eight faces of the octahedron. The problem is to find how many of the small tetrahedra are equivalent to the volume of the octahedron. The large tetrahedron is similar to the small one and is constructed in such a way that all its edges are double those of the small one. The large tetrahedron is in some sense 'twice as big' as the smaller, but the two is the scale factor for length: the volume is eight times as big and is therefore equivalent to eight of the small tetrahedra. It immediately follows that the octahedron has the same volume as four of the tetrahedra and also that a square-based pyramid with faces made up of the same equilateral triangles is twice the volume of the small tetrahedron.

This last observation provides a simple way of finding a formula for the volume of a tetrahedron, as follows:

Let the length of the edges be d.

Then, from the octahedron, it can be seen that the height of the square-based pyramid is half the diagonal of the square, which is $\frac{1}{2}\sqrt{2}d$.

Volume of pyramid $= \frac{1}{3}$ base $\times$ height $= \frac{1}{3} \times d^2 \times \frac{1}{2}\sqrt{2}d = \dfrac{\sqrt{2}}{6}d^3$

Volume of tetrahedron $= \frac{1}{2}$ volume of pyramid $= \dfrac{\sqrt{2}}{12}d^3$

Finally it is an interesting exercise to make some square-based pyramids with equilateral triangles as faces and use them, together with some tetrahedra, to make a square-based pyramid which is 'twice as big'. This will require the equivalent of sixteen tetrahedra.

CONCLUSION

Similarity is one of the big important ideas in geometry with a wealth of applications to real situations as well as being a frequent feature of theorems, proofs and problems. Its direct link to the transformation of enlargement provides an alternative approach involving scale factors, which is a simpler idea to grasp initially than the more traditional approach through equal ratios. It also extends readily to problems involving areas and volumes in similar shapes and solids.

As with all areas of geometry new ideas should be accompanied by practical tasks. Accurate drawing, working with actual shapes and solids, making models and using dynamic geometry software in a variety of ways all have a valuable part to play in developing the essential intuitive feel for the ideas of enlargement and similarity.

The word similar has an everyday meaning which implies a certain sameness. This is a potential source of confusion because it is less precise than the mathematical meaning. In everyday language we may say that some shapes, for example a set of rectangles, are similar or the 'same shape' because they all have four sides and right angles. Mathematical similarity certainly requires figures to have the same number of sides and identical angles, but it also requires corresponding lengths to be in the same proportion. Proportionality is the key property of similarity and it is an idea that is a considerable source of difficulty. That is a major reason for linking similarity to enlargement and for introducing scale factors because they offer a more accessible approach than equal ratios. Emphasis should be given initially to situations which involve doubling and other simple whole-number scale factors, which make better immediate sense to many students. Successful use of fractional scale factors is obviously very dependent on having acquired a real understanding of fractions and fluency with their use. Situations involving halving are considerably simpler than those involving any other fraction.

A variety of examples which relate to familiar situations should be used alongside more traditional abstract configurations to develop understanding and fluency in determining scale factors and using them to calculate lengths, and at a later stage relating them to areas and volumes. The midpoint theorem and its generalization, the intercept theorem, provide powerful tools for solving problems and proving results. It is important to offer motivating examples which stimulate curiosity and have an aesthetic appeal, and which challenge students to think independently.

Chapter 8

The Theorem of Pythagoras

POSING A PROBLEM

It is a good teaching strategy to introduce a new idea or topic by posing a problem which students work on for themselves. The simplest right-angled triangle is one which is isosceles with two equal sides of unit length. It is not immediately obvious how to find the length of the hypotenuse, other than by measuring, but it is a problem that can be posed for students as a first step towards establishing the theorem of Pythagoras.

When the simple right-angled triangle is drawn on a square grid it is not difficult to spot the square on the hypotenuse shown in the left-hand diagram of Figure 8.1. The area of this square is readily seen to be 2 and that leads to the square root of 2 as the length of the hypotenuse. This is an ingenious and surprising way of arriving at the length, but that is because it is linked to the very remarkable result that we commonly refer to as the theorem of Pythagoras.

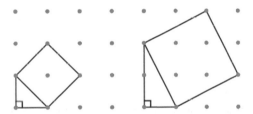

Figure 8.1 *How long is the hypotenuse?*

The idea of using the area of the square on the hypotenuse in this way, which is suggested by drawing right-angled triangles on a square grid, was familiar to the Babylonians and in China and India a long time before the time of Pythagoras. It can be extended readily to find the hypotenuse of other triangles when the other edges are of integer length. The right-hand diagram of Figure 8.1 shows a triangle with sides of 1 and 2 resulting in a square on the hypotenuse of area 5. In this case the area of the square will not be quite so obvious to students. They will need to use one of the two strategies for finding areas discussed at the beginning of Chapter 6, either dissecting the square into simpler shapes or surrounding it by a larger square and taking off the areas of the additional triangles formed.

A variety of examples similar to those in Figure 8.1 can be explored finding the area of the square on the hypotenuse and the length of the hypotenuse in each case. If results are tabulated systematically as in Figure 8.2, students can then seek the link between the area of the square and the lengths of the two sides. It is not difficult to see that the square on the hypotenuse is equal to the sum of the squares of the other two sides once the pattern in the additions shown in the table has been spotted. Further empirical reinforcement can be obtained by using the area-measuring facility of dynamic geometry software.

SIDES	SQUARE	SIDES	SQUARE	SIDES	SQUARE
1, 1	2 = 1 + 1	2, 1	5 = 4 + 1	3, 1	10 = 9 + 1
1, 2	5 = 1 + 4	2, 2	8 = 4 + 4	3, 2	13 = 9 + 4
1, 3	10 = 1 + 9	2, 3	13 = 4 + 9	3, 3	18 = 9 + 9
1, 4	17 = 1 + 16	2, 4	20 = 4 + 16	3, 4	25 = 9 + 16
1, 5	26 = 1 + 25	2, 5	29 = 4 + 25	3, 5	34 = 9 + 25

Figure 8.2 *Looking for the link between the square and the sides*

The numerical results certainly make Pythagoras' theorem seem very plausible. The result is summarized in Figure 8.3 as, $a^2 + b^2 = c^2$, where a and b are the two shorter sides of a right-angled triangle with a hypotenuse of length c. The result should be seen as a relationship between geometrical squares and not merely as an algebraic formula.

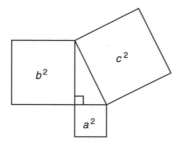

Figure 8.3 *Pythagoras' theorem: $a^2 + b^2 = c^2$*

Returning briefly to Figure 8.2, it is worth noting the presence of the square number 25 in the final column. That draws attention to the very special case of the 3, 4, 5 triangle and the possibility of other whole-number triples that can be the sides of a right-angled triangle. These triples offer plenty of scope for student investigation at different levels. While the 3, 4, 5 triangle is often used as a starting point for introducing Pythagoras' theorem, I would argue that the problem of finding the hypotenuse of the isosceles right-angled triangle is a more natural way to involve a diagram in which the square on the hypotenuse is meaningful and useful.

Students need to spend some time at an early stage working on simple numerical examples, calculating one side of a right-angled triangle given the other two. This will extend their familiarity with the theorem and help them to see what a powerful tool it is before investigating further why such a remarkable result should be true. The calculations should be straightforward, but a common source of difficulty is that of deciding whether to add or subtract, resulting in confusion between a pair of examples involving the same numbers, like those shown in Figure 8.4. This difficulty arises because students try to remember a procedure rather than sense what it means by referring back to the diagram and thinking what will be a sensible answer. It is useful to juxtapose examples like those in the Figure 8.4 to help them see that in one case the solution must be greater than 5 and in the other case less than 5.

It is important to stress that Pythagoras' theorem is a result concerning areas of squares and that it can be shown to be true geometrically for any triangle regardless of whether the lengths are integers. One of the ways mentioned above in conjunction with Figure 8.1 for calculating the

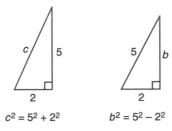

$$c^2 = 5^2 + 2^2 \qquad b^2 = 5^2 - 2^2$$

Figure 8.4 *Pythagoras' theorem: to add or subtract?*

area of the square on the hypotenuse is to surround the square with a larger square. This procedure is shown in the left-hand diagram of Figure 8.5. The diagram can be seen as four congruent right-angled triangles surrounding a square and the triangles can be translated to the positions shown in the right-hand diagram. It is then clear that the sum of the areas of the two shaded squares on the right is equal in area to the square on the hypotenuse on the left. This provides a neat and simple pictorial proof of Pythagoras' theorem, although we should assure ourselves that the shaded shape on the left is in fact a square, perhaps by engaging in a dialogue like the following:

T: How do you know it is a square?
A: It has four equal sides.
T: How do you know they are equal?
B: It is always the hypotenuse of the triangle and the four triangles are congruent.
T: What else do you need to show?
C: That the angles are right angles.
T: How can you show that?
D: Look at the angles at the bottom. The two angles from the triangle add up to 90°, so the other angle must be 90°.

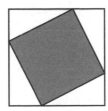 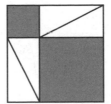

Figure 8.5 *A pictorial proof of Pythagoras' theorem*

Finally, before examining some more formal ways of proving Pythagoras' theorem in the next section, Figure 8.6 shows Perigal's dissection. This is an ingenious way of dissecting one of the smaller squares into four pieces which fit together with the other smaller square to make the square on the hypotenuse. Constructing the dissection is straightforward. Lines parallel and perpendicular to the hypotenuse are drawn through the centre of the square on the left to divide it into the required four parts. Students will find it instructive to make their own version of the dissection, perhaps choosing their own dimensions for the initial triangle so that a variety of examples are produced. It is also interesting to display the dissection using dynamic geometry software so that the effect of varying the triangle can be demonstrated.

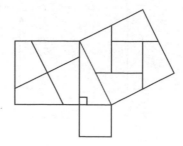

Figure 8.6 *Perigal's dissection*

PROVING PYTHAGORAS' THEOREM

Pythagoras' theorem appears famously as Proposition 47 in Book 1 of Euclid (Heath 1967) and it is presumed that this version of the proof, shown in Figure 8.7, originated with Pythagoras. To modern eyes the way the argument is presented makes it difficult to follow, but the proof is very ingenious and it is therefore worth finding ways of making it more accessible.

The essence of the proof is to show that the two smaller squares are respectively equal in area to the two rectangles into which the square on the hypotenuse is divided by dropping a perpendicular from the vertex of the triangle. Referring to the diagram reproduced in Figure 8.8, the proof can be presented as follows:

- Triangle FBC is half the area of square $ABFG$ and triangle ABD is equal to half the area of rectangle $BDLM$, because in each case they have the same base and height.
- Triangles FBC and ABD are congruent, since two sides and the included angle are equal as follows:

$$FB = AB \text{ (sides of square)}$$
$$BC = BD \text{ (sides of square)}$$
$$\angle FBC = \angle ABD \ (\angle ABC + 90°)$$

- It follows that square $ABFG$ and rectangle $BDLM$ are equal in area.
- A similar argument then applies to the other square and its corresponding rectangle.
- Hence, the two smaller squares are equal in area to the square on the hypotenuse.

The conventional written form of a proof can often be a barrier to understanding. This is illustrated by the style of Euclid, but it is still a characteristic of much written mathematics. The style should be brief, but sufficient, so that the whole argument is clear as well as the justification for the details of each step. Using colour in diagrams, and in written statements, to highlight particular features is a valuable way of making the explanation of a proof both more attractive and easier to follow. If the diagram is displayed using dynamic geometry software there is also the possibility of moving the configuration to show that the argument is still valid if its essential features are retained. For instance in Figure 8.8, the point A can be constrained to move on a hidden circle which has BC as diameter so that the angle at A remains a right angle.

PROPOSITION XLVII.

THEOREM.—*If a triangle* (ABC) *be right-angled*, the square which is constructed upon the side (BC) subtending the right angle is equal in area to the sum of the squares constructed upon the sides (AB and AC) which form the right angle.

CONSTRUCTION. *On the sides* AB, BC, *and* AC, *construct the squares* BG, BE, *and* CH (a); *through* A *draw* AL *parallel to* BD (b), *and join* AD *and* FC.

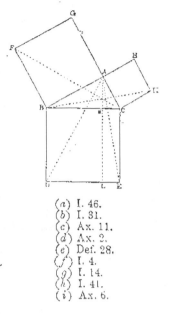

DEMONSTRATION. Because the angles FBA and CBD are both right angles (a), therefore they are equal (c); add to both the angle ABC, and the angle FBC is equal to ABD (d). Because the sides FB and BC are respectively equal to AB and BD (e), and the angle FBC to the angle ABD, therefore the triangle FBC is equal to the triangle ABD (f). Because the angles GAB and BAC are both right angles, therefore GA and AC are in the same straight line (g). Now the parallelogram BL is double of the triangle ABD, because they are on the same base BD and between the same parallels BD and AL (h); and the square GB is double of the triangle FBC, being on the same base FB and between the same parallels FB and GC (h). But the doubles of equals are equal to one another (i), and *therefore the parallelogram* BL *is equal in area to the square* GB. And in the same manner, by joining AE and BK, it may be proved that *the parallelogram* CL *is equal in area to the square* CH. *Therefore the whole square* BDEC *is equal in area to the two squares* BG *and* CH.

(a) I. 46.
(b) I. 31.
(c) Ax. 11.
(d) Ax. 2.
(e) Def. 28.
(f) I. 4.
(g) I. 14.
(h) I. 41.
(i) Ax. 6.

Figure 8.7 *Pythagoras' theorem: Proposition 47 from Book 1 of Euclid* (taken from a version of Euclid's *Elements* by Henry Law (1855))

A variant on Euclid's proof is to use a sequence of transformations to show that the corresponding squares and rectangles are equal. In Figure 8.9, which shows the steps for one square and rectangle, a shear is followed by a 90° rotation and then by another shear. Each transformation leaves the area invariant. Showing that the initial and final positions of the rotation are correct requires the same argument as that for the congruent triangles above. This proof is particularly effective if it is demonstrated with an animated sequence of diagrams constructed with dynamic geometry software and displayed on Microsoft Powerpoint.

It is interesting to compare these arguments to one using similar triangles to show that the corresponding squares and rectangles have equal areas. Figure 8.10 shows an enlarged version of the right-angled triangle alongside the left-hand diagram with a shaded square and its corresponding rectangle. With the sides denoted as shown on the diagram it is necessary to show

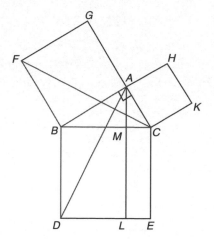

Figure 8.8 *Pythagoras' theorem: an alternative approach to Euclid's proof*

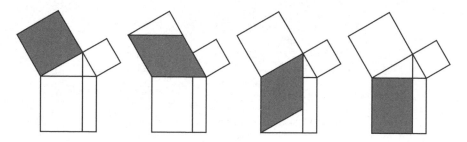

Figure 8.9 *Shearing and rotation to prove Pythagoras' theorem*

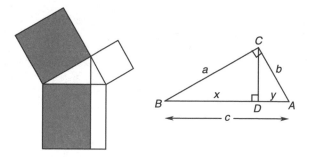

Figure 8.10 *Using similar triangles to prove Pythagoras' theorem*

that, a^2, the area of the square, is equal to cx, the area of the rectangle. Since triangles ABC and CBD are similar, we can use equal ratios to say:

$$\frac{a}{c} = \frac{x}{a} \quad \Rightarrow \quad a^2 = cx$$

In the same way, triangles ABC and ACD are similar giving:

$$\frac{b}{c} = \frac{y}{b} \quad \Rightarrow \quad b^2 = cy$$

Putting these two results together we have proved Pythagoras' theorem:

$$a^2 + b^2 = cx + cy = c(x + y) = c^2$$

This proof can be presented in a slightly different form using trigonometry either by deriving the pairs of equal ratios by expressing each of cos$A$ and cos$B$ as ratios in two different ways from the similar triangles or, alternatively, by proceeding as follows:

$$x = a \cos B \text{ and } y = b \cos A \quad \Rightarrow \quad c = a \cos B + b \cos A$$

Multiplying both sides by c gives: $c^2 = ac \cos B + bc \cos A$

$$a = \cos B \text{ and } b = c \cos A \quad \Rightarrow \quad c^2 = ac \cos B + bc \cos A = a^2 + b^2$$

As a final example of the rich variety of proofs of Pythagoras' theorem, Figure 8.11 uses a right-angled triangle *OCD* where *C* is a variable point on a semicircle with centre *O* and *D* is the

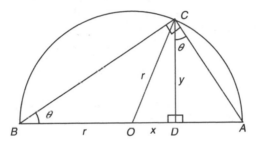

Figure 8.11 *A proof of Pythagoras' theorem using tangents*

foot of the perpendicular from *C* to the diameter *AB*. The sides of triangle *OCD* are denoted by the variables x, y and r. The equal angles at *B* and *C* in the similar right-angled triangles *BDC* and *CDA* are denoted by θ. Using these two triangles to express tan θ in two different forms, which are equated, leads directly to a neat proof of Pythagoras' theorem:

$$\tan \theta = \frac{y}{r+x} = \frac{r-x}{y} \quad \Rightarrow \quad (r+x)(r-x) = y^2 \quad \Rightarrow \quad x^2 + y^2 = r^2$$

A TRIGONOMETRICAL INTERLUDE

Trigonometry is another powerful tool which is linked to the idea of similar triangles and is frequently used in conjunction with Pythagoras' theorem in solving problems. Sine, cosine and tangent are commonly introduced to students as ratios, but there are considerable advantages, as I have argued in French (2002b), in starting with cosine and sine as the coordinates of points on a circle of unit radius. They are then defined, in the case of acute angles, as the lengths of the sides of a right-angled triangle with unit hypotenuse. This is illustrated by the left-hand diagram of Figure 8.12. The right-hand diagram shows how other right-angled triangles can then be seen as enlargements of a triangle with unit hypotenuse.

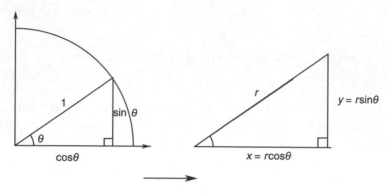

ENLARGEMENT WITH SCALE FACTOR *r*

Figure 8.12 *Defining cosine and sine*

   The extension to angles greater than 90° becomes a more natural and straightforward step and the right-hand diagram shows how viewing cosine and sine in this way links directly to finding the components of a vector, linking Cartesian and polar coordinates and understanding the parametric form for the equation of a circle. Moreover, Pythagoras' theorem applied to the left-hand diagram provides immediate confirmation of an important trigonometrical identity:

$$\cos^2 \theta + \sin^2 \theta = 1$$

   Tangent can be defined as in Figure 8.13 by extending the line segment *OP* to a point *T* where it meets the tangent to the circle at *R*. The length *RT* along the tangent is then defined as the

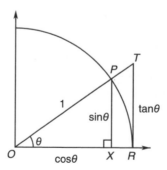

Figure 8.13 *Defining tangent*

trigonometric tangent, showing that there is a link between the geometric and trigonometric meanings of the word. The right-angled triangles *OXP* and *ORT* are similar with an enlargement scale factor which is the reciprocal of cosθ. This provides the definition of secant and shows how tangent is linked to cosine and sine. Pythagoras' theorem then gives us another identity which is similar in form to $\cos^2 \theta + \sin^2 \theta = 1$:

$$OT = \frac{1}{\cos\theta} = \sec\theta \quad \text{and} \quad RT = \frac{\sin\theta}{\cos\theta} = \tan\theta \quad \Rightarrow \quad 1 + \tan^2 \theta = \sec^2 \theta$$

An additional observation to make here is that tan θ is also the gradient of the line OT, since OR is of unit length. This useful fact provides an alternative way of seeing the link to cosine and sine.

The cosine rule is a generalization of Pythagoras' theorem. If the right angle is varied, while keeping the two sides on either side of it constant in length, the third side increases or decreases, as shown in Figure 8.14, as the angle at C increases or decreases. At the same time the square of the length of the side c is therefore more or less than $a^2 + b^2$ depending on whether angle C is more or less than 90°. The cosine rule includes the term $2ab \cos C$ which makes the necessary adjustment to Pythagoras' theorem.

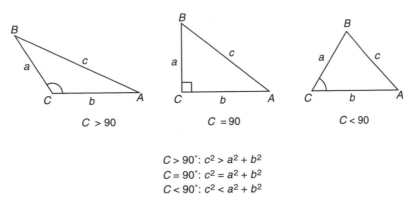

$$C > 90°: c^2 > a^2 + b^2$$
$$C = 90°: c^2 = a^2 + b^2$$
$$C < 90°: c^2 < a^2 + b^2$$

Figure 8.14 *Linking Pythagoras' theorem and the cosine rule*

The cosine rule is usually proved by applying Pythagoras' theorem to two right-angled triangles obtained by constructing one altitude of a general triangle. An alternative more geometric proof uses a generalization of the shearing and rotation proof of Pythagoras' theorem, which was discussed previously in conjunction with Figure 8.9. A triangle with squares on each side is shown in Figure 8.15. Each square is subdivided into two rectangles by one of the

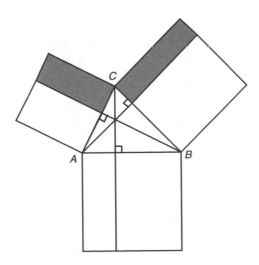

Figure 8.15 *The cosine rule*

altitudes of the triangle. Pairs of these rectangles can be shown to be equal in area either by simple trigonometry or by using two shears and a rotation as in the earlier Pythagoras proof. The areas of the shaded pair of rectangles in the figure are given by $ab \cos C$. By considering the two rectangles which form the lower square, it then follows that:

$$c^2 = (a^2 - ab \cos C) + (b^2 - ab \cos C) = a^2 + b^2 - 2\,ab \cos C$$

SOME PROBLEMS USING PYTHAGORAS' THEOREM

Pythagoras' theorem is a result that is constantly needed in solving geometrical problems and proving significant results. Although these frequently require the use of algebra or trigonometry, it is always necessary to identify appropriate triangles and to take account of other geometrical features in arriving at solutions. Four very different examples are discussed in this section from the rich variety of examples that will be found in school textbooks and elsewhere.

Webster (2003) describes a surprising result based on the configuration with squares on the three sides of a triangle. The three shaded triangles between the squares are equal in area to the triangle in the middle. This is a simple result to prove by expressing the area of triangle ABC as $\frac{1}{2}\,ab \sin C$. Since the angle at C in the upper shaded triangle is $180 - C$, the area of that triangle is $\frac{1}{2}\,ab \sin(180 - C)$, which is also equal to $\frac{1}{2}\,ab \sin C$. The other shaded triangles can be shown to have the same area as triangle ABC in a similar way.

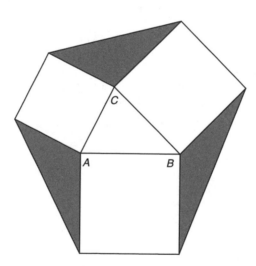

Figure 8.16 *Surprising equal areas*

Schumann and Green (1994, p. 263) draw attention to a remarkable property of the three squares on the sides of a right-angled triangle configuration shown in Figure 8.17. When the square on the hypotenuse is reflected in the hypotenuse, one of the upper vertices of the reflected square always lies on the edge of one of the smaller squares. It is particularly impressive when this is demonstrated with dynamic geometry software. The result is easily explained by noting that the triangles ABC and ADE are congruent, because they have two equal sides and equal

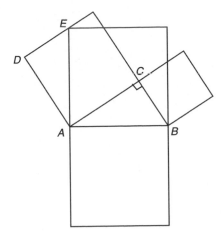

Figure 8.17 *A reflected square*

angles at A. A similar argument applies when the other upper vertex of the reflected square lies on the right-hand square.

A method that can be used for determining the radius of an arc of a circle or a circle if the centre is inaccessible so that a direct measurement cannot be made is shown in Figure 8.18. The diagram could represent a wheel touching the ground at the point A and resting against the

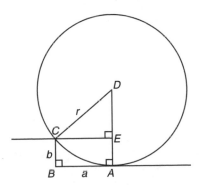

Figure 8.18 *Finding the radius*

edge of a curb or a block of wood at C. The same configuration with a pair of lines, AB and BC, at right angles could be used in relation to any arc of a circle. If the two lengths AB and BC, denoted by a and b, are measured, the radius can be calculated. Applying Pythagoras' theorem to the right-angled triangle CDE, we have:

$$r^2 = (r - b)^2 + a^2 \quad \Rightarrow \quad 2br = a^2 + b^2 \quad \Rightarrow \quad r = \frac{a^2 + b^2}{2b}$$

Apollonius' theorem provides a relationship between the lengths of the medians and the lengths of the sides of a triangle. In Figure 8.19, the point D is the midpoint of the side AB of triangle ABC. Using the usual notation, the sides BC and AC are denoted by a and b, with d as

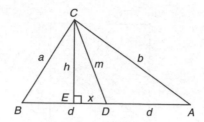

Figure 8.19 *Apollonius' theorem*

the length of *BD* and *AD* and *m* as the length of the median *CD*. CE is an altitude of the triangle with *CE* and *DE* in the right-angled triangle *CDE* denoted by *h* and *x* respectively.

Applying Pythagoras' theorem to the three right-angled triangles in the diagram gives:

$$\text{Triangle } CDE: x^2 + h^2 = m^2$$
$$\text{Triangle } BCE: (d - x)^2 + h^2 = a^2$$
$$\text{Triangle } ACE: (d + x)^2 + h^2 = b^2$$

Adding the second and third equations and then substituting from the first gives the relationship between the four lengths *a*, *b*, *d*, and *m* which is known as Apollonius' theorem and can be used to calculate the lengths of the medians:

$$a^2 + b^2 = [(d - x)^2 + h^2] + [(d + x)^2 + h^2]$$
$$= 2d^2 + 2x^2 + 2h^2$$
$$= 2d^2 + 2m^2$$
$$= 2(d^2 + m^2)$$

If the third side, AB, of the triangle is denoted by *c* in the conventional way, the result can be stated in the form:

$$m^2 = \tfrac{1}{2}(a^2 + b^2) - \tfrac{1}{4}c^2.$$

Adding together the corresponding results for each of the three medians, denoted here by *l*, *m*, and *n*, we arrive at another interesting result which is that the sum of the squares of the medians is $\tfrac{3}{4}$ of the sum of the squares of the sides:

$$l^2 + m^2 + n^2 = \tfrac{3}{4}(a^2 + b^2 + c^2).$$

CONCLUSION

The theorem of Pythagoras is one of the most famous and remarkable theorems in mathematics with a wide range of applications of both practical and mathematical significance. Students need to know what the theorem says, where it comes from and how to use it. It is easy to concentrate on the first and the third and to neglect the second and yet it is important to explore how the result can be achieved in a variety of ways both empirical and deductive. This helps to generate an intuitive feel for the result if it is accompanied by the necessary fluency with relevant calculations, including the use of algebra and trigonometry. It also gives a valuable experience of the application of a range of strategies and ideas and helps to develop the critical skills of identifying the key features of a configuration and of sensing where to place that crucial additional line which is so often the key to solving a problem.

There are a multitude of different proofs of the Pythagoras' theorem and each draws on different ideas, so that seeing them reinforces different aspects of geometry as well as stimulating interest. The proofs that have been considered in this chapter have involved areas, congruence, transformations, similarity and trigonometry all of which are important and need to be seen in a wide variety of different contexts. Students should encounter a number of different proofs of the theorem during their study of geometry, not because they need to be able to remember and reproduce them, but because they should add to their understanding of the theorem, reinforce many important concepts and strategies and add generally to the richness of their geometrical experience.

Chapter 9

The Circle

CHORDS AND TANGENTS

The left-hand diagram of Figure 9.1 shows a sequence of parallel lines cutting a circle. This can be demonstrated readily by moving a straight-edge on a diagram drawn on paper or on a board or, perhaps more effectively, on a screen using dynamic geometry. The focus of attention is on the chord – the line segment AB, where A and B are the points of intersection between the line and the circle. As the line sweeps across the circle, AB increases in length, reaching a maximum when it is a diameter, and then decreasing until it becomes a tangent when it touches the circle in a single point where A and B coincide. In the right-hand diagram of Figure 9.1, a diameter has been added perpendicular to the parallels. This draws attention to the fact that any chord is bisected by such a perpendicular diameter and that the tangent is perpendicular to the radius through its point of contact.

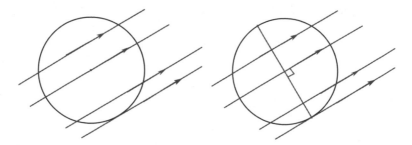

Figure 9.1 *Parallel lines intersecting a circle*

An isosceles triangle is formed when each end of a chord is joined to the centre of the circle. Figure 9.2 illustrates the two essential properties of a chord in a circle which follow from the properties of isosceles triangles and take the form of two converse statements:

- the line joining the midpoint of a chord to the centre of the circle is perpendicular to the chord
- a line through the centre of a circle perpendicular to a chord bisects the chord

The presence of isosceles triangles in circles is a vital property to draw upon when exploring the geometry of a circle and is used extensively in proving results in the subsequent sections of this chapter. In addition the right-angled triangles formed by the perpendicular bisector of chords can be used for a variety of calculations involving lengths and angles using Pythagoras' theorem and trigonometry.

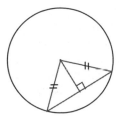

Figure 9.2 *The chord properties of a circle*

The key property that a tangent to a circle is perpendicular to the radius through the point of contact is a limiting case of the chord properties. Accurately constructing a tangent to a circle requires the use of this perpendicularity property, but is not a very interesting paper and pencil exercise. The result is more interesting if posed as a problem with dynamic geometry by asking students how to draw a tangent to a circle that can then be moved to any position round the circle as illustrated by Figure 9.3.

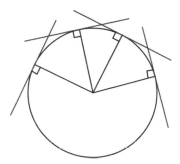

Figure 9.3 *Moving a tangent round a circle*

Rotating a line about a point outside a circle, as shown in the left-hand diagram of Figure 9.4, gives a different perspective on tangents by drawing attention to two properties:

- from any point outside a circle there are two tangents which are equal in length
- the line from the centre of a circle to a point outside the circle bisects the angle between the two tangents from that point

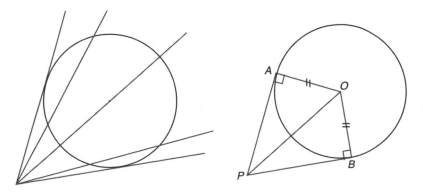

Figure 9.4 *A rotating line intersecting a circle*

The right-hand diagram of Figure 9.4 shows the pair of triangles *OAP* and *OBP* which are congruent because they are both right-angled, share a common hypotenuse *OP* and have equal radii *OA* and *OB* as sides. The two properties above follow from this congruence.

Figure 9.5 shows another interesting exercise to extend understanding of tangents. The problem is to determine how many common tangents there are to a pair of circles in different positions. The diagrams show the various possibilities. The case of three circles provides a much more challenging task for students to consider.

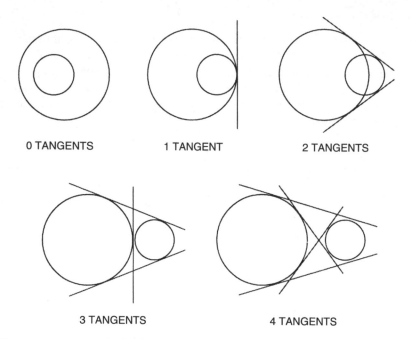

Figure 9.5 *Common tangents to a pair of circles*

THE ANGLE IN A SEMICIRCLE

In Figure 9.6 the line segment *AB* is the diameter of a semicircle and *P* is a point on the semicircle. It is easy to demonstrate that angle *APB* is a right angle by drawing *P* in various positions on a semicircle and measuring angle *APB* either with a protractor or using a set square. This can be done much more dramatically using dynamic geometry with *P* as a point that can be moved round the semicircle.

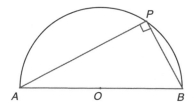

Figure 9.6 *Angle in a semicircle*

A first step towards making sense of a formal proof of the right-angle result is to do some calculations with angles. To do this it is necessary to draw in the radius OP as shown in Figure 9.7, thereby creating two isosceles triangles, OAP and BOP. Then if angle OAP is given all the other angles in the two triangles can be calculated readily using the angle properties of isosceles triangles. Results for various values of the angle OAP are shown in the table of Figure 9.7. Creating such a table with a spreadsheet is a useful task because a general formula for each column has to be determined. It is easy to spot that the sum of corresponding pairs of angles in the first and last columns is 90° in each case. Besides the obvious fact that the angles in the middle pair of columns have a sum of 180°, students will also observe that those in the third column are twice those in the first and similarly for the second and last columns. This is an example where the exterior angle of a triangle is equal to the sum of the opposite pair of angles in the special case of isosceles triangles. It also anticipates the important result that the angle subtended by an arc at the centre of a circle is twice the angle at the circumference subtended by the same arc.

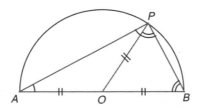

$\angle OAP = \angle OPA$	$\angle AOP$	$\angle BOP$	$\angle OBP = \angle OPB$
10°	160°	20°	80°
20°	140°	40°	70°
30°	120°	60°	60°
40°	100°	80°	50°
50°	80°	100°	40°
60°	60°	120°	30°

$$\angle OPA + \angle OPB = 90°$$

Figure 9.7 *Angle in a semicircle*

The result can easily be proved by arguing in the same way as above, but with a general angle. If the two pairs of equal angles, measured in degrees, are denoted respectively by θ and ϕ as shown in Figure 9.8, then angle BOP is 2θ and $\phi = \frac{1}{2}(180 - 2\theta) = 90 - \theta$. It then follows that angle APB is $\theta + 90 - \theta = 90$. An alternative approach is to observe that the sum of the angles in the large triangle APB is $2\theta + 2\phi = 180$, from which we can immediately see that $\theta + \phi = 90$.

The angle in a semicircle property is only one of the linked set of results that are commonly referred to as the circle theorems, which are discussed in the next section of this chapter. It is worth considering this result separately before the other results because it is relatively easy to understand and it arises in a wide variety of geometrical situations. To illustrate this variety the theorem is applied in what follows to some very different problems.

One of the important properties of tangents considered in the first section of this chapter is that two tangents can be drawn from an external point to a circle and the distances from the

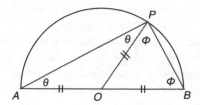

Figure 9.8 *Angle in a semicircle*

points of contact to that point are equal. In order to construct these tangents it is necessary to find the position of the points of contact and to do that we make use of the property that a tangent is perpendicular to the radius through the point of contact. To carry this out on paper with straight-edge and compasses is not a very exciting task, but it comes to life if the challenge is to make it work on a computer screen using dynamic geometry, because the final result can be manipulated by moving the external point and varying the position and radius of the circle. That provides a very robust test as to whether the construction has been carried out correctly.

In the left-hand diagram of Figure 9.9, *P* is the external point and *O* is the centre of the circle and we require a point *A* on the circle so that angle *OAP* is a right angle. We want a right angle and we know that the angle in a semicircle is a right angle. Thus, if we construct a semicircle with *OP* as diameter by finding the midpoint of *OP* as its centre, then its point of intersection with the original circle is the required point of contact and we can construct the tangent. Indeed, if we complete the whole circle we have both points of contact and can then construct both tangents.

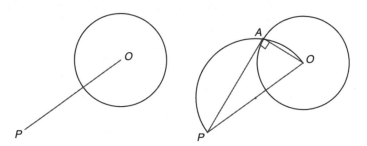

Figure 9.9 *Constructing a tangent to a circle*

Figure 9.10 shows two circles which intersect at *A* and *B*. Their centres are denoted by *C* and *D* and *AC* and *AD* are produced to give diameters *AP* and *AQ*. The three points *P*, *B* and *Q* in

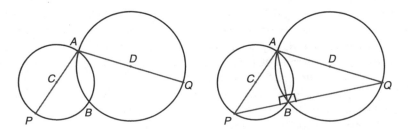

Figure 9.10 *Proving three points are collinear*

the left-hand diagram certainly look as though they are collinear. The problem is to prove that this is so. It clearly makes sense as a first step to join *PB* and *QB*. The difficulty for students is to see what step to take next. They should be encouraged to think back from what it is they are trying to show, which should focus attention on the angle at B and the need to show that angle *PBQ* is 180°. The clue is to draw in the line *AB*, because we then see, as the right-hand diagram shows, that the angles *ABP* and *ABQ* are both right angles because each is an angle in a semicircle.

Figure 9.10 has another interesting feature which takes us back to the ideas of Chapter 7. The centres *C* and *D* are midpoints of the sides *AP* and *AQ* of triangle *APQ* so that the midpoint theorem tells us that *PQ* is twice the length of *CD* and that these two line segments are parallel.

The third example illustrated by Figure 9.11 is more algebraic. *P* is point on a semicircle with centre *O* drawn on diameter *AB*. *C* is the foot of the perpendicular from *P* to *AB*. The two

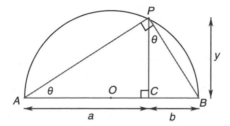

Figure 9.11 *Comparing the geometric and arithmetic mean*

lengths *AC* and *BC* are denoted by *a* and *b* and the perpendicular PC is denoted by *y*. Because angle *APB* is a right angle we can easily show that angles *CAP* and *CPB* are equal, denoted by θ in the diagram, and hence that triangles *CAP* and *CPB* are similar. Since these two triangles are right-angled, the simplest way of linking the lengths of corresponding sides is to use trigonometry, in this case the tangent of angle θ:

$$\tan \theta = \frac{y}{a} = \frac{b}{y} \quad \Rightarrow \quad y^2 = ab \quad \Rightarrow \quad y = \sqrt{ab}$$

We see from this that *y* is the geometric mean of *a* and *b* or, to express this in a different way, *a*, *y* and *b* are consecutive terms in a geometric sequence. For example, if a population doubled from 1 million to 2 million over a 50-year period at a steady rate, the population after 25 years, the halfway point, would be $\sqrt{2}$ or approximately 1.4 million.

The arithmetic mean is given by $\frac{1}{2}(a + b)$ and this is 1.5 million in our example. This is greater than the geometric mean, a fact that is always true unless the two numbers are equal. Figure 9.11 makes it clear geometrically why this is so, because $\frac{1}{2}(a + b)$ is half the diameter which is, of course, the radius of the semicircle and the radius is clearly always going to be greater than the perpendicular *PC*, unless *C* coincides with the centre *O* in which case *a* = *b*.

As a final application of the angle in a semicircle theorem we turn to trigonometry where the diagram shown in Figure 9.12 provides a pictorial proof of the identities known as the double-angle formulae. If the radius of the semicircle is taken as 1 and the angle *OAP* as θ, then the angle *COP* is the exterior angle of the isosceles triangle and is therefore equal to 2θ. Using either triangle *ABP* or the isosceles triangle *OAP* we can show that *AP* is of length 2 cos θ. We can

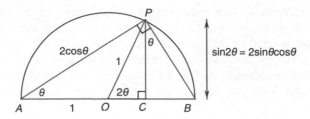

Figure 9.12 *Trigonometry: the double-angle formulae*

then determine the length of PC in two different ways: using triangle OCP it is sin 2 θ, whereas using triangle ACP it is 2 sin θ cos θ. We have proved the identity sin 2 θ = 2 sin θ cos θ in the case where θ is an acute angle.

Since the length OC in triangle OCP is cos 2 θ, it is possible in a similar way to prove two identities for cos 2 θ:

$$\cos 2\ \theta = 2 \cos^2 \theta - 1 \text{ and } \cos 2\ \theta = 1 - 2 \sin^2 \theta.$$

By adding and subtracting these two results, two further identities are obtained:

$$\cos 2\ \theta = \cos^2 \theta - \sin^2 \theta \text{ and } 1 = \cos^2 \theta + \sin^2 \theta$$

These examples illustrate the ubiquity and power of this simple result that the angle in a semicircle is a right angle. They are not so much applications to be remembered and certainly should not all be encountered within the space of a few lessons. Rather they should arise in appropriate contexts as part of the continuing task of helping students to understand mathematical arguments and to appreciate the links and connections between mathematical ideas.

THE CIRCLE THEOREMS

The theorem concerning the angle in a semicircle is one of a family of linked results known as the circle theorems. Logically it is not the first of these, because it can be derived from the theorem that relates the angle at the centre to angles at the circumference subtended by the same arc. However, as suggested above there are good reasons to introduce it before the other circle theorems and then at a later stage place it in that broader context.

Dynamic geometry software has a facility for measuring angles and that is very useful for exploring geometrical properties because the measures change as points on the diagram are moved. This is particularly effective in the case of the angle at the centre theorem. This states that the angle at the centre of a circle is twice the angle at the circumference subtended by, or standing on, the same arc. Figure 9.13 displays an example from a dynamic geometry screen where the angle at the centre is clearly twice the angle at the circumference. Varying the point P or the other points or the radius of the circle will create a host of other confirming examples, although there will be some occasions when the rounding of the measures should cause questions to be asked about whether the result is approximately or exactly true. There is a clear need for proof – measuring is not sufficient.

The usual proof, illustrated in Figure 9.14, is based on isosceles triangles. In the left-hand diagram, with the line PO produced to some point C, the two angles AOC and BOC are external

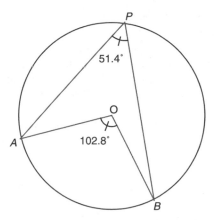

Figure 9.13 *Angles at the centre and circumference*

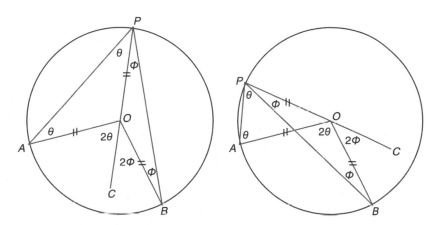

Figure 9.14 *Proving the angle at the centre theorem*

angles of the isosceles triangles *AOP* and *BOP*. The equal angles of these two triangles are denoted by θ and ϕ respectively and it is easy to show that the two external angles at *O* are then 2θ and 2ϕ. Since the angle at the circumference, *APB*, is $\theta + \phi$ and the angle at the centre, *AOB*, is $2\theta + 2\phi$, it is clear that *AOB* is twice *APB* as required.

However, there are more possibilities to consider because the configuration of lines could be like that of the right-hand diagram in Figure 9.14, where *P* has been moved anti-clockwise round the circle so that the line *BP* passes below *O*, crossing *OA* at some point. In this case, angle *APB* is $\theta - \phi$ and the angle *AOB* is $2\theta - 2\phi$. Moving *P* clockwise so that *AP* intersects *OB* will result in angles of $\phi - \theta$ and $2\phi - 2\theta$.

P may also be in a position where *AP* passes through the centre *O* so that the diagram is like that for the angle in a semicircle with angle ϕ becoming zero and the relevant angles being just θ and 2θ (or ϕ and 2ϕ if *BP* passes through *O* and θ is zero). Another possibility is that *P* may be moved so that it lies between *A* and *B*, on the minor arc. In that case the angle at the centre is the reflex angle at *O*, but the same arguments will apply.

Four circle theorems, shown in Figure 9.15, are immediate consequences of the angle at the centre theorem:

- the angle in a semicircle is a right angle because the angle at the centre is 180° and the corresponding angle at the circumference is 90°
- the angles in the same segment (or angles subtended by the same arc), denoted here by θ, are equal because each is half the corresponding angle at the centre
- the opposite angles, denoted here by θ and ϕ, of a cyclic quadrilateral add up to 180°, because each is half of an angle at the centre and the two corresponding angles at the centre add up to 360°
- each exterior angle of a cyclic quadrilateral is equal to the corresponding opposite interior angle, which is an immediate consequence of the previous theorem

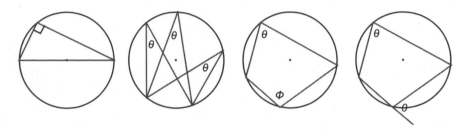

Figure 9.15 *Four more circle theorems*

Understanding and using these results together with the angle at the centre theorem is greatly enhanced if their interrelationship is appreciated. One of the great advantages of dynamic geometry over static diagrams is that the links can be displayed dynamically by moving points round a circle to illustrate each result and to show how one result leads to another.

We often assume that the converse of a theorem is true, but strictly we ought to be sure before we make that assumption. As an example, it is often useful to use the fact that the opposite angles of a quadrilateral are supplementary to show that the four vertices are concyclic or, in other words, that they lie on a cyclic quadrilateral. We can prove this by supposing that the vertices of a quadrilateral *ABCD* with the angles at *A* and *C* supplementary are not concyclic, as shown in Figure 9.16. If the circle through the points *A, B* and *D* is constructed the point *C* will lie either inside or outside the circle. In the figure it has been taken to be outside, but the argument is the same with it inside. With *E* as the point where the line *BC* meets the circle, we know that the angles *BED* and *BAD* are supplementary because the quadrilateral *ABED* is certainly cyclic. However, that would mean that angles *BED* and *BCD* were equal and that is clearly impossible, so the original assumption that the quadrilateral was not cyclic is incorrect, thereby proving that the converse theorem is in fact true.

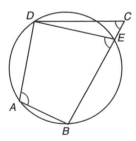

Figure 9.16 *Proving the converse of the cyclic quadrilateral theorem*

There is one further circle theorem that needs separate consideration, namely the alternate segment theorem, shown in Figure 9.17. The first diagram illustrates the theorem, which states that the angle between a tangent and a chord is equal to the angle in the alternate segment – the angles marked as *θ* in the diagram. The other three diagrams then show how angle *APB*, as the angle in the major segment determined by the chord *AB*, remains constant as *P* is moved. In some respects the alternate segment theorem can be seen as a sort of limiting case of angles in the same segment in that the angle *APB* becomes the angle between the tangent at *A* and the chord *AB* when *P* is moved to coincide with *A*.

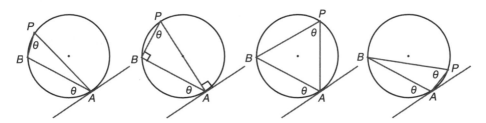

Figure 9.17 *The alternate segment theorem*

The second diagram in the sequence provides us with the usual proof. When *P* is such that *AP* becomes a diameter, the presence of the right angle between tangent and radius and in the semicircle makes it clear why the two angles *θ* are equal.

Awareness of relevant properties and theorems is necessary both for solving geometrical problems and for generating proofs, but it is obviously not sufficient, because it is all too common an experience for both students and teachers to fail to see something which is obvious once it is pointed out. There is often not an immediately direct and obvious way of solving a geometrical problem, because the solution may involve several different ideas or may depend on inserting a critical line. In some respects algebraic problems can seem to be more straightforward because you can rapidly decide on the variables and write down some equations to solve. With geometry problems it is often necessary to 'play around' with the problem, looking at it in different ways until a solution strategy begins to emerge. In the example that follows I have attempted to indicate the sort of ideas that might emerge as attempts are made to arrive at a solution. These suggest ways that a teacher can encourage students to think about problems.

The left-hand diagram of Figure 9.18 shows a typical problem where some angles have to be determined. A circle is inscribed in triangle *ABC* and the triangle *PQR* is formed by joining the

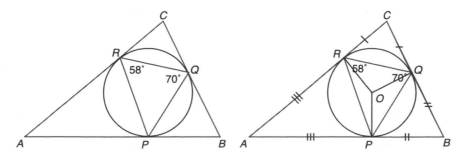

Figure 9.18 *Find the angles of triangle ABC*

points of contact. The problem is to find the angles of triangle ABC. The teacher's task then is to help the student who does not immediately see an obvious way of proceeding. One useful strategy is to forget about the immediate question and see what properties of the diagram might be relevant. Here are some thoughts that may arise for this example:

- the sides of the big triangle are tangents to the circle
- two tangents can be constructed from an external point to a circle
- there are three isosceles triangles therefore (the equal sides have been indicated in the right-hand diagram of Figure 9.18)
- each isosceles triangle has a pair of equal angles
- the alternate segment theorem gives various pairs of equal angles
- each tangent makes a right angle with the radius at the point of contact (these radii have been included in the right-hand diagram)
- if lines from the centre are joined to the points of contact angles at the centre of the circle are created, so the angle at the centre theorem might be useful
- there are three kites
- these kites are cyclic quadrilaterals because each has an opposite pair of right angles

In the process of making these observations a way through the problem may begin to emerge and can be explored. One possibility might be to use letters to represent some of the unknown angles and to set up some equations, but while this can be successful let us restrict our considerations to geometrical approaches. Here is one way of proceeding:

Using the alternate segment theorem: $\angle APR = 70°$.

Then from isosceles triangle APR (or by using the alternate segment theorem again): $\angle ARP = 70°$

Hence, $\angle PAR = 180° - 140° = 40°$.

In the same way $\angle BPQ = \angle BQP = 58°$ and hence from triangle BPQ $\angle PBQ = 180° - 116° = 64°$.

The three angles of triangle ABC are therefore 40°, 64° and 76°.

An alternative approach is based on the final three observations in the list above:

$\angle POR = 140°$, because it is twice $\angle PSR$, using the angle at the centre theorem.

$\angle PAR = 180° - 140° = 40°$, since the angle sum of the kite $APSR$ is 360° and its angles at P and R are right angles because they are between a radius and a tangent.

The other angles can be determined in a similar way.

It is important in the classroom to do more than present neat solutions to problems in the hope that students learn unconsciously how to solve problems themselves. Clearly seeing good solutions is necessary as a way of building up experience of a variety of facts and strategies, but students need to solve problems for themselves. In order to do that successfully they need strategies and explanations of solutions which are accompanied by discussion about what prompts the thinking at each step.

SOME INTERESTING RESULTS USING THE CIRCLE THEOREMS

The left-hand diagram of Figure 9.19 show a regular heptagon and on the right we have a regular curved heptagon which is the shape of twenty-pence and fifty-pence coins in the United Kingdom. The middle diagram shows how the curved arcs which form the edges of the curved heptagon are constructed. Each arc has its centre at the opposite vertex of the polygon. The interesting property of a regular curved heptagon is that its diameter is constant, where the diameter is defined as the greatest width from any point. Unlike the diameter of a circle, the diameter of a regular curved heptagon does not necessarily pass through the centre of the heptagon. The problem is to find a formula for the circumference of the curved heptagon in terms of *d* the diameter.

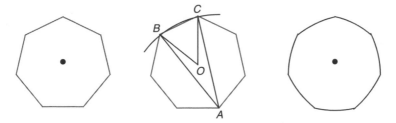

Figure 9.19 *Circumference of a regular curved heptagon*

Referring to the middle diagram again it is clear that we need to find the length of an arc like *BC* and that means that we need to know angle *BAC*. The diagram shows the secret: *BAC* is an angle at the circumference standing on the arc *BC* of the circle which circumscribes the polygon. Angle *BOC* is the angle at the centre standing on the same arc and is easy to calculate because it is $\frac{1}{7}$ of 360° or $\frac{1}{7}$ of 2π in radians. It is simpler to work in radians as follows:

$$\text{Angle at centre} = \frac{2\pi}{7} \quad \Rightarrow \quad \text{Angle at circumference} = \frac{\pi}{7}$$

$$\text{Arc length} = \frac{\pi d}{7} \quad \Rightarrow \quad \text{Circumference of curved heptagon} = 7 \times \frac{\pi d}{7} = \pi d$$

The remarkable fact is that the circumference of the regular curved heptagon is the same as that of a circle with same diameter. It is instructive to construct that circle on the same diagram as the heptagon to compare the two, but the diagram needs to be large to distinguish the curves.

Figure 9.20 shows two diagrams which illustrate two results involving cyclic quadrilaterals. In the left-hand diagram, the cyclic quadrilateral *ABCD*, with *CB* produced to *E*, has been constructed so that *AB* bisects the angle *DBE*. The problem is to show that the triangle *ACD* is isosceles. Since angle properties are the key feature of configurations of this kind, a sensible strategy would be to try to show that the two angles denoted by *c* and *d* in triangle *ACD* are equal. From the information given about the angle bisector we know that the angles marked as *a* and *b* are equal. We need to make a link between this fact and what we have to show. That hinges upon making some appropriate observations about equal angles in the configuration, but we are helped by identifying the initial facts and the ultimate goal. In this case the links are fairly immediate, giving a proof as follows:

a = d (exterior angle of a cyclic quadrilateral equal to opposite interior angle)

b = c (angles in the same segment)

Since *a = b*, because *AB* bisects angle *DBE*, then *c = d*, proving that triangle *ACD* is isosceles.

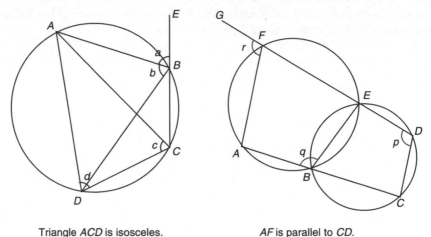

Triangle *ACD* is isosceles.   *AF* is parallel to *CD*.

Figure 9.20 *Two results involving cyclic quadrilaterals*

The right-hand diagram of Figure 9.20 shows two intersecting circles with cyclic quadrilaterals, *ABEF* and *BCDE*, sharing the common chord. The problem is to show that the two edges *AF* and *CD* are parallel. One way of proving that a pair of lines are parallel is to show that an appropriate pair of angles are equal. With the line *DF* produced to *G*, we can see that the angles denoted by *p*, *q* and *r* are equal applying the exterior angle property of a cyclic quadrilateral twice. Hence, since angles *p* and *r* are equal, it follows that the two lines *AF* and *CD* are parallel.

Figure 9.21 shows Miquel's remarkable six-circle theorem, which is discussed in Goddijn (2003) with an example of a students' proof. A ring of four circles are constructed so that the outer set of four intersection points lie on a common circle. The remarkable fact is that the inner

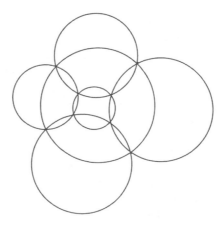

Figure 9.21 *Miquel's six-circle theorem*

set of four intersection points also lie on a circle. It is fascinating to create the configuration with dynamic geometry software and observe the effect of varying the circles.

The proof is surprisingly simple and elegant. Sets of four intersection points form quadrilaterals, which are shown in Figure 9.22 without the circumscribing circles. If the four outer quadrilaterals are cyclic then the four pairs of angles denoted by *a, b, c* and *d* are equal because of the exterior angle property. If the outer quadrilateral is cyclic, then $a + b + c + d = 180°$ from which it immediately follows that the inner quadrilateral is cyclic also.

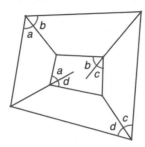

Figure 9.22 *Six cyclic quadrilaterals*

As a final bonus, if the centres of the initial ring of four circles lie on the outer circle, then the inner quadrilateral is a rectangle, a result that readers are invited to explore for themselves.

CONCLUSION

The circle theorems provide an excellent example of a family of linked results which provide a valuable source of examples of both traditional angle-finding problems and surprising results which encourage a search for proofs. They do not provide a lot of immediately obvious real-world applications, but they are rich in intrinsic interest and have a way of arising in unlikely ways like proving trigonometrical identities or finding the circumference of a fifty-pence coin.

Learning to work with the circle theorems brings together many aspects of learning to think geometrically. Success in solving problems and appreciating and generating proofs requires both a knowledge of facts and a range of strategies for producing appropriate chains of reasoning. An element of creative flair is often involved, but students should be given advice about how to think constructively and creatively when faced with problems.

When embarking on a geometrical problem or proof it is often a valuable strategy to forget about the immediate data of the problem and to spend some time exploring the configuration in an open way, noting either mentally or in writing as many of its properties as possible. This often sparks off suitable lines of thoughts, but at the least it provides a background familiarity and a source of ideas for a more systematic approach to the actual problem. Sketching several different versions of the configuration or exploring it with dynamic geometry can be very useful, as can highlighting particular features in colour. Many proofs involve parallel lines and their related angle properties or their link to proportionality through the intercept theorem. The secret is often to add a key line or two which may be a parallel line or sometimes a line which creates a triangle that is congruent or similar to an existing triangle in the diagram.

When teachers (and textbooks) explain how a problem is solved, or present a proof of a result, the way it is discussed can be very significant. Clearly it is useful to ask students questions at each stage of the process to elicit ideas and to check on understanding, but it is also important to give them some sense of where ideas come from. Each step should not be presented as though it were obvious with no indication as to what prompted it. Students who offer a suggestion should frequently be asked what made them think of an idea, as well as asking them to justify it. It is certainly valuable to develop the art of reviewing the whole argument at intervals – to 'see the wood for the trees' as the saying goes – looking back at the starting points and looking forward to where the argument is leading. Reviewing the argument in this way is also a good tactic when we are stuck – reminding us of 'what we know' and 'what we want', to quote the useful advice given in Mason (1988).

The final stage in solving a problem or finding a proof is to communicate the argument in a suitably succinct written form. Much mathematical writing aimed at novices is too verbose and dense and does not always offer a good model for students to emulate. The use of three-letter notation can be a barrier and there are considerable advantages, wherever possible, to use single letter variables for lengths and angles to clarify arguments. It is a good idea to set out key statements on separate lines with the justification alongside and it is important to make the initial assumptions and the final result clear. It is often useful to indicate the general form of the argument at the beginning. Students need constant encouragement and help to produce clear written arguments. With the increasing availability of word processors with facilities to create and edit mathematical expressions it should in the future become easier to ask students to produce a first draft of the solution of a problem or a proof. They can then be asked to redraft their account following discussion and advice about their mathematical accuracy and their written style in the same way that students are expected to produce more than one draft of an essay in other subject areas. Other forms of written communication such as creating posters for classroom display or Powerpoint presentations offer attractive alternative incentives to produce clear, suitably illustrated written arguments.

This summary has highlighted three stages in solving geometrical problems:

- an initial exploratory stage to understand what the problem is about, to generate ideas and to try out alternative solution strategies
- a deductive stage where formal arguments are developed
- a final stage where the thinking is communicated in a suitable public form

All three stages are important and need time and thought given to them. It is all to easy to spend too high a proportion of time on the second stage, neglecting the messy first stage and failing to offer constructive advice about how to communicate effectively, particularly in a written form.

Chapter 10

Linking Geometry and Algebra

COORDINATES AND GRAPHS

The simple idea of denoting a point by referring to its distances from a pair of fixed axes is profoundly important because it provides a link between algebra and geometry by enabling us to describe curves by equations. Not only does this mean that the power of algebraic thinking can be used in solving geometrical problems, but also that geometrical ideas can provide a source of insight for algebraic problems.

Students encounter this link when they first observe that the coordinates of the points on a straight line display a simple pattern, as shown by the example of Figure 10.1. The observed fact that the y coordinate is always one more than the x coordinate leads to the equation of the straight line as $y = x + 1$. Subsequent investigation, along the lines that I have discussed in French (2002b), extends the ability to move between a set of coordinates, typically in the form of a table of values, and the equation of the line and to reverse the process by generating coordinates from an equation. Graphical calculators and computer graph-plotting software provide a valuable aid for exploring graphs of all kinds.

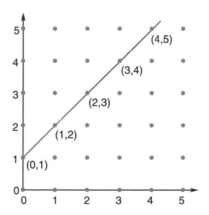

Figure 10.1 *Coordinates and a straight-line graph*

The idea of gradient is one of the key properties that emerges from an early investigation of straight-line graphs. A straight-line graph like that shown in Figure 10.1 prompts two obvious questions:

- what other equations give straight lines parallel to $y = x + 1$?
- what other equations give straight lines that cross the y axis at 1?

The first requires the realization that the number 1, the constant term, has to be varied and the second draws attention to the role of the coefficient of x. Thus begins the process of coming to understand that any straight line has an equation of the form $y = mx + c$, where m is the gradient and c is the intercept on the y axis. Such a formal statement is not, however, appropriate in the early stages of learning about graphs when it is more important to develop the sense that varying the two parameters influences the position of the line in relation to the axes.

Looking at equations of the form $y = mx$, as shown in Figure 10.2 avoids the distraction of the constant term and enables attention to be focused on the idea of gradient and how it is measured. Starting from a diagram with $y = x$ and $y = 2x$, Figure 10.2 can be built up through a dialogue like the following:

T: How could we get a steeper straight line through the origin?
A: $y = 3x$?
T: Where does that go on the diagram?
B: It goes through 3.
T: Where is the 3?
C: Through 3 when x is 1.
T: So, what are the coordinates of that point?
A: (1, 3)
    [The line $y = 3x$ is plotted and further discussion ensues concerning steeper lines.]
T: And how could we get a straight line that is less steep than $y = x$?
B: $y = \frac{1}{2} x$
T: Good, so the number that goes with x tells us how steep the line is. Why then is it 2 with $y = 2x$?
C: Because you go 1 along and 2 up.
T: And $y = \frac{1}{2} x$?
D: You go 2 along and 1 up.

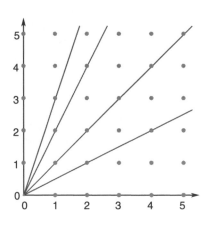

$y = x, y = 2x, y = 3x$ and $y = \frac{1}{2}x$

Figure 10.2 *Straight lines through the origin*

Here we have the essence of the idea of gradient as distance up 'over' distance along, the ratio that used to be seen in road signs that showed steep hills as 1 in 5. That has been somewhat obscured by the practice of indicating steep hills by percentages so that 1 in 5 becomes 20%, but that can be interpreted as 20 metres up for 100 metres along. Mathematical gradients have the added complication that they can be negative to denote a slope that leans the opposite way, but that is not a major source of difficulty when the underlying idea of gradient is understood, provided that negative numbers are familiar and do not act as a barrier.

Textbooks frequently present gradient in the context of the coordinate plane as a formula to be remembered, as follows:

$$\text{gradient of line joining points } (x_1, y_1) \text{ and } (x_2, y_2) = \frac{y_2 - y_1}{x_2 - x_1}.$$

Such a formula, particularly if it is introduced at too early a stage, makes an essentially simple idea look complicated. Rather than require students to remember such a formula, which divorces the idea from its geometrical context, it is much better to encourage them to use a simple verbal description like 'distance up over distance along' or 'increase in y over increase in x'. They can then work out the gradient in any particular situation by making a quick sketch which displays the two lengths involved. If for some particular reason a formula is required, it can be worked out when needed on the basis of the understanding that has been developed.

The same observation about formulas applies to the question of finding the distance between two points whose coordinates are given. This does not need a specific formula: it is simply an application of Pythagoras' theorem, which again requires a quick sketch to determine the lengths in the x and y directions, the same idea as the distances along and up needed to find the gradient. An example for two particular points, like that shown in Figure 10.3, summarizes the ideas and serves better as a memory aid than general formulae for general points.

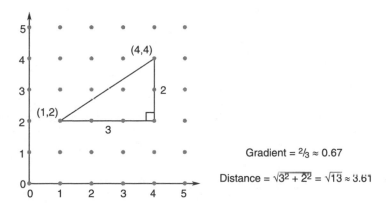

Figure 10.3 *Gradient and length of a line joining two points*

A good example which brings together the two ideas is to find the distance and gradient of a road between two places on a map whose grid references and spot heights are given. Besides linking various mathematical ideas the problem also provides a link between mathematics and geography. The grid reference system on maps produced by the Ordnance Survey in the United Kingdom is based on kilometre squares which are thought of as being divided into 100 smaller squares. A six-figure grid reference like 913538 denotes a point whose coordinates are (913, 538), where the units are tenths of a kilometre which are the lengths of the edges of these notional small squares. As an example let us consider the calculations necessary to find the horizontal distance and the gradient between the point 913538 at height 132 metres and the point 931526 at a height of 59 metres:

Difference in x coordinates $= 931 - 913 = 18$

Difference in y coordinates $= 538 - 526 = 12$

Distance between points $= \sqrt{18^2 + 12^2} = \sqrt{468} \approx 21.63$

The distance is approximately 2163 metres, since units are tenths of a kilometre.

Difference in spot heights in metres $= 132 - 59 = 73$

$$\text{Gradient} = \frac{73}{2163} \approx 0.034$$

The gradient is approximately 3.4% or about 1 in 30.

It is also important, at some stage, to make the link between gradient and tangent as a means of determining the angle of slope. In this example involving grid references the angle of slope, θ, is given by $\tan \theta \approx 0.034$ which gives a value of about $1.9°$.

Alongside the obvious fact that two lines which are parallel have the same gradient, the relationship between the gradients of a pair of perpendicular lines is important. This result can easily be established by looking at several particular cases as in the first two diagrams of Figure 10.4 and then generalizing in the third diagram.

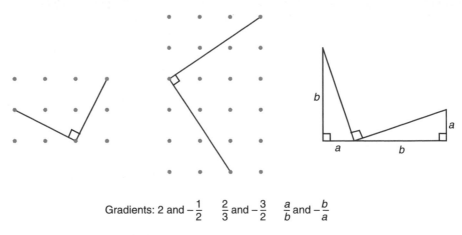

Gradients: 2 and $-\dfrac{1}{2}$　　$\dfrac{2}{3}$ and $-\dfrac{3}{2}$　　$\dfrac{a}{b}$ and $-\dfrac{b}{a}$

Figure 10.4 *Gradients of perpendicular lines*

It is easy to spot that the product of the two gradients is -1 or, to express it in a different way, that the gradient of one is the negative reciprocal of the other. The result is usually expressed as $m_1 m_2 = -1$, where m_1 and m_2 are the gradients of the two perpendicular lines. It is equivalent to the fact that the scalar product of two perpendicular vectors is zero, a very important idea that is discussed in the Chapter 12.

Another useful procedure is to find the point that divides a line joining two points in a given ratio. The midpoint is a special case found by taking the mean of the x and y coordinates. Again, understanding how the general procedure can be worked out from first principles is more important than just remembering a formula and this should be reinforced by starting with simple numerical examples. Figure 10.5 illustrates the case where a point P divides the line

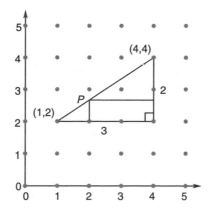

Figure 10.5 *A point P dividing a line in the ratio 1:2*

joining the points (1,2) and (4,4) in the ratio 1:2. Constructing line segments parallel to the two sides of the triangle creates two smaller similar triangles whose edges are in the ratio 1:2. From this the x and y coordinates of P can be found as follows:

$$x = 1 + \tfrac{1}{3} \text{ of } 3 = 2 \quad \text{and} \quad y = 2 + \tfrac{1}{3} \text{ of } 2 = 2\tfrac{2}{3}.$$

The method is applied below to two general points (x_1, y_1) and (x_2, y_2) to find the midpoint, the point that divides the line in the ratio 1:2 and, finally, the point which divides the line segment in the ratio $\lambda : \mu$. These examples build on the procedure used above and are examples of how students can be introduced to results, which are progressively more general, by working with a procedure from first principles:

Midpoint of the line joining (x_1, y_1) and (x_2, y_2):

$$x = x_1 + \tfrac{1}{2}(x_2 - x_1) = \tfrac{1}{2}(x_1 + x_2) \quad \text{and} \quad y = y_1 + \tfrac{1}{2}(y_2 - y_1) = \tfrac{1}{2}(y_1 + y_2).$$

Point dividing the line joining (x_1, y_1) and (x_2, y_2) in the ratio 1:2:

$$x = x_1 + \tfrac{1}{3}(x_2 - x_1) = \tfrac{2}{3}x_1 + \tfrac{1}{3}x_2 \quad \text{and} \quad y = y_1 + \tfrac{1}{3}(y_2 - y_1) = \tfrac{2}{3}y_1 + \tfrac{1}{3}y_2$$

Point dividing the line joining (x_1, y_1) and (x_2, y_2) in the ratio $\lambda : \mu$:

$$x = x_1 + \frac{\lambda}{\lambda + \mu}(x_2 - x_1) = \frac{\lambda x_2 + \mu x_1}{\lambda + \mu} \quad \text{and} \quad y = y_1 + \frac{\lambda}{\lambda + \mu}(y_2 - y_1) = \frac{\lambda y_2 + \mu y_1}{\lambda + \mu}.$$

Formidable formulae like the last ones above look much simpler to students when the parameters are given values relating to simple cases. Specific cases, like the first two, are easier to recall and provide a pattern from which the general result can be derived.

As an example using the ideas of this section, Figure 10.6 shows a quadrilateral which has been defined by the coordinates of its four vertices. The diagram suggests that the quadrilateral may have a pair of parallel sides and that there are simple relationships between the lengths of the sides. It is easy to show that the gradients of the sides AB and CD are both equal to -1, so that the sides are parallel and the quadrilateral is a trapezium. Using Pythagoras' theorem the lengths of these parallel sides are found to be $\sqrt{8}$ and $\sqrt{2}$ and we can see that AB is twice the

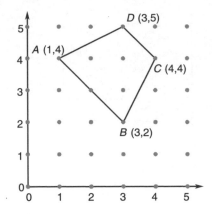

Figure 10.6 *The properties of a quadrilateral*

length of *CD*, because $\sqrt{8} = 2\sqrt{2}$. Calculating the lengths of the other two sides shows that they are both equal to $\sqrt{5}$, so that the trapezium is isosceles. Moreover the diagram shows readily that the diagonals are equal in length and that their point of intersection at (3, 4) divides each in the ratio 2:1, the same as the ratio of *AB* to *CD*. This agrees, of course, with the result that would be obtained using the formulae discussed above for finding a point that divides a line segment in a given ratio. Figure 10.6 is an accurately plotted diagram, but in practice problems like this can be solved by referring to a diagram that has been sketched by hand so that it looks approximately right.

This section has focused on the link between the coordinates of points on a straight line and its equation together with some basic procedures related to position, distance and gradient. Understanding of these important ideas is reinforced when they are illustrated with simple diagrams using small integers for the coordinates of the points involved. Familiar ideas like Pythagoras' theorem, gradient and the properties of similar triangles can then be readily applied. This understanding is hindered if there is too early an emphasis on remembering and attempting to apply formulae whose derivation and purpose is often not fully appreciated.

LOCUS

One of the powerful features of coordinate geometry is its use in determining algebraically the locus of a set of points subject to some conditions. The conditions lead to an equation involving a general point (x,y) which is the equation of the curve that forms the locus. Many equations of standard curves can be obtained in this way as well as solutions to a variety of locus problems.

Two simple examples are illustrated by Figure 10.7. In the first case the problem is to find the locus of a set of points that are equidistant from two given points. This is the perpendicular bisector of the line segment joining the points. Its equation can be found in a number of ways, but it is particularly instructive to find it by equating the distances of a general point denoted by (x,y) from the two given points. Pythagoras' theorem enables us to find expressions for the squares of the two distances. Simplification of the resulting equation then gives the equation of the required line as shown below:

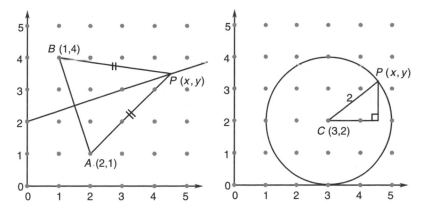

Figure 10.7 *Two locus problems*

$$AP^2 = BP^2$$
$$(x-2)^2 + (y-1)^2 = (x-1)^2 + (y-4)^2$$
$$-4x - 2y + 5 = -2x - 8y + 17$$
$$6y = 2x + 12$$
$$y = \tfrac{1}{3}x + 2$$

In the second case the locus is the set of points at a fixed distance from a given point. That, of course, is the definition of the circle with the result being the equation of a circle. In the example the points are at a distance of 2 units from the point (3,2) and the simplest form of the equation of a circle is found immediately as a direct application of Pythagoras' theorem:

$$CP^2 = (x-3)^2 + (y-2)^2 = 4$$

This generalizes readily to give the general equation for a circle with radius *r* and centre (*a,b*):

$$(x-a)^2 + (y-b)^2 = r^2$$

An interesting problem where the nature of the locus is not immediately obvious from geometrical considerations is to find the locus of a point where the distances from two given points are in the ratio 2:1. In Figure 10.8 the points O and *A*, the origin and (6, 0), are taken as the two points and a general point *P* is such that *OP* = 2*AP*. The problem can be explored initially by constructing a set of concentric circles as shown in the diagram with centres at the points *O* and *A*. Points are identified at the intersections of appropriate circles to fulfil the ratio condition. The diagram shows that these points appear to lie on a circle. We can prove that the locus really is a circle by considering a general point, like that denoted by *P*, and using the relationship between the lengths to obtain the equation of the circle as follows:

$$4AP^2 = OP^2$$
$$4((x-6)^2 + y^2) = x^2 + y^2$$
$$3x^2 - 48x + 144 + 3y^2 = 0$$
$$x^2 - 16x + 48 + y^2 = 0$$
$$(x-8)^2 + y^2 = 16$$

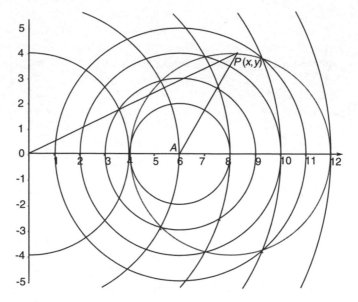

Figure 10.8 *A locus problem*

This gives a circle with centre (8,0) and radius 4 which corresponds to the circle in the diagram passing through the intersection points of pairs of corresponding circles. The argument can be readily extended to any pair of points to show that the locus is always a circle for any ratio except when the ratio is 1:1. In that very simple case the locus is the perpendicular bisector of the line segment joining the points.

TRANSFORMING GRAPHS

Understanding the way in which graphs can be transformed is an invaluable aid to sketching and interpreting graphs and the functions they represent. A familiarity with the properties of some simple transformations provides an important link between algebra and geometry. The important transformations in this respect are translations and stretches in the x and y directions and, to a lesser extent, reflections in the two axes.

Translations are best illustrated by their effects on the graph of $y = x^2$ and stretches by their effects on $y = \sin x$ or $y = \cos x$, as shown in Figure 10.9. Examples like these are discussed at length in French (2002b) and are a standard feature in school textbooks. A graphical calculator

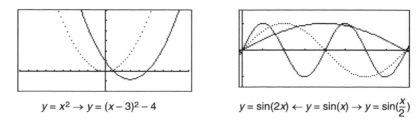

$$y = x^2 \rightarrow y = (x-3)^2 - 4 \qquad\qquad y = \sin(2x) \leftarrow y = \sin(x) \rightarrow y = \sin(\tfrac{x}{2})$$

Figure 10.9 *Translations and stretches*

or a graph-plotting software package provide an excellent means of exploring transformations in relation to graphs: the diagrams in both Figures 10.9 and 10.10 come from screens produced on a graphical calculator.

The circle provides a very good example of the application of both these transformations. The left-hand diagram of Figure 10.10 shows the circle $x^2 + y^2 = 1$, which has centre at the origin

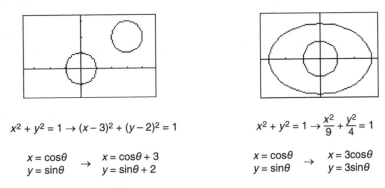

$$x^2 + y^2 = 1 \rightarrow (x-3)^2 + (y-2)^2 = 1$$

$$x^2 + y^2 = 1 \rightarrow \frac{x^2}{9} + \frac{y^2}{4} = 1$$

$$\begin{aligned} x &= \cos\theta \\ y &= \sin\theta \end{aligned} \quad \rightarrow \quad \begin{aligned} x &= \cos\theta + 3 \\ y &= \sin\theta + 2 \end{aligned}$$

$$\begin{aligned} x &= \cos\theta \\ y &= \sin\theta \end{aligned} \quad \rightarrow \quad \begin{aligned} x &= 3\cos\theta \\ y &= 3\sin\theta \end{aligned}$$

Figure 10.10 *Translating and stretching a circle*

and unit radius. When it is translated by 3 units in the x direction and 2 units in the y direction the equation becomes. $(x-3)^2 + (y-2)^2 = 1$. Clearly the 3 and the 2 are the x and y coordinates of the centre of the circle. The equation prompts some useful questions:

T: What happens when $x = 3$?
A: You get $(y-2)^2 = 1$.
T: What does that tell you?
B: $y = 3$, because $y - 2 = 1$.
T: What does this tell you about the circle?
C: The point (3, 3) is at the top of the circle.
T: What about the point at the bottom of the circle?
A: That is (3, 1).
T: How does that come from the equation?
B: The negative square root: when $y - 2 = -1$, you get $y = 1$.
T: What happens when $y = 2$?
C: You get the points on the left and right of the circle: (2, 2) and (4, 2).

Stretches have the much more dramatic effect of transforming circles into either ellipses or circles of different sizes in the special case of enlargement. The right-hand diagram of Figure 10.10 shows the same initial circle stretched by a factor of 3 in the x direction and factor 2 in the y direction. In each case a pair of parametric equations, given in terms of a parameter θ, is shown below the diagram, and this provides a simple route to the Cartesian equation through Pythagoras' theorem in its important trigonometrical form: $\cos^2\theta + \sin^2\theta = 1$.

The importance of circles as geometric figures is abundantly obvious. Being able to represent them in an algebraic form with equations provides another tool for dealing with problems while providing a crucial link with Pythagoras' theorem which is also of such fundamental importance in mathematics. The simple action of stretching a circle leads to the ellipse, a curve which has many interesting properties and applications, which provide the focus of the next section.

THE ELLIPSE

One way of generating an ellipse as a locus, often referred to as the 'slipping ladder', is shown in the left-hand diagram of Figure 10.11. The line AB – the ladder – is of constant length, with the point B moving along the x axis and the point A moving along the y axis. The locus of the point P is an ellipse. This can be proved easily by letting $AP = a$ and $BP = b$. Then, if the ladder makes an angle θ with the ground and P has coordinates (x,y), we have $x = a \cos \theta$ and $y = b \sin \theta$, the parametric equations of an ellipse, where $2a$ and $2b$ are the lengths of the major and minor axes respectively. Besides the locus it is also interesting to observe the envelope of lines, shown in the right-hand diagram of Figure 10.11, created by the positions of the ladder as it moves.

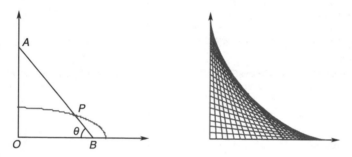

Figure 10.11 *The slipping ladder*

The same idea was used in the past in drawing offices in a device for drawing ellipses known as the ellipsograph or Trammel of Archimedes. A description of this will be found in Cundy and Rollett (1961). It is also worth noting that 'up and over' garage doors use variations on the 'slipping ladder' principle, so that the locus of a general point on such a door is an ellipse. Figure 10.12 shows the locus of the foot of such a door as it is opened or closed. Many of the ideas in this section are based on an article which was inspired by the properties of these 'up and over' doors: French (1999a).

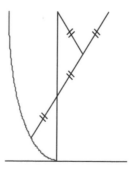

Figure 10.12 *Up and over garage door*

The most familiar way of drawing an ellipse uses two pins and a piece of string. Pins are placed at two points, F_1 and F_2, as shown in Figure 10.13, and the ends of a length of string are tied to the pins so that it lies slack between them. The string is then held taut with a pen which is moved, keeping the string taut, to plot the locus.

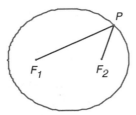

Figure 10.13 *Drawing an ellipse with two pins and a piece of string*

The two points where the pins are placed are the foci of the ellipse. Varying the positions of these two foci varies the shape of the ellipse. When they coincide the locus is a circle and as they are moved apart it becomes a wider and thinner ellipse, tending towards a straight line when the string is stretched taut between them.

Figure 10.14 shows how to demonstrate this locus with dynamic geometry software. A circle is drawn with its centre at one focus, F_1, and its radius equal to the length of the string, which is also the length of the major axis of the ellipse. Taking Q as a general point on this circle, we have to find a P on the line segment QF_1 such that $PQ = PF_2$. It then follows that $PF_1 + PF_2 = QF_1$, the radius of the circle, which is constant. The position of P is then found as the point where the perpendicular bisector of QF_2 cuts the line segment QF_1. The locus of P is an ellipse and the perpendicular bisector used in the construction is the tangent to that ellipse.

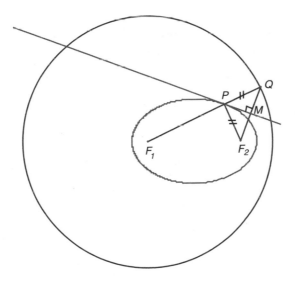

Figure 10.14 *The ellipse as the locus of a point where the sum of its distances to the foci is constant*

Dynamic geometry software is invaluable as a means of showing loci in a dramatic way. There is great value in the thinking that leads to the method of construction and in the possibility of varying the parameters. In this case the positions of the foci and the radius of the circle can be moved to see how the locus varies.

An interesting question that follows from this is to prove that the locus is, in fact, the same curve as the ellipse that comes from the 'stretched circle', described through its parametric equations in the previous section. It is easy to verify that the length of the string is equal to the length of the major axis, denoted by 2*a*, by observing what happens when the two segments of the string overlap. This can be written as:

$$PF_1 + PF_2 = 2a$$

In Figure 10.15 the origin is taken halfway between the two foci, since this is obviously the centre of the ellipse. *P*, the general point on the ellipse, has coordinates (x,y) and the coordinates of the foci are denoted by $(-ae,0)$ and $(ae,0)$. *e* is the eccentricity of the ellipse, which takes values between 0 and 1 corresponding to the two extremes of a circle and a straight line. Thus, the ellipse of Figure 10.15 has an eccentricity of about $\frac{1}{2}$.

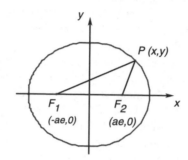

Figure 10.15 *Ellipse with foci*

We can now find expressions for the two lengths PF_1 and PF_2 and use them to find the equation of the ellipse. Using Pythagoras' theorem the lengths are given by:

$$PF_1^2 = (x + ae)^2 + y^2 \quad \text{and} \quad PF_2^2 = (x - ae)^2 + y^2$$

Subtracting these two equations gives the simple result:

$$PF_1^2 - PF_2^2 = 4aex.$$

Since this is a difference of two squares, and we know that $PF_1 + PF_2 = 2a$, it follows by dividing that:

$$PF_1 - PF_2 = 2ex.$$

Solving $PF_1 + PF_2 = 2a$ and $PF_1 - PF_2 = 2ex$ as a pair of simultaneous equations then gives expressions for the two lengths PF_1 and PF_2:

$$PF_1 = a + ex \quad \text{and} \quad PF_2 = a - ex.$$

Finally, substituting for PF_1 in $PF_1^2 = (x + ae)^2 + y^2$ gives:

$$(a + ex)^2 = (x + ae)^2 + y^2$$
$$a^2 + 2aex + e^2x^2 = x^2 + 2aex + a^2e^2 + y^2$$
$$a^2(1 - e^2) = x^2(1 - e^2) + y^2$$

Dividing both sides by $a^2(1 - e^2)$ gives $\dfrac{x^2}{a^2} + \dfrac{y^2}{a^2(1 - e^2)} = 1$.

However, $y = \pm b$ when $x = 0$, where b is half the length of the minor axis. It follows therefore that $a^2(1 - e^2)$ is equal to b^2. On substituting b^2, we have the familiar Cartesian equation for an ellipse:

$$\frac{x^2}{a^2} + \frac{y^2}{b^2} = 1.$$

In many textbooks the ellipse is defined as the locus of a point which moves so that there is a constant ratio (the eccentricity) between its distance from a fixed point (a focus) to its distance from a fixed line (a directrix). This relationship can be expressed as $PF_1 = ePD$, where D is a point on the directrix, and the equation of the ellipse can be derived from it. However, this is perhaps a rather obscure starting point. Another possibility is to define an ellipse as a section of a cone. That is intuitively appealing, but unfortunately it does not lead to a particularly straightforward way of deriving the equation of the curve. In the case of the parabola, however, the equation can be derived by viewing the curve as the section of a cone in a reasonably straightforward way and that idea introduces the next section.

THE PARABOLA

Students commonly first encounter the parabola in the context of learning about functions and graphs as the curve given by the equation $y = x^2$. The geometric properties of the curve are frequently given little emphasis because algebraic applications take priority, although some students may return to the parabola when they study the properties of conic sections as part of coordinate geometry. The link with the cone, which was the original source of the parabola in Greek mathematics, is often only mentioned in passing and yet it is an interesting application of geometrical ideas to derive the equation of the parabola from the cross section on a plane parallel to the slant edge.

The left-hand diagram of Figure 10.16 shows a cone ABC with the slant edge making an angle θ with the base. O is a point on AC with the length CO denoted by d. A cross section OPQ is created by a plane parallel to the slant edge, where PQ is a chord perpendicular to the diameter AB of the base. With PQ meeting AB at the point M, OM is the axis of the parabola, which is parallel to the slant edge CB.

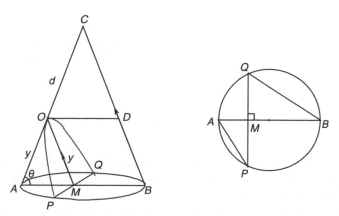

Figure 10.16 *Parabola as a cross section of a cone*

Taking O as the origin and OM as the y axis, the point P has coordinates (x,y), where $x = PM$ and $y = OM$. The right-hand diagram shows the circle forming the base of the cone. The problem is to show that y is proportional to x^2. We proceed as follows:

- $x^2 = AM.BM$ from the similar right-angled triangles AMP and BMQ.
- $AM = 2y\cos\theta$, because triangle OAM is isosceles and therefore $OA = y$.
- $BM = 2d\cos\theta$, because triangle COD is isosceles and $OD = BM$.
- Hence, $x^2 = 4dy\cos^2\theta$ which gives $y = \dfrac{x^2}{4d\cos^2\theta}$.

The curve $y = x^2$ is given by the particular case where $4d\cos^2\theta = 1$, which arises most simply when $d = 1$ and the angle θ is 60°. The curved surface of a cone with that angle is the same as a semicircle with the slant edge as radius, so it is easy to produce a model of the cone to show the source of the parabolic cross section.

The parabola has traditionally been defined as the locus of a point whose distance from a fixed point, the focus, is equal to its distance from a fixed line, the directrix. Using this definition it is simple to derive the equation of the parabola, but first let us see how it enables us to construct a parabola. Figure 10.17 shows a set of parallel lines with a set of concentric circles, whose centre lies on one of the lines and whose radii are multiples of the distance between the lines. The points of intersection between each line and a corresponding circle determine a parabola. Inspection of each of these points shows that they are equidistant from the centre of the circles and from the directrix.

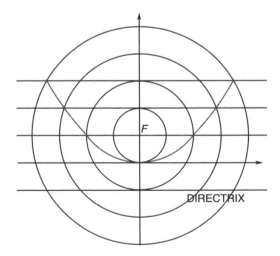

Figure 10.17 *Intersecting circles and lines to give a parabola*

Figure 10.18 gives a method, based on the focus directrix definition, for constructing a parabola as a locus. This can be demonstrated very effectively using dynamic geometry software and the diagram can be used both to derive the equation of the curve and to investigate some of its properties. The focus, F is taken as a point on the y axis. The directrix is constructed as a line parallel to the x axis the same distance below the axis as F is above. D is then taken as a variable point on the directrix and a line constructed through D perpendicular to the directrix. The

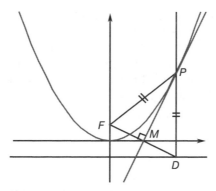

Figure 10.18 *Constructing a parabola*

parabola is the locus of a set of points, denoted here by P, which are equidistant from F and D. That means that triangle PFD is isosceles.

The point P is obtained by constructing the perpendicular bisector of FD, the base of the isosceles triangle, and finding where it intersects the perpendicular line through D. If the point D is moved along the directrix, thereby varying the x coordinate of P, the locus of P is a parabola as shown. No written description can do justice to the effect of demonstrating by moving the point D using dynamic geometry software. The reader is strongly urged to try out this simple construction and to explore its possibilities with students. This is an excellent example of the way in which the availability of software tools can make mathematical ideas both more accessible and more exciting.

Having constructed the diagram it is straightforward to determine the equation of the parabola. The coordinates of the focus are taken as $(0, f)$ and the point D on the directrix is then $(x, -f)$ with (x, y) as the coordinates of P. Equating the squares of the equal lengths PF and PD then leads to the equation of the parabola as follows:

$$PF^2 = PD^2$$
$$(y + f)^2 = x^2 + (y - f)^2$$
$$4fy = x^2$$
$$y = \frac{x^2}{4f}$$

The simplest case where the parabola has the equation $y = x^2$ is obtained when $f = \frac{1}{4}$. It is instructive to observe the effect of varying the position of the point F to see the resulting variation in the parabolic locus.

One surprising feature of the diagram is that the perpendicular bisector of the base of the isosceles triangle appears to be the tangent to the parabola at the point P and moreover the point M, where it cuts the base, lies on the x axis. The latter fact is easy to prove by noting the two congruent triangles which have M as a common vertex. Showing that the line MP is tangent is more interesting. The distance from any point on the line MP is equidistant from both D and F, but the distance from any point other than P to the directrix is less than its distance from the directrix, so the point P is the only point on the line that lies on the parabola. The line is therefore the tangent because there would, apart from the special case of the origin where the x axis is the tangent, be two points of intersection if it crossed the parabola.

The other noteworthy feature of the Figure 10.18 is that it shows clearly the significance of the focus as the point in a parabolic reflector from which a light source generates parallel light rays or conversely the point to which a parallel beam converges. This happens because the angle of incidence between the light ray and the tangent at the point where it hits the reflector is equal to the angle of reflection. The equality of the three angles between the straight lines meeting at the point *P* in the diagram explains why this is so.

CONCLUSION

Harnessing the power of algebra to solve geometric problems through the use of a coordinate system and the resulting representation of straight lines and curves by equations was a major breakthrough in the development of mathematics and is associated with the name of Descartes. The availability of powerful computer software and sophisticated graphical calculators complements that power as a way of helping to make these ideas accessible to a wide range of students in accessible and stimulating ways.

Both algebra and sophisticated technological tools have dangers in their different ways in that they can act as barriers to seeing the underlying geometrical ideas if they are used at a level of sophistication that is beyond the student at their particular stage of development. In the case of algebra this happens when remembering complicated looking formulae takes precedence over understanding the underlying ideas that they represent so that simple problems which should be approached in simple ways become unnecessarily difficult. With computers and calculators which handle complexity so readily it is easy to generate diagrams and graphs which hide the important geometrical ideas that students have to master if they are to come to understand that complexity. It is also very easy for mathematical ideas to become lost through attempting to use too wide a range of commands within a software package or graphical calculator.

A number of important teaching and learning points emerge from this chapter which has looked at the application of algebra to geometry through the key idea that a straight line or curve can be represented by an equation with reference to a system of coordinates:

- Situations described in terms of coordinates or equations of curves need to be portrayed with a diagram rather than seen as a purely algebraic or numerical exercise. For most purposes it is not necessary to draw such diagrams accurately, because their purpose is to suggest a way of solving a problem or to give some idea of the magnitude of a numerical answer or the form of the equation of a curve.
- Formulae for standard procedures such as finding the distance between two points or the gradient of a line should not be introduced at too early a stage. Particular procedures are often understood and remembered more readily through simple numerical examples which encapsulate the essential idea.
- Locus is a valuable idea both in establishing the equations of standard curves and in solving more general problems. This requires an ability to formulate a relationship, usually involving lengths in a suitable algebraic form, then to carry out some simplification and finally to check and interpret the solution. As with all problems where algebra is used, it is important to give sufficient time and consideration to the important first stage of formulation and the last stage of checking and interpretation, rather than concentrate exclusively on the more mechanical aspects of the solution.

- Variety of approach is important both in providing different insights and ways of looking at an idea and in helping students to see the great richness of interconnections and applications of geometrical ideas. Curves like the ellipse and parabola, and the hyperbola and others that have not been considered here, each have a range of applications and interesting properties and each benefits form being looked at from both an algebraic and a geometrical perspective.

One of the barriers to learning both geometry and algebra successfully is that both involve making sense of what often looks complicated, whether it be figures with an array of lines and curves or symbolic arguments. Linking algebra and geometry brings two sources of complication together which may make the situation even more difficult for the learner. On the other hand bringing these two different ways of looking at problems together is a source of greater insight and stimulation and has contributed greatly to the development of mathematics since the time of Descartes.

Chapter 11

Polyhedra

THE REGULAR POLYHEDRA

Polyhedra are an attractive aspect of three-dimensional geometry which can provide a range of challenges for students at all levels. A school geometry course should give all students the opportunity to construct a range of polyhedra, including each of the five regular polyhedra illustrated in Figure 11.1, and to examine their properties and the links between them.

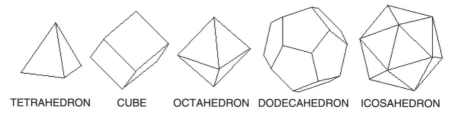

TETRAHEDRON   CUBE   OCTAHEDRON DODECAHEDRON ICOSAHEDRON

Figure 11.1 *The five regular polyhedra*

The traditional mode of construction is to use a net : details will be found in the classic book by Cundy and Rollett (1961) and in good school textbooks, as well as other sources such as Wenninger (1971). An alternative, and in many ways more instructive, way of making poly-hedra is to use individual polygons as the building blocks. Polygons can be cut out from card, or sets of interlocking plastic polygons are available from some educational suppliers. The Mathematical Activity Tiles (MATs) produced by the Association of Teachers of Mathematics and described in Pinel (1993), which were referred to in Chapter 3, are made of thick card and are a particularly attractive and useful medium for working with polyhedra.

The fact that there are only five regular polyhedra is in itself surprising and can be demon-strated readily when polyhedra are constructed with individual polygons. The argument follows the lines of Proposition 18 of the final book, Book XIII, of Euclid's *Elements* (see Heath 1967). A regular polyhedron is one where each of the faces is an identical regular polygon, so we can consider each of the regular polygons in turn to see what polyhedra constructed from each are possible as follows:

- 3 equilateral triangles at each vertex gives a regular tetrahedron (4 faces).
- 4 equilateral triangles at each vertex gives a regular octahedron (8 faces).
- 5 equilateral triangles at each vertex gives a regular icosahedron (20 faces).
- 6 or more equilateral triangles at a vertex are not possible, because the angle sum at the vertex is 360° or more.
- 3 squares at each vertex gives a cube, or a regular hexahedron (6 faces).

- 4 or more squares at a vertex are not possible, again because the angle sum at the vertex is 360° or more.
- 3 regular pentagons at each vertex give a regular dodecahedron (12 faces).
- 4 or more regular pentagons at a vertex are not possible and 3 or more regular polygons with 6 or more sides are also not possible, because of the constraint imposed by the angle sum at the vertex.

This is a simple example of a proof by exhaustion where all the possibilities are considered. Although it is not completely rigorous as a proof, because it is necessary to argue why each of the polyhedra is both possible and unique, it is very convincing and more than sufficient at an elementary level. Besides providing a simple way of identifying all the possibilities it also gives a good feel as to why the number is so surprisingly limited to just five.

The other surprising and important elementary property of polyhedra which can be established at an elementary level is the relationship between the number of vertices (V), edges (E) and faces (F) known as Euler's formula:

$$V - E + F = 2$$

The table of Figure 11.2 gives values of V, E and F for a variety of simple polyhedra. Including a column for $V+F$ makes it easy to spot the relationship between the three variables.

	V	E	F	$V + F$
Triangular prism	6	9	5	11
Cube	8	12	6	14
Pentagonal prism	10	15	7	17
Tetrahedron	4	6	4	8
Square-based pyramid	5	8	5	10
Pentagonal pyramid	6	10	6	12
Octahedron	6	12	8	14
Dodecahedron	20	30	12	32
Icosahedron	12	30	20	32

Figure 11.2 *Vertices, edges and faces for some common polyhedra*

A number of interesting patterns are evident in the numbers in the table. With prisms and pyramids there are very simple linear relationships between the number of edges, n, of the cross section and the base respectively, and the values of V, E and F.

$$\text{Prisms: } V = 2n, \quad E = 3n, \quad F = n + 2$$
$$\text{Pyramids: } V = n + 1, \quad E = 2n, \quad F = n + 1$$

Each relationship can be explained readily by reference to the properties of the configuration involved and, moreover, these results can be used in a simple way to prove Euler's formula for prisms and pyramids as follows:

$$\text{Prisms: } V - E + F = 2n - 3n + (n + 2) = 2$$
$$\text{Pyramids: } V - E + F = (n + 1) - 2n - (n + 1) = 2$$

It is also significant that the cube and octahedron have identical values for E and that the values of V and F are swapped. The same is true for the dodecahedron and icosahedron, and for each of the pyramids V and F take the same value so swapping them makes no difference. The pairs of polyhedra are duals and pyramids are self-dual. For example, a regular octahedron is formed if the midpoints of adjacent faces of a cube are joined as shown in Figure 11.3. Likewise a cube is formed if the midpoints of adjacent faces of a regular octahedron are joined. There is a similar relationship between the dodecahedron and icosahedron and for pyramids, where joining the midpoints of faces gives a pyramid of the same kind.

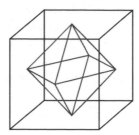

Figure 11.3 *Octahedron in a cube*

The relationship between V, E and F is not in any way related to whether the polygons constituting the various polyhedra are regular. The values of the variables given, for example, for the cube would hold equally well for a cuboid or a parallelepiped or any other polyhedron with 6 faces with 4 edges each.

While a full proof of Euler's formula is not appropriate at an elementary level, it can be made very plausible by seeing that any polyhedron is equivalent to a connected network of lines on a sphere. Removing one of the lines either reduces each of E and F by 1 or, if the line is a 'loose end', it reduces each of E and V by 1. In each case the value of $V - E + F$ is unchanged. This process of removing edges can be continued until a single vertex and no edges remain, with the whole surface of the sphere constituting a single face. Since $V - E + F = 2$ for this simple configuration it seems reasonable that it should hold for any network on the sphere that can be created by reversing the removal process described above.

It is tempting to suppose that Euler's formula applies to all polyhedra, but it is necessary to be clear how a polyhedron is defined. An entertaining and detailed discussion of the difficulties of formulating and proving the formula will be found in the book *Proofs and Refutations* by Lakatos (1976). A simple example makes it clear that things can easily go wrong. Suppose that a cube has a square hole from the top to the bottom face as shown in Figure 11.4. Note that there

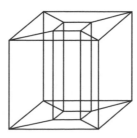

Figure 11.4 *A polyhedron with a hole*

are edges on the top and bottom surfaces joining the corners of the hole to the vertices of the cube to ensure that all the edges are connected. We then find on counting vertices, edges and vertices that $V - E + F = 16 - 32 + 16 = 0$, which is not at all what we might have expected.

The earlier talk of spheres may seem to be moving away from polyhedra and into the realms of topology, but it is not difficult in an elementary way to appreciate the equivalence between a polyhedron and a network of lines on a sphere and to see that holes could be introduced into conventional polyhedra and that would be equivalent to a network on a doughnut or torus. To make things even more intriguing try drawing networks on a Moebius strip which has one face, one edge and one vertex (necessary if we define an edge as a line joining two vertices). Euler's formula for a network on a Moebius strip must therefore be $V - E + F = 1$.

SOME PROPERTIES OF THE CUBE

At first sight a cube seems a simple shape, but it has many interesting properties and there are many questions that can be asked about it. An obvious starting point is the construction of a cube using a net. Figure 11.5 shows several different configurations of squares that are known as

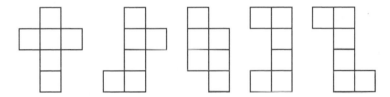

Figure 11.5 *Which hexominoes are nets of a cube?*

hexominoes. The left-hand one is the usual net used for constructing a cube, but of the others two will serve as a net, but two will not. It is a good exercise in spatial thinking to ask students to identify which hexominoes are nets of a cube and which are not. Another simple exercise is to identify one vertex of a net and ask students to say which other vertices will coincide with it when the net is folded up. For some students it will be appropriate to investigate these problems by cutting out the nets and attempting to fold them; for others it should be a mental exercise in visualizing what would happen if folding was attempted. A more demanding exercise is to find all the 35 possible hexominoes and determine how many of them are nets of a cube. This problem and others concerning hexominoes are discussed at length by Gardner (1965) in the wider context of polyominoes in an interesting chapter in *Mathematical Puzzles and Diversions*.

Coloured interlocking cubes provide an attractive medium for looking at properties of cubes in a very different way from questions prompted by a single cube. They provide a context for posing problems which require visualization as well as requiring combinatorial or algebraic thinking. A three by three cube with two colours used for alternate cubes, as shown in Figure 11.6, is an interesting configuration which can stimulate many questions like the following:

- How many black cubes are there?
- How many white cubes are there?
- What colour is the cube in the middle?
- How many cubes can you see in the picture and how many are hidden?

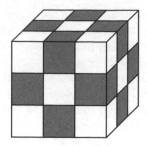

Figure 11.6 *How many cubes of each colour in this 3 by 3 cube?*

- How many cubes are coloured on 0, 1, 2 and 3 faces respectively if it is only the exposed faces that are coloured?
- Could you make a cube like this with a hole in the middle using 13 pairs of cubes where each pair has one of each colour?
- What is the minimum number of plane cuts needed to release the middle cube?

Each of these questions involves an element of visualization combined with reasoning and a systematic approach together with opportunities for students to communicate their thinking, as in the following dialogue about the first three questions.

T: How many black cubes are there?
A: 13.
T: How did you get that answer?
A: 4 on the top layer, 4 on the bottom and 5 in the middle layer.
T: So, how many white cubes are there then?
B: 14. There are 5 each on the top and bottom and 4 in the middle layer.
T: Is there a different way of doing it?
C: You could take 13 away from 27.
T: Why 27?
C: Because there are 27 cubes altogether.
T: What colour is the cube in the middle?
D: Black.
T: How do you know?
D: Because it is white in the middle on the top, so the cube below has to be black.

The final question about the number of plane cuts is particularly intriguing. An interesting discussion will be found in Buxton (1981) where he shows how a dialogue with a student eventually leads to a breakthrough. The critical insight is to see that there must be at least six plane cuts to release the middle cube because each face has to be parted from an adjoining cube.

Another aspect of the cube is to consider its symmetry. At first sight this seems obvious and not particularly interesting. Determining the planes of symmetry is straightforward: the question is equivalent to asking how the cube can be cut to give two pieces which are mirror images. There are three planes that cut the cube in half to form two cuboids. Each of these planes cuts four faces of the cube in half, so with twelve faces there must be three such planes. Alternatively, plane cuts can be made diagonally across faces. In this case there are six planes, because there are two such planes for each pair of opposite faces. Since there are three pairs of opposite faces that gives six planes. Another way of looking at this is to note that each of these diagonal planes involves two opposite edges of the cube. Since there six opposite pairs of edges, there must be twelve planes. These questions may seem very straightforward, but each requires an element of visualization and an element of reasoning to arrive at an answer.

Rotational symmetry offers further challenges. Figure 11.7 shows the three distinct ways in which an axis of rotational symmetry can be placed. In each case we can ask what the order of rotational symmetry is and how many possible positions there are for the axis. The question about positions for each of the three cases is respectively linked to the number of faces, edges and vertices.

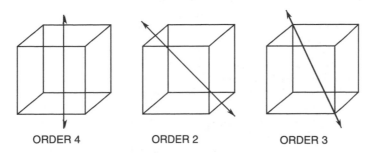

ORDER 4   ORDER 2   ORDER 3

Figure 11.7 *Rotational symmetry of the cube*

The third case, where the axis of rotational symmetry passes through an opposite pair of vertices is particularly striking, because we do not immediately expect a cube to display order 3 rotational symmetry. It is worth holding a pair of opposite vertices between thumb and fingertip and then turning the cube to see the symmetry. It is also worth viewing the cube along the line of the axis to see that there is a hexagonal cross section. This is illustrated by the three diagrams of Figure 11.8. The left-hand diagram shows the cube with an axis of rotational symmetry and the middle diagram shows the hexagonal cross section when the cube is viewed along the axis.

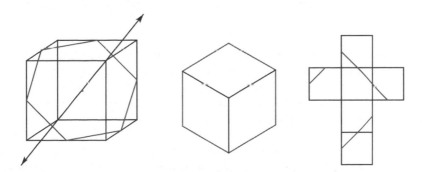

Figure 11.8 *Hexagon in a cube*

The right-hand diagram of Figure 11.8 shows a net of a cube with the diagonal lines which form the edges of the hexagonal cross section joining midpoints of edges. It is a challenging exercise for students to decide for themselves where to place these diagonal lines on the net. If the lines are drawn on a card net and the parts beyond the lines are cut off and discarded, the resulting net will fold up to give half a cube with the hexagon exposed. The model can be improved by making a card hexagon to fit into the empty face. Two such models will fit together to make a complete cube.

THE REGULAR TETRAHEDRON

The fact that a cube has rotational symmetry of order three suggests the presence of equilateral triangles. Joining alternate vertices of the hexagon in the middle diagram of Figure 11.8 will result in the triangle formed by the diagonals of the square faces as shown in the left-hand diagram of Figure 11.9. That triangle prompts some obvious questions:

T: What can you tell me about the triangle drawn on the cube?
A: It is equilateral.
T: How do you know that?
B: Because the sides are equal?
T: Why are they equal?
C: Because each side is the diagonal of a square.
T: Yes, but why does that make them equal?
D: All the square faces are identical, so all the diagonals are the same length.

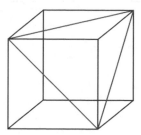 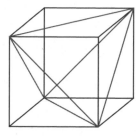

Figure 11.9 *Equilateral triangle and regular tetrahedron in a cube*

If some further diagonals are included, as shown in the right-hand diagram, a regular tetrahedron is created within the cube. This leads to a number of interesting classroom tasks.

- Construct an open-topped cube and construct a regular tetrahedron which just fits inside. This involves calculating the length of the diagonal of a face of the cube to give the length of the edge of the tetrahedron. When the two polyhedra have been constructed it is always comes as a surprise that the tetrahedron will actually fit into the cube, because it looks too big. Indeed fitting it in is an interesting puzzle for the uninitiated!
- Construct a regular tetrahedron and then construct four smaller tetrahedra to sit on the faces to complete the cube. These smaller tetrahedra have one face which is an equilateral triangle and three faces which are right-angled isosceles triangles obtained by cutting square faces of the cube in half. Starting with the edge length of the regular tetrahedron it is a simple matter to calculate the lengths required.
- Determine what fraction of the volume of the cube is occupied by the tetrahedron. This involves seeing that each of the small tetrahedra is one sixth of the volume of the cube, using the standard result that the volume of a pyramid is one third of the area of the base multiplied by the height. Four of these tetrahedra therefore occupy two thirds of the volume of the cube and the regular tetrahedron must therefore occupy one third of the cube. Using this fact it is then possible to show that the volume of a regular tetrahedron with edges of length a is $\frac{1}{12}\sqrt{2}a^3$.

The result for the volume of a regular tetrahedron was derived in a different way in Chapter 7, where the link between the tetrahedron and the octahedron was discussed in conjunction with similarity in three-dimensional contexts. Four regular tetrahedra placed on four of the faces of a regular octahedron form a regular tetrahedron with dimensions that are double those of the smaller tetrahedra as shown in Figure 11.10. It follows from this that the volume of a regular octahedron is four times the volume of a regular tetrahedron with the same edge length. Using the formula for a regular tetrahedron derived above, the volume for an octahedron with edges of length a is $\frac{1}{3}\sqrt{2}a^3$.

Figure 11.10 *Four tetrahedra and an octahedron*

A related task is to compare the volumes of a square-based pyramid with triangular faces that are equilateral and a similar square-based pyramid whose edges are twice as long. It is easy to see that four such small pyramids will form the base of the larger pyramid as shown in left-hand diagram of Figure 11.11. The spaces between adjacent pyramids can be filled with regular tetrahedra. This striking fact follows because a regular tetrahedron fits precisely between two adjacent square-based pyramids. Looking at the gap between the pyramids it is clear that there are four vertices which can be joined to make a tetrahedron. The line joining the upper vertices of the two pyramids is the same as the edge lengths, because the vertices are each vertically above the centres of the respective square bases and the distance between these centres is the same as the length of the edges of the square. Thus all the edges of the tetrahedron are the same length and it is therefore regular.

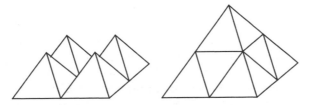

Figure 11.11 *Similar square-based pyramids*

A square-based pyramid can be placed on top to complete the similar, but larger, pyramid, and another inverted square-based pyramid will fill the space immediately below the top pyramid. In total there are six pyramids and four tetrahedra, so the four tetrahedra are equivalent to two pyramids. Two square-based pyramids with their bases placed together make a regular octahedron so this result links with the earlier result. All this is very difficult to follow from two-dimensional pictures and does serve to illustrate very forcibly the need for students to work with three-dimensional objects in order to make sense of such arguments.

Constructing models is a valuable and attractive activity in itself, but it also provides a variety of interesting geometrical results and relationships to explore. The results may not be particularly important in themselves, but they do provide valuable opportunities to develop reasoning skills in a geometrical context.

THE RHOMBIC DODECAHEDRON

The left-hand diagram of Figure 11.12 shows a square-based pyramid within a cube formed by joining the centre of the cube to the four vertices of one of the square faces. It is not difficult to see that six of these pyramids fit together to make the cube, since one can be constructed on each of the six square faces. This provides a further confirmation of the fact that the volume of a pyramid is one third the area of the base multiplied by the height, because the height of these pyramids is half the height of the cube.

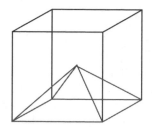
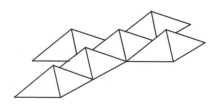

Figure 11.12 *Square-based pyramid in a cube*

Constructing six of these pyramids and fixing them to a standard net of a cube of suitable size provides a nice model which fits together very neatly if the net for the pyramids has been designed correctly. The critical requirement is to calculate the length of the sloping edges given the edges of the square base. The simplest way to do that is to calculate the length of the longest diagonal of the cube and then halve it.

One intriguing feature of this configuration is that it can be reversed so that the pyramids point outwards rather than inwards from the square faces of the cube. Corresponding pairs of isosceles triangles form rhombuses because they are in the same plane. Since there is one such rhombus for each of the edges of the cube, the resulting polyhedron is known as a rhombic dodecahedron. It is depicted in the top diagram of Figure 11.13

In the bottom left-hand diagram all the shorter diagonals have been included and they simply form the cube upon which the rhombic dodecahedron is based. In the bottom right-hand diagram all the longer diagonals have been included and it is interesting to observe that they form a regular octahedron. This is an enlargement of the octahedron formed by joining the midpoints of the faces of the cube which was depicted previously in Figure 11.3.

A final remarkable property of the rhombic dodecahedron is that it tessellates in three dimensions. This is a direct consequence of the way that it is constructed on the faces of a cube. Since, rather obviously, a cube tessellates, then the same must be true of a rhombic dodecahedron. If the students in a class are each asked to make a rhombic dodecahedron using the

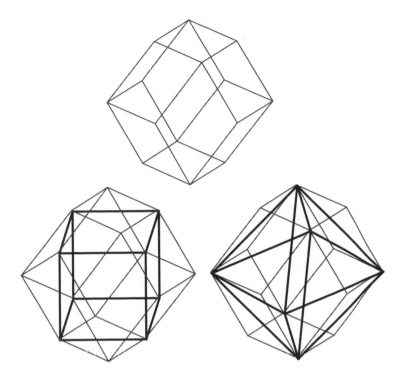

Figure 11.13 *Rhombic dodecahedron*

same dimensions, they will be truly impressed when they see how all their models fit together so neatly.

THE REGULAR DODECAHEDRON AND ICOSAHEDRON

Counting the faces, edges and vertices of a regular dodecahedron and the regular icosahedron referring to actual models is a small, but worthwhile task for students. Both polyhedra have 30 edges, but the dodecahedron has 12 faces and 20 vertices whereas the icosahedron has 12 vertices and 20 faces. This means that they are a dual pair of polyhedra such that an icosahedron is obtained by joining the centres of adjacent faces of a dodecahedron and vice versa. Both polyhedra are simple to construct: nets can either be found in the books mentioned earlier in the chapter or, as a more challenging task, students can devise their own. Alternatively,

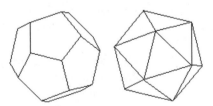

Figure 11.14 *A regular dodecahedron and a regular icosahedron*

and perhaps more instructively, models can be made using plastic or card triangles and pentagons.

As with the other polyhedra discussed in this chapter there are a variety of classroom tasks which relate to regular dodecahedra and icosahedra, although these are inevitably more demanding than activities involving simpler solids. The two examples which follow involve constructing dissections of a regular icosahedron:

- Construct two pentagonal pyramids using 5 equilateral triangles and a regular pentagon and then construct a pentagonal anti-prism using 10 equilateral triangles and 2 regular pentagons. An anti-prism is like an ordinary prism, except that the opposite ends are linked with triangles instead of rectangles so that the two ends while parallel are oriented differently. In this case the anti-prism is the central slice of a regular icosahedron: adding the two pentagonal pyramids completes the icosahedron.
- Construct a different polyhedron using 10 equilateral triangles and 2 regular pentagons. The result is rather like a thick wedge with the two pentagons sharing a common edge and the triangles filling the space between. This wedge-shaped polyhedron combines with the two pentagonal pyramids to produce a regular icosahedron again which means that the two polyhedra constructed with 10 equilateral triangles and 2 regular pentagons are equal in volume.

Many people would erroneously argue that the two polyhedra referred to above have the same volume because they are constructed with an identical set of polygons, namely 10 equilateral triangles and 2 regular pentagons. It is a common misconception that equal surface area implies equal volume, similar to the false notion that equal perimeter implies equal area. Such errors are very persistent and are not helped by exceptional cases like this one where an incorrect argument gives a correct answer. A good counter-example is illustrated in Figure 11.15. This shows two cuboids, which can be constructed with interlocking cubes. The surface area is 22 in both cases, but the volumes of 5 and 6 are clearly not the same!

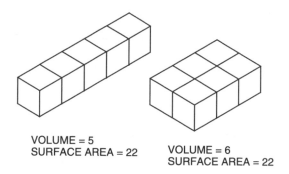

VOLUME = 5
SURFACE AREA = 22

VOLUME = 6
SURFACE AREA = 22

Figure 11.15 *Surface area and volume of cuboids*

Another remarkable feature of the icosahedron is its link to the golden rectangle. In Chapter 7 the ratio between the length of the diagonal and the length of the edge of a regular pentagon is shown to be the golden ratio, which is given by $\frac{1}{2}(1 + \sqrt{5})$ and has a value of approximately 1.62. Regular pentagons appear within a regular icosahedron as the cross section which is the base of the pentagonal pyramid associated with each vertex. If you examine a regular icosahedron you will see that opposite pairs of edges are parallel. Lines joining corresponding pairs of vertices at the ends of these edges are the diagonals of regular pentagons and therefore the rectangles defined by opposite pairs of edges are golden rectangles. The 12 vertices of the icosahedron define three mutually perpendicular golden rectangles, as shown in Figure 11.16. It is a simple matter to make three identical golden rectangles with card and make slots in them so that they fit together to show a regular icosahedron in this way.

Figure 11.16 *Three golden rectangles to form a regular icosahedron*

The standard design for a football, sometimes referred to as a bucky ball, is based on a polyhedron which has 32 faces made up of 12 regular pentagons and 20 regular hexagons. This polyhedron, depicted in Figure 11.17 is a truncated regular icosahedron: each of its vertices has been cut off to reveal a face which is a regular pentagon. It is a straightforward matter for students to construct a bucky ball using card or plastic pentagons and hexagons. It is clearly more demanding to devise a net to construct the polyhedron. Counting the number of edges and vertices is a useful small task. These results, together with the fact that there are 32 faces can then be used to verify that Euler's formula is satisfied.

Figure 11.17 *Bucky ball*

One form of the element carbon has molecules made up of 60 atoms of carbon arranged in the form of a bucky ball. It was discovered in 1985 by Sir Harry Kroto, professor of chemistry at the University of Sussex and two Americans, Robert Curl and Richard Smalley, from Rice University at Houston in Texas. This form of carbon was named buckminsterfullerene after the

American architect Buckminster Fuller, who designed the geodesic dome. The internet is a valuable source of information about buckminsterfullerene and geodesic domes.

As I have noted the bucky ball is a truncated regular icosahedron. It is also one of a family known as Archimedean polyhedra, of which there are 13 excluding prisms. All the faces are regular polyhedra, but not all of the same kind, and all the vertices are congruent. A number of these are obtained by truncating the regular polyhedra and these open up further possibilities for construction and calculation. As examples Figure 11.18 shows two truncations of a cube. In the left-hand case triangular faces have been revealed by plane cuts through the midpoints of each set of mutually perpendicular edges. The resulting polyhedron is known as a cuboctahedron and has 6 square faces and 8 triangular faces. Interestingly it is the dual of the rhombic dodecahedron. The right-hand diagram shows a truncated cube where the corners have been cut off to reveal equilateral triangles in such a way that the remaining part of each square face is a regular octagon. In both cases it is worth verifying that Euler's formula is satisfied and to calculate what fraction the volume is of the original cube.

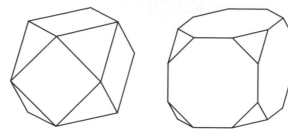

Figure 11.18 *Two truncated cubes*

CONCLUSION

Polyhedra have an immediate aesthetic appeal and constructing them is both a pleasurable and an instructive activity. There are a number of attractive books on the subject and there are many fascinating interactive websites where the properties of polyhedra can be readily explored by changing their orientation or superimposing them. Two good examples of such websites are:

www.shef.ac.uk/~pm1nps/courses/groups/plato.html

www.divideo.it/personal/todesco/java/polyhedra/theApplet.html

Constructing polyhedra should be more than an exercise in cutting out a pre-drawn net or following a set of detailed instructions for the design of a net. Designing a net is a valuable geometrical task in itself and polyhedron models should be used as the basis for further discussion and investigation. This should include seeing why there are only five regular polyhedra, discovering the surprising simplicity of Euler's formula, looking at the symmetry of a variety of polyhedra, posing some questions about volume and exploring the ways in which some of the different solids are related.

It is perhaps unfortunate that polyhedra are often categorized as part of recreational mathematics when they are such a rich topic to investigate and have links to so many other areas of mathematics. This chapter has tried to show something of this wealth of possibilities and how it can fruitfully be explored in the classroom at different levels.

Chapter 12

Vector Geometry

TRANSLATIONS AND VECTORS

Vectors are used to represent any mathematical entity which has both magnitude and direction, as opposed to scalars, which just have magnitude. They have a wide range of applications in mathematics and physics particularly in connection with mechanics where key concepts like velocity, acceleration and force are all examples of vector quantities. In the context of geometry they represent displacements and this provides a simple way to introduce this powerful idea. Vectors are depicted very simply as arrows which clearly have a length, or magnitude, and a direction. In the early stages of learning about vectors in geometry it makes sense to restrict considerations to two dimensions, but the great beauty of vectors is that all the ideas extend readily to provide a powerful tool for looking at three-dimensional problems.

Initially at school level vectors arise naturally as a means of describing translations. In the triangles of Figure 12.1, the bottom right-hand vertices are denoted by O, P and Q and we can

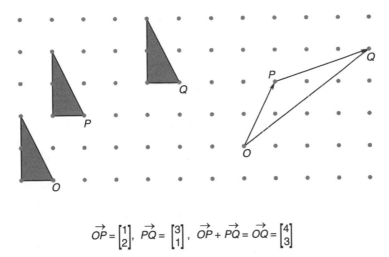

$$\vec{OP} = \begin{bmatrix} 1 \\ 2 \end{bmatrix}, \ \vec{PQ} = \begin{bmatrix} 3 \\ 1 \end{bmatrix}, \ \vec{OP} + \vec{PQ} = \vec{OQ} = \begin{bmatrix} 4 \\ 3 \end{bmatrix}$$

Figure 12.1 *Combining two translations*

see that the translation taking O to P involves moving 1 unit to the right and 2 units upwards, whereas in going from P to Q the translation is 3 units to the right and 1 upwards. If we move directly from O to Q, then the translation is 4 units to the right and 3 upwards, obtained by adding the respective components of the two separate translations. This leads naturally to the notion of adding two vectors. The figure gives two of the common symbolic forms used for vectors: an arrow over a pair of letters denoting points emphasizes the direction aspect and distinguishes from a pair of letters denoting a length, whereas the column vector form provides a simple means of displaying the two components. It is important to distinguish between vectors and coordinates and writing vectors in a column format helps in making that distinction.

The underlying idea of adding two vectors is exemplified geometrically by the triangle law shown in Figure 12.1. The arrows representing a pair of vectors are placed end on and the single equivalent vector is the sum or resultant. This idea is clarified by using vectors as a way of describing translations: a pair of successive translations is equivalent to a single translation. It is further emphasized by looking at particular cases where the translations are represented by column vectors.

Figure 12.2 draws attention to two further important points. The first concerns the equality of vectors: all vectors with the same magnitude and direction are equivalent or, alternatively, all vectors with identical components are equivalent. The two pairs of vectors representing the opposite pairs of sides of the parallelogram are therefore equivalent as shown. Secondly, the operation of adding vectors is commutative, because the order in which the vectors are added does not matter. This gives the parallelogram law, where the resultant is the vector representing the diagonal of a parallelogram, as an alternative formulation to the triangle law for adding vectors.

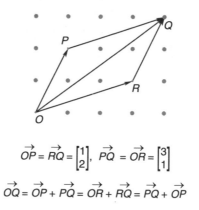

$$\vec{OP} = \vec{RQ} = \begin{bmatrix} 1 \\ 2 \end{bmatrix}, \ \vec{PQ} = \vec{OR} = \begin{bmatrix} 3 \\ 1 \end{bmatrix}$$

$$\vec{OQ} = \vec{OP} + \vec{PQ} = \vec{OR} + \vec{RQ} = \vec{PQ} + \vec{OP}$$

Figure 12.2 *Pairs of equivalent vectors*

Notation for vectors is potentially confusing because a number of different forms are in common use. The arrow over a pair of letters is a useful initial notation, but it soon becomes more convenient to move to denoting vectors by single letters, which are customarily printed in bold. There are advantages also in using the double-letter notation in bold without the arrow above. This is the convention that is followed in the rest of this chapter. However, there is a difficulty here because it is difficult to use 'bold' in a hand written form. The usual way round this is to underline the vectors, writing OP or p in place of **OP** and **p**, but it has to be acknowledged that this is a further potential source of confusion to students in the early stages.

The idea of subtracting vectors seems to follow on naturally from addition as illustrated by Figure 12.3, which continues to use the same positions of the points *O*, *P* and *Q* as in the previous examples. While this is mathematically a straightforward logical deduction from the addition of vectors, it is a much more difficult and abstract idea than addition, because it does not have quite the same immediate intuitive appeal, even though it is reinforced by the subtraction of the components of column vectors.

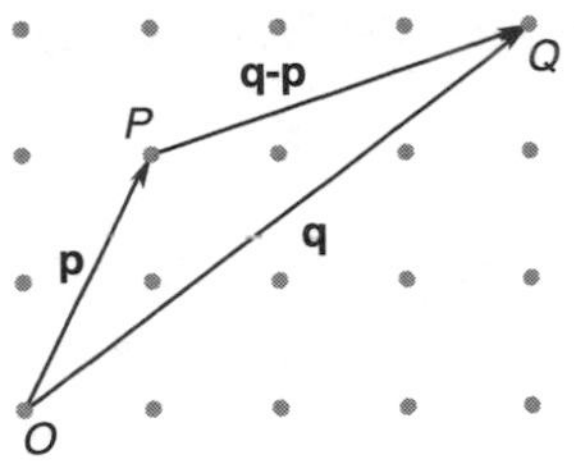

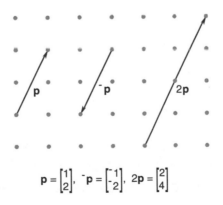

$$OP = p = \begin{bmatrix} 1 \\ 2 \end{bmatrix}, \quad OQ = q = \begin{bmatrix} 4 \\ 3 \end{bmatrix}$$

$$OP + PQ = OQ \Rightarrow PQ = OQ - OP = q - p = \begin{bmatrix} 3 \\ 1 \end{bmatrix}$$

Figure 12.3 *Subtracting vectors*

The idea of a 'negative vector', discussed below, where the arrow is reversed provides an alternative way of looking at subtraction of vectors by invoking the triangle law for addition in a different way. Referring back to Figure 12.3, we can say:

$$PQ = PO + OQ = ^-p + q = q - p$$

However, the final step here can only make good sense if the necessary algebraic understanding is secure.

Multiplying a vector by a scalar is a much more straightforward idea illustrated by some simple examples in Figure 12.4. The key point is that the magnitude of the vector changes, whereas the direction is unchanged unless the multiplier is a negative number, in which case the direction is reversed. This simple idea is very useful in a geometrical context: if two line segments are described by the vectors **p** and *k***p** where *k* is a scalar constant, then the segments are parallel and one is *k* times longer than the other.

$$p = \begin{bmatrix} 1 \\ 2 \end{bmatrix}, \quad ^-p = \begin{bmatrix} ^-1 \\ ^-2 \end{bmatrix}, \quad 2p = \begin{bmatrix} 2 \\ 4 \end{bmatrix}$$

Figure 12.4 *Multiplying a vector by a scalar*

Since a vector can be characterized either by its magnitude and direction or by its components in two perpendicular directions it is obviously necessary to be aware of the relationship between these different variables and to be able to change from one form to the other. This involves the routine use of Pythagoras' theorem and trigonometry. The essential results are summarized in Figure 12.5.

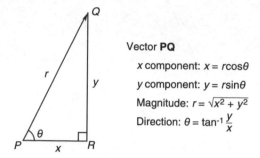

Vector **PQ**

x component: $x = r\cos\theta$

y component: $y = r\sin\theta$

Magnitude: $r = \sqrt{x^2 + y^2}$

Direction: $\theta = \tan^{-1}\dfrac{y}{x}$

Figure 12.5 *Linking the magnitude, direction and components of a vector*

VECTORS APPLIED TO GEOMETRICAL PROBLEMS

There is always a danger of confusion between coordinates and the column vector form of a vector. The two ideas have much in common, but are distinct, although we sometimes wish to fix the position of a vector by referring to the position vector of a point with reference to a specified origin and then the distinction is very slight. However, we have to work with both ideas and Figure 12.6 shows a typical problem involving a quadrilateral, which is specified in terms of the coordinates of its vertices.

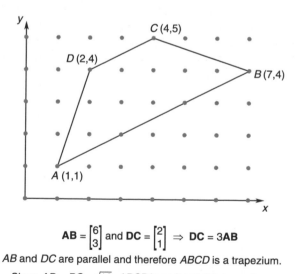

$$\mathbf{AB} = \begin{bmatrix} 6 \\ 3 \end{bmatrix} \text{ and } \mathbf{DC} = \begin{bmatrix} 2 \\ 1 \end{bmatrix} \Rightarrow \mathbf{DC} = 3\mathbf{AB}$$

AB and *DC* are parallel and therefore *ABCD* is a trapezium.

Since $AD = BC = \sqrt{10}$, *ABCD* is an isosceles trapezium.

Figure 12.6 *What can you say about this quadrilateral?*

The midpoint theorem has been discussed previously in Chapter 7 in conjunction with enlargement and similarity. Vectors provide a different perspective on the theorem illustrating the simple principles that arise from the equivalence of vectors. In Figure 12.7, **a** and **b** are used to

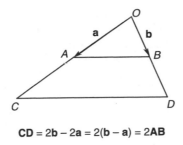

$$\mathbf{CD} = 2\mathbf{b} - 2\mathbf{a} = 2(\mathbf{b} - \mathbf{a}) = 2\mathbf{AB}$$

Figure 12.7 *The midpoint theorem*

denote vectors representing line segments from the vertex O to A and B, the midpoints of two sides. When the line segments AB and CD are expressed as vectors it is clear from the vector expressions that the lines are parallel and that one is twice the length of the other.

The fact that the diagonals of a parallelogram bisect each other can be established using vector methods as shown in Figure 12.8. Expressions are obtained for the midpoints of the diagonals OC and AB in terms of the two vectors $\mathbf{a}$ and $\mathbf{b}$. Since the expressions are equal they must refer to the same point, showing that each diagonal is bisected by the other. It is worth noting here that the midpoint of AB is given by the vector $\frac{1}{2}(\mathbf{a} + \mathbf{b})$, which is a useful general result for the midpoint, or mean point, of a line segment.

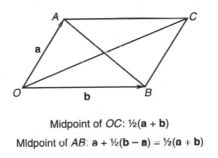

Midpoint of OC: $\frac{1}{2}(\mathbf{a} + \mathbf{b})$

Midpoint of AB: $\mathbf{a} + \frac{1}{2}(\mathbf{b} - \mathbf{a}) = \frac{1}{2}(\mathbf{a} + \mathbf{b})$

Figure 12.8 *The diagonals of a parallelogram bisect each other*

The approach to this last example is a prelude to the idea of vector equations of lines which provide a more general way of dealing with problems involving the intersection of lines and provide a first step towards the important application of vector methods to geometry in three dimensions.

VECTOR EQUATIONS OF LINES

The Cartesian equation of a line is dependent on a coordinate system with a pair of perpendicular axes. Vector equations are more flexible in that they provide a way of describing a line in two dimensions in terms of a pair of non-parallel vectors. This readily extends to three dimensions with three vectors which must be linearly independent, which implies that they are not coplanar and no two of them are parallel.

In Figure 12.9, **a** is the position vector of a point on the line and **b** is a vector in the direction of the line. The position vector of any point on the line is then given by **r** = **a** + *t***b** where **r** is used to denote a general point on the line and *t* is a parameter which generates multiples of the vector **b**. In the figure, various values of the parameter are displayed against the corresponding points on the line.

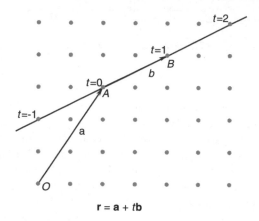

Figure 12.9 *The vector equation of a line*

It is interesting to see how the vector equation is linked to the corresponding Cartesian equation of the line. Referring to the line in Figure 12.9 with the grid points placed at unit intervals the vector equation, which is equivalent to a pair of parametric equations, leads to the Cartesian equation as follows:

$$\begin{bmatrix} x \\ y \end{bmatrix} = \begin{bmatrix} 2 \\ 3 \end{bmatrix} + t \begin{bmatrix} 2 \\ 1 \end{bmatrix} \quad \Rightarrow \quad \begin{array}{l} x = 2 + 2t \\ y = 3 + t \end{array} \quad \Rightarrow \quad y = \tfrac{1}{2}x + 2$$

In three dimensions the vector equation is much more useful because a line has to be specified by a pair of Cartesian equations. The vector equation is a compact way of writing a set of parametric equations, where each point on the line is specified by a single value of the parameter.

As an example of the application of the vector equation of a line, we can look at a proof that the medians of a triangle are concurrent and are each divided in the ratio 2:1 by their point of intersection. This result has been proved in Chapter 7 in a far simpler way, but a vector proof is nonetheless instructive. Figure 12.10 shows the triangle *ABC* with *E* and *F* as the midpoints of the sides *AC* and *AB*. The vectors **AE** and **AF** are denoted by **e** and **f**. The values of the parameters at the point of intersection can then be determined as follows:

> Vector equation of line *EB*:   **r** = **e** + *t*(2**f** − **e**)
> Vector equation of line *FC*:   **r** = **f** + *s*(2**e** − **f**)
> Equating coefficients of **e**:   1 − *t* = 2*s*
> Equating coefficients of **f**:   2*t* = 1 − *s*
> Solving: $s = t = \tfrac{1}{3}$

Both parameters have a value of $\tfrac{1}{3}$ which implies that the point of intersection divides each of the two medians in the ratio 2:1. Since the same argument would apply to any pair of medians, it follows that the three medians meet at a common point.

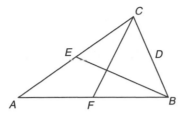

Figure 12.10 *The medians of a triangle are concurrent*

A more sophisticated way of looking at the problem is to take an origin O at some point outside the plane of the triangle and denote the vectors **OA, OB** and **OC** by **a, b** and **c** respectively, so that the midpoints E and F are represented by $\frac{1}{2}(\mathbf{a} + \mathbf{c})$ and $\frac{1}{2}(\mathbf{a} + \mathbf{b})$. Then the previous argument becomes as follows:

Vector equation of line EB: $\mathbf{r} = \frac{1}{2}(\mathbf{a} + \mathbf{c}) + s(\mathbf{b} - \frac{1}{2}(\mathbf{a} + \mathbf{c}))$
Vector equation of line FC: $\mathbf{r} = \frac{1}{2}(\mathbf{a} + \mathbf{b}) + t(\mathbf{c} - \frac{1}{2}(\mathbf{a} + \mathbf{b}))$
Equating coefficients of **a**: $\frac{1}{2} - \frac{1}{2}s = \frac{1}{2} - \frac{1}{2}t$
Equating coefficients of **b**: $s = \frac{1}{2} - \frac{1}{2}t$
Equating coefficients of **c**: $\frac{1}{2} - \frac{1}{2}s = t$
Solving: $s = t = \frac{1}{3}$

Substituting the value of s or t gives $\mathbf{r} = \frac{1}{3}(\mathbf{a} + \mathbf{b} + \mathbf{c})$ as the position vector of the point of intersection, the point which is commonly known as the centroid of the triangle.

THE SCALAR PRODUCT

The scalar product is commonly introduced by giving a definition, without indicating where the idea has come from. In keeping with the idea of making the purpose for any new idea clear at an early stage, and also because it is good to encourage students to work on problems which lead to new ideas, the scalar product can be introduced by posing the problem of finding the angle between two vectors. It is often useful to start with a particular case and then generalize, so we begin by finding the angle between the vectors **a** and **b** in Figure 12.11.

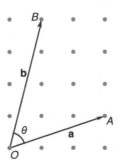

Figure 12.11 *The angle between two vectors*

Since it is a simple matter to find the lengths of the three sides of triangle OAB using Pythagoras' theorem, the angle can be determined using the cosine rule as follows:

$$\mathbf{a} = \begin{bmatrix} 3 \\ 1 \end{bmatrix} \text{ and } \mathbf{b} = \begin{bmatrix} 1 \\ 4 \end{bmatrix} \quad \Rightarrow \quad \mathbf{c} = \mathbf{AB} = \begin{bmatrix} -2 \\ 3 \end{bmatrix}$$

$$a = \sqrt{10},\ b = \sqrt{17} \text{ and } c = \sqrt{13}$$

Cosine rule: $13 = 27 - 2\sqrt{10}\sqrt{17}\cos\theta \quad \Rightarrow \quad \cos\theta = \dfrac{7}{\sqrt{10}\sqrt{17}} \quad \Rightarrow \quad \theta \approx 57.5°$

This provides a pattern for an argument to determine the angle between two general vectors, **a** and **b**:

$$\mathbf{a} = \begin{bmatrix} a_1 \\ a_2 \end{bmatrix} \text{ and } \mathbf{b} = \begin{bmatrix} b_1 \\ b_2 \end{bmatrix} \quad \Rightarrow \quad \mathbf{c} = \mathbf{AB} = \begin{bmatrix} b_1 - a_1 \\ b_2 - a_2 \end{bmatrix}$$

$$a = \sqrt{a_1^2 + a_2^2},\ b = \sqrt{b_1^2 + b_2^2} \text{ and } c = \sqrt{(b_1 - a_1)^2 + (b_2 - a_2)^2}$$

Cosine rule: $c^2 = a^2 + b^2 - 2ab\cos\theta$

$$\Rightarrow \quad (b_1 - a_1)^2 + (b_2 - a_2)^2 = a_1^2 + a_2^2 + b_1^2 + b_2^2 - 2ab\cos\theta$$

$$\Rightarrow \quad ab\cos\theta = a_1 b_1 + a_2 b_2$$

The last statement enables us to calculate the angle for any vectors **a** and **b** without doing all the intermediate calculations using the cosine rule. Because of its significance the terms on each side of the equation are referred to as the scalar product of the vectors and they are written in a special way as **a.b**. Thus, we have a definition of scalar product:

$$\mathbf{a.b} = ab\cos\theta = a_1 b_1 + a_2 b_2$$

It is important to note that the definition readily extends to three dimensions because the argument based on the cosine rule applies equally when the vectors have three components. Although the definition has arisen from the problem of finding the angle between two vectors, its importance extends far beyond that, because it has the highly useful property of being zero when the two vectors are perpendicular:

$$\mathbf{a.b} = 0 \quad \Leftrightarrow \quad \mathbf{a} \text{ is perpendicular to } \mathbf{b} \text{ if neither is a zero vector.}$$

It is worth noting, because the connection is often not made, that this result is equivalent to saying that the product of the gradients, m_1 and m_2, of two perpendicular lines is minus one. This is shown as follows:

$$\mathbf{a.b} = 0 \quad \Leftrightarrow \quad \begin{bmatrix} 1 \\ m_1 \end{bmatrix} \cdot \begin{bmatrix} 1 \\ m_2 \end{bmatrix} = 0 \quad \Leftrightarrow \quad m_1 m_2 + 1 = 0 \quad \Leftrightarrow \quad m_1 m_2 = -1$$

The two examples which follow show some geometrical situations where the scalar product is useful. In the rhombus *OABC* of Figure 12.12, the sides *OA* and *BC* are equal and parallel and may therefore be denoted by the same vector **a**. The same is true of the sides *OB* and *AC* denoted here by **b**. We can show that the diagonals are perpendicular by showing that the scalar product of the vectors representing them is zero. Since **OA**=a and **AC**=b, it follows that **OC**=a+b and **BA**=a−b. Then, the scalar product is given by:

$$\mathbf{OC.BA} = (\mathbf{a} + \mathbf{b}).(\mathbf{a} - \mathbf{b}) = \mathbf{a.a} + \mathbf{b.a} - \mathbf{a.b} - \mathbf{b.b} = a^2 - b^2$$

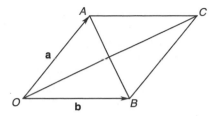

Figure 12.12 *The diagonals of a rhombus are perpendicular*

Since *a* and *b* denote the magnitudes of the vectors **a** and **b** and these are the lengths of the sides of the rhombus which are equal, we know that *a* and *b* are equal. It then follows that the scalar product **OC.BA** is zero and therefore that the diagonals are perpendicular. It is also immediately clear that the rhombus is the only type of parallelogram whose diagonals are perpendicular, because it is only when *a* and *b* are equal that the scalar product is zero.

While this is most certainly not the simplest way of proving that the diagonals of a rhombus are perpendicular, it is instructive as an exercise in applying the algebra of vectors to a geometrical context. Multiplying out the brackets draws attention to the commutative property satisfied by the scalar product and to the fact the scalar product of a vector with itself is the square of its magnitude.

An altitude is a perpendicular height of a triangle. Any triangle has three altitudes, corresponding to taking each of the three sides as base. Showing that the altitudes of a triangle are concurrent, as illustrated by Figure 12.13, requires a different style of argument with vectors.

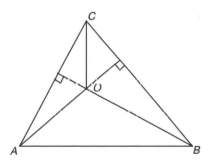

Figure 12.13 *The altitudes of a triangle are concurrent*

As with the concurrence of medians in the previous section, we have to start by considering the intersection of two of the altitudes and then show that the line from this point to the other vertex is the third altitude. So, let the altitudes from *A* and *B* meet at *O* and denote the vectors **OA**, **OB** and **OC** by **a**, **b** and **c**. We know that *OA* is perpendicular to *BC* and *OB* is perpendicular to *CA*, and so we have two scalar products that are zero. From these we can make some deductions as follows:

$$\mathbf{OA.BC} = 0 \quad \Rightarrow \quad \mathbf{a.(c - b)} = 0 \quad \Rightarrow \quad \mathbf{a.c = a.b}$$
$$\mathbf{OB.CA} = 0 \quad \Rightarrow \quad \mathbf{b.(a - c)} = 0 \quad \Rightarrow \quad \mathbf{a.b = b.c.}$$

It follows from these two statements that the scalar products **a.c** and **b.c** are equal and from that we can make further deductions as follows:

$$\mathbf{a.c} = \mathbf{b.c} \quad \Rightarrow \quad \mathbf{a.c} - \mathbf{b.c} = 0 \quad \Rightarrow \quad \mathbf{c.(a-b)} = 0 \quad \Rightarrow \quad \mathbf{OC.BA} = 0.$$

This seems to suggest that OC is perpendicular to BA and is therefore the other altitude. However, it could be that $\mathbf{OC}$ is a zero vector. In that exceptional case the points O and C coincide and the angle at C is a right angle. The concurrence is obviously true for a right-angled triangle, because two of the sides are altitudes, so we are safe in concluding that the altitudes are concurrent in any triangle.

GEOMETRY IN THREE DIMENSIONS

The real power of vectors in geometry comes when they are applied to figures in three dimensions. Problems with cubes provide a good starting point because the difficulties involved in visualizing the relationship between lines can be eased by making frequent reference to an actual model of a cube. In the classroom it makes sense for every student to have a cube that they can refer to. A simple portable model can be made from a square of paper or thin card and four paper clips as described in Figure 12.14.

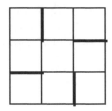

- Subdivide a square into 9 equal squares.
- Cut along the bold lines.
- Fold so that the middle square is the base and pairs of outer squares overlap to form the four vertical faces.
- Secure the faces with paper clips.

Figure 12.14 *A simple model of a cube*

The cube of Figure 12.15 shows triangle *BGE* created by joining three vertices, which has been referred to previously in Chapter 11. To prove that this triangle is equilateral we can find the angle between two sides using the scalar product of the vectors representing the sides. It is convenient to let the edges of the cube be of unit length and to let *OA*, *OC* and *OD* be the x, y and z axes respectively. To do that it is necessary to find the two vectors. The vector **EG,** for example, can be found by noting how we can move from E to G by taking a step of one unit in the negative x direction, one unit in the y direction and no units in the z direction. That gives us:

$$\mathbf{EG} = \begin{bmatrix} -1 \\ 1 \\ 0 \end{bmatrix}, \mathbf{EB} = \begin{bmatrix} 0 \\ 1 \\ -1 \end{bmatrix} \text{ with } EG = EB = \sqrt{2}.$$

It then follows that: $\cos\theta = \dfrac{\mathbf{EG.EB}}{EG \times \mathrm{EB}} = \frac{1}{2} \quad \Rightarrow \quad \theta = 60°.$

The same argument applies to any other pair of vectors representing sides of the triangle and so the triangle is equilateral. Clearly it is much simpler to show that the triangle is equilateral by showing that the lengths of its sides are equal, but it is often instructive to see how a new idea like scalar products does produce results that make sense in simple situations.

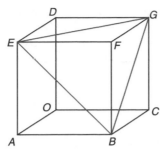

Figure 12.15 *A triangle in a cube*

A less immediately obvious property is that the line *OF* is perpendicular to the plane determined by the equilateral triangle. To show that is true we can show that the scalar products of **OF** with the vectors representing two of the sides are both zero. This raises two important issues that need to be discussed with students: how there can be an angle when two lines are skew, which means that they do not intersect, and why it is necessary and sufficient to consider the angle that *OF* makes with only two of the sides. The calculations are straightforward:

$$\mathbf{OF} = \begin{bmatrix} 1 \\ 1 \\ 1 \end{bmatrix} \Rightarrow \mathbf{OF.EG} = \begin{bmatrix} 1 \\ 1 \\ 1 \end{bmatrix} \cdot \begin{bmatrix} -1 \\ 1 \\ 0 \end{bmatrix} = 0, \text{ and } \mathbf{OF.EB} = \begin{bmatrix} 1 \\ 1 \\ 1 \end{bmatrix} \cdot \begin{bmatrix} 0 \\ 1 \\ -1 \end{bmatrix} = 0$$

Since **OF** is perpendicular to the plane of triangle *BGE*, it is the normal vector to the plane and that is directly involved in the equation of the plane. A cross section of a cube like this triangle provides a particularly convenient way to introduce both vector and Cartesian equations of a plane. With λ and μ as two parameters, any point, *P*, on the plane containing triangle *BGE* is given by:

$$\mathbf{OP} = \mathbf{OE} + \lambda\mathbf{EG} + \mu\mathbf{EB} \quad \text{or} \quad \begin{bmatrix} x \\ y \\ z \end{bmatrix} = \begin{bmatrix} 1 \\ 0 \\ 1 \end{bmatrix} + \lambda\begin{bmatrix} -1 \\ 1 \\ 0 \end{bmatrix} + \mu\begin{bmatrix} 0 \\ 1 \\ -1 \end{bmatrix}$$

If we form the scalar product of both sides of this equation with the normal vector **OF**, we neatly eliminate the parameters and obtain the Cartesian equation. Since **EG.OF**=0 and **EB.OF**=0, we have:

$$\mathbf{OP.OF} = \mathbf{OE.OF} + \lambda\mathbf{EG.OF} + \mu\mathbf{EB.OF} = \mathbf{OE.OF},$$

Substituting the column vectors then gives the usual form of the Cartesian equation of a plane, where the coefficients of the three variables are the normal vector:

$$\begin{bmatrix} z \\ y \\ z \end{bmatrix} \cdot \begin{bmatrix} 1 \\ 1 \\ 1 \end{bmatrix} = \begin{bmatrix} 1 \\ 0 \\ 1 \end{bmatrix} \cdot \begin{bmatrix} 1 \\ 1 \\ 1 \end{bmatrix} \quad \Rightarrow \quad x + y + z = 2$$

This simple example provides a prelude to introducing the general Cartesian equation of a plane, but it is worth exploring a little further before introducing further complications. Firstly it helps students to appreciate the role of the normal vector to see it in reality with their own cube. An equilateral triangle of appropriate size can be cut out of card to represent triangle *BGE* and a cocktail stick or knitting needle used for the normal vector. In order to construct the model with cube, triangle and normal vector it is necessary to know where **OF** cuts the triangle, so a little calculation is needed involving the vector equation of the line *OF*:

$$\text{Equation of line } OF: \quad \begin{bmatrix} x \\ y \\ z \end{bmatrix} = t \begin{bmatrix} 1 \\ 1 \\ 1 \end{bmatrix}$$

Substituting in $x + y + z = 2$: $3t = 2 \implies t = \tfrac{2}{3}$

Coordinates of point of intersection: $(\tfrac{2}{3}, \tfrac{2}{3}, \tfrac{2}{3})$

The point is the intersection of the medians of the equilateral triangle. Fitting cube, triangle and normal vector together successfully gives life to what would otherwise be rather dry and abstract calculations. A simple practical exercise like this increases motivation and insight.

Another point for discussion is to consider parallel planes like that containing triangle *ACD* and those through the points *O* and *F*. Comparing these reinforces the idea of the normal vector as a way of showing the orientation of the plane. This is a more complicated idea than that of the direction of a line, which in two directions is linked to the gradient. Gradient alone is not sufficient in three dimensions – we need to be able to distinguish not only between going north and south up a 1 in 5 slope, but all the directions in between!

For a final problem let us return to the cube where six diagonals on the square faces form a regular tetrahedron as shown in Figure 12.16. This surprising configuration has been discussed

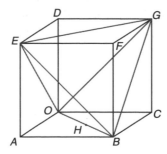

Figure 12.16 *A tetrahedron in a cube*

previously in Chapter 11, but here we will use a scalar product to calculate the dihedral angle – the angle between two adjacent faces. To avoid halves let us suppose the cube has edges of length 2 and that *H* is the centre of the base. Then angle *EHG* is the dihedral angle which can be calculated from the scalar product of the two vectors **HE** and **HG** as follows:

$$\mathbf{HE} = \begin{bmatrix} 1 \\ -1 \\ 2 \end{bmatrix} \text{ and } \mathbf{HG} = \begin{bmatrix} -1 \\ 1 \\ 2 \end{bmatrix} \implies HE = HG = \sqrt{6}$$

$$\cos\theta = \frac{\mathbf{HE.HG}}{HE \times HG} = \tfrac{2}{6} = \tfrac{1}{3} \implies \theta \approx 70.5°$$

CONCLUSION

Vectors provide a very powerful tool for solving geometrical problems, particularly in three dimensions where vector equations often take a simpler form than the corresponding Cartesian equations. They do, of course, have applications in a wide variety of fields besides geometry, but their origins are geometrical. Geometry provides an obvious context at any level for developing their properties and learning to use them effectively. Column vectors can be introduced at an early stage in secondary school as a way of describing translations. When two vectors are equal they have both the same magnitude and the same direction and this tells us not only the relationship between the lengths of two line segments, but also that they are parallel. Much can be accomplished simply on the basis of addition, subtraction and multiplication by scalars, but the scalar product, which is a more abstract idea, is a valuable tool to develop because it provides such a neat test of perpendicularity. At a later stage the vector product is a another useful idea, but that goes beyond the scope of this book.

This book has presented a variety of ways of looking at geometry, some taking a symbolic algebraic form, as with coordinates, equations of curves and vectors, and others purely geometrical in the style of Euclid. Students need to experience this variety of approaches and to see alternative ways of looking at problems of all kinds. Success with geometry is dependent on establishing a sound intuitive feel for geometrical objects through appropriate practical tasks, so that the essentially deductive nature of geometry can proceed from a familiarity with simple properties and relationships. Geometry provides an excellent medium for developing mathematical thinking through solving problems and learning to appreciate and generate proofs. The subject is immensely rich in surprising theorems and intriguing problems, and it has the added strong attraction of its immediate visual appeal. All this goes to make geometry a most attractive and challenging subject to teach and learn and one that lies very much at the heart of mathematics.

Bibliography

Adey, P. and Shayer, M. (1994) *Really raising standards: Cognitive intervention and academic achievement*. London and New York: Routledge.

Alexanderson, G. L. and Seydel, K. (1978) 'Kurschak's tile', *Mathematical Gazette* **62**, 192–6.

Andrews, P. and Sinkinson, A. (2000) 'Continuity, Coherence and Curricular Entitlement', *Mathematics Teaching*, **172**, 52–5.

APU (1987) *Topics No. 3: Lines and Angles*. London: Assessment of Performance Unit.

Askew, M. and Wiliam, D. (1995) *Ofsted Reviews of Recent Research: Recent Research in Mathematics Education 5–16*. London: HMSO.

Balacheff, N. (1988) 'Aspects of Proof in Pupils' Practice of School Mathematics', in Pimm, D. (ed.) *Mathematics, Teachers and Children*. London: Hodder & Stoughton.

Barnard, T. (2002) 'Starting Points and End Points', *Mathematics in School* **31**(3), 23–6.

Bolt, B. (1991) *Mathematics meets Technology*. Cambridge: Cambridge University Press.

Boyer, C. B. and Merzbach, U. C. (1991) *A History of Mathematics* (2nd edn). New York: John Wiley.

Buxton, L. (1981) *Do you panic about maths?* London: Heinemann.

Chazan, D. (1993) 'High School Geometry Students' Justifcation for Their Views of Empirical Evidence and Mathematical Proof', *Educational Studies in Mathematics* **24**(4), 359–87.

Cockcroft, W. (1982) *Mathematics Counts: Report of the Committee of Enquiry into the Teaching of Mathematics*. London: HMSO.

Cooper, B. (1985) *Renegotiating Secondary School Mathematics*. London: Falmer.

Cundy, M. and Rollett, A. P. (1961) *Mathematical Models*. Oxford: Oxford University Press.

Davis, P. J. and Hersh, R. (1983) *The Mathematical Experience*. Harmondsworth: Penguin.

Davis, R. B. (1984) *Learning Mathematics*. Beckenham: Croom Helm.

de Villiers, M. D. (1998) 'An Alternative Approach to Proof in Dynamic Geometry', in Lehrer, R. and Chazan, D. *Designing Learning Environments for Developing Understanding of Geometry and Space*. Mahwah, NJ: Lawrence Erlbaum Associates.

de Villiers, M. D. (1999) *Rethinking Proof with the Geometer's Sketchpad*. Emeryville, CA: Key Curriculum Press.

DfEE/QCA (1999) *Mathematics: the National Curriculum for England*. London: Department for Education and Employment/Qualifications and Curriculum Authority.

DfEE (2001) *Key Stage 3 National Strategy. Framework for Teaching Mathematics, Years 7, 8 and 9*. London: Department for Education and Employment.

Dickson, L., Brown, M. and Gibson, O. (1984) *Children Learning Mathematics: a Teacher's Guide to Recent Research*. Eastbourne: Holt, Rinehart & Winston.

Duval, R. (1998) 'Geometry from a Cognitive Point of View', in Mammana, C. and Villani, V. *Perspectives on the Teaching of Geometry for the 21st Century*. Dordrecht, Boston and London: Kluwer.

Fauvel, J. and Gray, J. (1987) *The History of Mathematics: a Reader*. London: Macmillan.

Fielker, D. (1973) 'A Structural Approach to Primary School Geometry', *Mathematics Teaching*, **63**, 12–16.

Fischbein, E. (1982) 'Intuition and Proof', *For the Learning of Mathematics*, **3**(2), 9–24.

Frederickson, G. N. (1997) *Dissections: Plain and Fancy*. Cambridge: Cambridge University Press.

French, D. (1988) 'Reflections on a Cube', *Mathematics in School*, **17**(4), 30–3.

French, D. (1992) 'A Number and its Cube', *Mathematics in School*, **21**(2), 38–41.

French, D. (1998) 'Dissecting a Dodecagon', *Mathematics in School*, **27**(1), 18–19.

French, D. (1999a) 'Up and Over', *Mathematics in School*, **28**(2), 6–8.

French, D. (1999b) 'Parabolic Reflectors', *The Mathematical Gazette*, **83**(497), 237–44.

French, D. (2002a) 'An Octagon in a Square', *Mathematics in School*, **31**(2), 23–5.

French, D. (2002b) *Teaching and Learning Algebra*. London: Continuum.

French, D. (2003a) 'Van Schooten's theorem', in Pritchard, C. (ed.) *The Changing Shape of Geometry*. Cambridge: Cambridge University Press.

French, D. (2003b) 'Regular Pentagons and the Fibonacci Sequence', in Pritchard, C. (ed). *The Changing Shape of Geometry*. Cambridge: Cambridge University Press.

French, D. and Bibby, N. (2003) 'Pythagoras Extended: a Geometric Approach to the Cosine Rule', in Pritchard, C. (ed.) *The Changing Shape of Geometry*. Cambridge: Cambridge University Press.

French, D. and Stripp, C. (eds) (1997) *Are You Sure? Learning about Proof*. Leicester: The Mathematical Association.

Gal, H. and Vinner, S. (1997) 'Perpendicular Lines – What is the Problem?' *Proceedings of the 21st Conference of the International Group for the Psychology of Mathematics Education*. University of Helsinki.

Gardner, M. (1965) *Mathematical Puzzles and Diversions*. Harmondsworth: Penguin.

Gardner, M. (1966) *More Mathematical Puzzles and Diversions*. Harmondsworth: Penguin.

Goddijn, A. (2003) 'Miquel's Six Circle Theorem', in Pritchard, C. (ed.) *The Changing Shape of Geometry*. Cambridge: Cambridge University Press.

Godfrey, C. and Siddons, A.W. (1903) *Elementary Geometry*. Cambridge: Cambridge University Press.

Goldenburg, E. P., Cuoco, A. A. and Mark, J. (1998) 'A Role for Geometry in General Education', in Lehrer, R. and Chazan, D. *Designing Learning Environments for Developing Understanding of Geometry and Space*. Mahwah, NJ: Lawrence Erlbaum Associates.

Hart, K.M. (ed.) (1981) *Children's Understanding of Mathematics: 11–16*. London: John Murray.

Heath, T. L. (1967) *The Thirteen Books of Euclid's Elements*. New York: Dover Publications.

Holt, J. (1958) *How Children Fail*. Harmondsworth: Penguin.

Howson, A.G. (1973) 'Milestone or Millstone', *The Mathematical Gazette*, **58**, 258–66.

Howson, A.G. (1982) *A History of Mathematics Education in England*. Cambridge: Cambridge University Press.

Howson, G. (1991) *National Curricula in Mathematics*. Leicester: The Mathematical Association.

Hoyles, C. (1997) 'The Curricular Shaping of Students' Approaches to Proof', *For the Learning of Mathematics*, **17**(1), 7–16.

Hoyles, C., Foxman, D. and Küchemann, D. (2002) *A Comparative Study of Geometry Curricula*. London: QCA.

Inhelder, B. and Piaget, J. (1958) *The Growth of Logical Thinking*. London: Routledge & Kegan Paul.

Inhelder, B., Piaget, J. and Szeminska, K. (1960) *The Child's Conception of Geometry*. London: Routledge & Kegan Paul.

Jones, K. (1998) 'Deductive and Intuitive Approaches to Solving Geometrical Problems', in Mammana, C. and Villani, V. *Perspectives on the Teaching of Geometry for the 21st Century*. Dordrecht, Boston and London: Kluwer.

Kaiser, G., Lunn, E. and Huntley, I. (1999) *International Comparisons in Mathematics Education*. London: Falmer Press.

Kerslake, D. (1979) 'Visual Mathematics', *Mathematics in School*, **8**(2), 34–5.

Küchemann, D. (1981) 'Reflections and Rotations', in Hart, K. M. (ed.) *Children's Understanding of Mathematics: 11–16*. London: John Murray.

Lakatos, I. (1976) *Proofs and Refutations*. Cambridge: Cambridge University Press.

Lehrer, R. and Chazan, D. (1998) *Designing Learning Environments for Developing Understanding of Geometry and Space*. Mahwah, NJ: Lawrence Erlbaum.

Ma, Liping (1999) *Knowing and Teaching Elementary Mathematics*. Mahwah, NJ: Lawrence Erlbaum.

Mammana, C. and Villani, V. (1998) *Perspectives on the Teaching of Geometry for the 21st Century*. Dordrecht, Boston and London: Kluwer.

Mason, J. (1988) *Learning and Doing Mathematics*. London: Macmillan.

Mathematical Association (1923) *A First Report on the Teaching of Geometry in Schools*. London: G. Bell & Sons.

Mathematical Association (1938) *A Second Report on the Teaching of Geometry in Schools*. London: G. Bell & Sons.

NCTM (1989) *Curriculum and Evaluation Standards for School Mathematics*. Reston, VA: National Council of Teachers of Mathematics.

NCTM (1991) *Professional Standards for Teaching Mathematics*. Reston, VA: National Council of Teachers of Mathematics.

NCTM (1999) *Developing Mathematical Reasoning in Grades K-12: 1999 Yearbook*. Reston, VA: National Council of Teachers of Mathematics.

NCTM (2000a) *Learning Mathematics for a New Century: 2000 Yearbook*. Reston, VA: National Council of Teachers of Mathematics.

NCTM (2000b) *Principles and Standards for School Mathematics*. Reston, VA: National Council of Teachers of Mathematics.

Nelsen, R. B. (1993) *Proofs without Words: Exercises in Visual Thinking*. Washington, DC: The Mathematical Association of America.

Nelsen, R. B. (2000) *Proofs without Words II: Exercises in Visual Thinking*. Washington, DC: The Mathematical Association of America.

Nickson, M. (2000) *Teaching and Learning Mathematics: a Teacher's Guide to Recent Research and its Application*. London: Cassell.

Oldknow, A. and Taylor, R. (2000) *Teaching Mathematics with ICT*. London: Continuum.

Pimm, D. (1987) *Speaking Mathematically*. London: Routledge & Kegan Paul.

Pimm, D. (1995) *Symbols and Meanings in School Mathematics*. London and New York: Routledge.

Pinel, A. (1993) *Mathematical Activity Tiles*. Southampton: Polygon Resources.

Polya, G. (1945) *How to Solve It*. Princeton, NJ: Princeton University Press.

Price, M. H. (1994) *Mathematics for the Multitude? A History of the Mathematical Association*. Leicester: The Mathematical Association.

Pritchard, C. (ed.) (2003) *The Changing Shape of Geometry*. Cambridge: Cambridge University Press.

RAND Mathematics Study Panel (2003) *Mathematical Proficiency for All Students:Towards a Strategic Research and Development Program in Mathematics*. Santa Monica, CA: RAND.

RS/JMC (2001) *Teaching and Learning Geometry 11–19*. London: Royal Society/Joint Mathematical Council.

Schumann, H. and Green, D. (1994) *Discovering Geometry with a Computer*. Bromley: Chartwell-Bratt.

Senk, S. L. and Thompson, D. R. (2003) *Standards-Based School Mathematics Curricula*. Mahwah, NJ: Lawrence Erlbaum.

Skemp, R. (1976) 'Relational and Instrumental Understanding', *Mathematics Teaching*, **77**, 20–6.

SMP (1965) *School Mathematics Project*, Book 1. Cambridge: Cambridge University Press.

SMP (1966) *School Mathematics Project*, Book 2. Cambridge: Cambridge University Press.

SMP (1968) *School Mathematics Project*, Book A. Cambridge: Cambridge University Press.

SMP (2000) *SMP Interact*, Book 1. Cambridge: Cambridge University Press.

Tall, D. (1991) *Advanced Mathematical Thinking*. Dordrecht, Boston and London: Kluwer.

van Hiele, P. M. (1986) *Structure and Insight*. Orlando, FL: Academic Press.

Webster, R. (2003) 'Bride's chair revisited', in Pritchard, C. (ed.) *The Changing Shape of Geometry*. Cambridge: Cambridge University Press.

Wenninger, M. J. (1971) *Polyhedron Models*. Cambridge: Cambridge University Press.

Index

Adey, P. and Shayer, M. 15, 18
Alexanderson, G. and Sydel, K. 51
alternate segment theorem 113, 117
analytic geometry 2, 7
Andrews, P. and Sinkinson, A. 11, 45
angle 17, 35–37, 43–46
Apollonius' theorem 101, 102
APU, *see* Assessment of Performance Unit
Archimedean polyhedra 148
Archimedes 67, 128
Area 18, 65–76
Assessment of Performance Unit 17
Association for Improvement of Geometrical
    Teaching 12
Association of Teachers of Mathematics 30, 136
ATM, *see* Association of Teachers of Mathematics
Autograph 24, 26

Babylonians 94
Balacheff, N. 23
Barnard, A. 7
Boyer, C. and Merzbach, U. 74
buckminsterfullerene 148
bucky ball 147
Buxton, L. 140

Cabri Geometry 24, 25, 27, 37, 41, 70
calculus 65, 69
Cavalieri's Principle 67, 74
China 91
chords 104–106
circle theorems 6, 104–118
circles 70–73
Cockcroft, W. 14
cognitive acceleration 15
computers 23, 28
concrete operations 15
congruence 14, 22, 23, 42, 47, 55–64, 103

constructions 55–64
Cooper, B. 13
coordinates 2, 119–124
cosine rule 99
cube 139–141
Cundy, M. and Rollett, A. 128, 136
curriculum 5–9, 63
Curriculum and Evaluation Standards (USA) 6

de Villiers, M. 8, 23
default 20
Department for Education and Employment 6
Descartes 2, 134, 135
DfEE, *see* Department for Education and
    Employment
dihedral angle 160
dilatation 77
dodecagon 51–53
dodecahedron 145–148
Duval, R. 8
dynamic geometry 1, 3, 4, 14, 24, 25, 41, 42, 45–47,
    52, 54–58, 62–64, 67, 78, 83, 90, 100, 104 106,
    110, 112, 117, 129, 132, 133

Euler's formula 137, 147, 148
ellipse 127–131
enlargement 1, 14, 77–90
Elementary Geometry 12, 14
Euclid's *Elements* 2, 12, 27, 56, 57, 94–96, 136,
    161

Fielker, D. 19
Fischbein, E. 16
formal operations 15
France 5, 7 14, 25
Frederickson, G. 52
French, D. 51, 77, 86, 97, 119, 126, 128
Fuller, Buckminster 148

Gal, H. and Vinner, S. 19
Gardner, M. 139
geodesic dome 148
Geometer's Sketchpad 24, 25, 41
Goddjin, A. 116
Godfrey, C. 12
Godfrey, C. and Siddons, A. 12, 14
golden ratio 87, 88, 146
Goldenburg, E., Cuoco, A. and Mark, J. 3
gradient 99, 119–122
graph plotting software 119, 126, 127, 134
graphical calculators 119, 126, 127, 134
graphs 119–135
Greeks 87, 131

habits of mind 3
Hart, K. 78
Heath, T. 56, 94
hexominoes 139
Howson, A. G. 12
Hoyles, C. 23
Hoyles, C., Foxman, D. and Küchemann, D. 5
Hungary 11

ICMI, *see* International Commission on
    Mathematical Instruction
icosahedron 8, 145–148
India 91
Inhelder, B. and Piaget, J. 15
intercept theorem 84–87
International Commission on Mathematical
    Instruction 6
intuition 16, 17, 29, 39, 55, 76
isometries 55

Japan 5, 7, 11, 14
JMC, *see* Joint Mathematical Council
Joint Mathematical Council 6

Kerslake, D. 19
Key Stage 3 National Strategy 14
Kroto, Sir Harry 147
Küchemann, D. 40
Kürschak's tile 51

Lakatos, I. 138
Lindgren's dissection 52

locus 124–126, 128, 129, 134
LOGO 10, 14, 24, 25, 35, 36, 39, 49, 50, 54

Mammana, C. and Villani, V. 6
Mason, J. 118
Mathematical Activity Tiles 30, 136
Mathematical Association 12, 13, 15
Mathematical Puzzles and Diversions 139
MathsNet 26, 27
matrices 2
MATs, *see* Mathematical Activity Tiles
midpoint theorem 1, 81–84, 109, 152,153
Miquel's six circle theorem 116, 117
misconceptions 17, 18, 31, 35, 40
Moebius strip 139

National Council of Teachers of Mathematics
    6, 14
National Curriculum for England 6, 14, 57
NCTM, *see* National Council of Teachers of
    Mathematics
Netherlands 5

octahedron 89, 90, 138, 143–145
Oldknow, A. and Taylor, R. 3
Omnigraph 21

parabola 131–134
pentagon 87, 88
Perigal's dissection 93, 94
perimeter 18, 65–76
Perry, Professor John 12
Piaget, J. 15
Pimm, D. 19, 20
Pinel, A. 30, 136
polygons 48–51
polyhedra 89, 90, 136–148
polyominoes 139
Price, M. 12
Principles and Standards for School Mathematics
    (USA) 6
Pritchard, C. 2
proof 1, 6, 59–64
Proofs and Refutations 138
proportionality 77, 78, 90
pure geometry 2
Pythagoras' theorem 3, 6, 7, 17, 91–103, 152

QCA, *see* Qualifications and Curriculum Authority
quadrilateral 1, 6, 46–48, 57, 62
Qualifications and Curriculum Authority 6

RAND 10, 11
reflection 14, 37, 38, 40–42, 55, 60, 61
rhombic dodecahedron 74, 144, 145
rotation 14, 18, 37, 38, 40–42, 55, 60, 95, 96
Royal Society 6

scalar product 122, 155–158
scale factor 14, 77–80
School Mathematics Project 14, 31
Schumann, H. and Green, D. 100
Senk, S. and Thompson, D. 6
shear 67, 69, 95, 96
shear 95, 96, 99, 100
similarity 14, 77–90, 103
Singapore 5, 7
Skemp, R. 10
SMP, *see* School Mathematics Project
spatial awareness 2, 16
sphere 74, 75
spreadsheet 81, 107
stages A, B and C 13, 16

stretch 126, 127
symmetry 7, 24, 32, 40–42, 52, 62
synthetic geometry 7

tangents 104 106
Teaching and Learning Algebra 77
tessellations 37–39, 48, 144
tetrahedron 89, 90, 136, 137, 142–144, 160
transformations 7, 14, 24, 37–39, 55, 60, 67, 95, 103
translation 37, 38, 55, 126, 127, 149–152
triangle numbers 2, 3
trigonometry 7, 9, 97–100, 103

United States 6, 14

vectors 2, 149–161
van Schooten's theorem 62, 63
volume 65–76, 88–90
volumes of revolution 75
Varignon's theorem 2, 8, 82
van Hiele, P. M. 15, 16, 30, 53

Webster, R. 100
Wenninger, M. J. 136